Political Tone

liberals rarely "liberate"

conservatives rarely "conserve" (Karen point
76-7
(restore mythic vision / "lost constitution")

Chicago Studies in American Politics

A SERIES EDITED BY BENJAMIN I. PAGE, SUSAN HERBST,
LAWRENCE R. JACOBS, AND JAMES DRUCKMAN

Also in the series:

Political Tone

How Leaders Talk and Why

RODERICK P. HART, JAY P.
CHILDERS, AND COLENE J. LIND

THE UNIVERSITY OF CHICAGO PRESS   CHICAGO AND LONDON

RODERICK P. HART holds the Allan Shivers Centennial Chair in Communication at the University of Texas at Austin and is the author or editor of a dozen books, including, most recently, *Political Keywords*. JAY P. CHILDERS is assistant professor in the Department of Communication Studies at the University of Kansas. He is the author of *The Evolving Citizen*. COLENE J. LIND is a PhD candidate in communication studies at the University of Texas at Austin.

The University of Chicago Press, Chicago 60637
The University of Chicago Press, Ltd., London
© 2013 by The University of Chicago
All rights reserved. Published 2013.
Printed in the United States of America

22 21 20 19 18 17 16 15 14 13   1 2 3 4 5

ISBN-13: 978-0-226-02301-4 (cloth)
ISBN-13: 978-0-226-02315-1 (paper)
ISBN-13: 978-0-226-02329-8 (e-book)

Library of Congress Cataloging-in-Publication Data

Hart, Roderick P., author.
    Political tone : how leaders talk and why / Roderick P. Hart, Jay P. Childers, and Colene J. Lind.
        pages cm. — (Chicago studies in American politics)
    Includes bibliographical references and index.
    ISBN 978-0-226-02301-4 (cloth : alkaline paper) — ISBN 978-0-226-02315-1 (paperback : alkaline paper) — ISBN 978-0-226-02329-8 (e-book) 1. Political oratory. 2. Politicians—Language. 3. Rhetoric—Political aspects. I. Childers, Jay P., 1974– author. II. Lind, Colene J., author. III. Title. IV. Series: Chicago studies in American politics.
    PN4193.P6H36 2013
    808.5'1—dc23

2012048344

⊗ This paper meets the requirements of ANSI/NISO Z39.48-1992 (Permanence of Paper).

Contents

PART I

Understanding Language

The Mysteries of Political Tone

People use words to make impressions on other people. It has always been thus. Within the first two years of life, we learn how to be hurtful and endearing, even with precious few words at our command. The years pass, relationships develop, our vocabularies thicken. By the time adulthood beckons, we have become rhetorical artists. By then we can do more work with fewer words by having learned language's vectoring potential. Others' words affect us in turn. What they say can heal our souls or crush our spirits. It has always been thus.

These principles also apply in politics, an arena with words aplenty. Savage words, destructive words, comforting words, inspiring words. Words from many tongues, words freshly coined. Legal words, monetary words, indeterminate words, suggestive words. Here, too, we learn to make fine discriminations, deciding that the Tea Party is "strident" and Barack Obama "reserved." We sense that Glenn Beck has the distinctive marks of the ex-addict: self-abasing superiority. We learn that Keith Olbermann's annoying glibness betrays his former job—that of the sports announcer. We discover that Newt Gingrich "pontificates" and Sarah Palin is "flighty." We learn that Joe Biden uses too many words and that some people distrust him as a result. We learn that Nancy Pelosi is "cold," Harry Reid "avuncular," Mike Huckabee "folksy," and Mitt Romney "bureaucratic." Word-sensitive Americans—which is to say most Americans—make observations like this each day and think nothing of it.

In this book, we think longer about such matters. We examine a wide swath of American rhetoric to determine how language affects our perceptions of others. We focus mostly on national politics, but only because it presents such an interesting tableau. We present some institutional analyses as well as some case studies—of Bill Clinton, George W. Bush,

Barack Obama, and Sarah Palin—because these four individuals have been especially adept at affecting people's values and attitudes. But how do they do so? Why did we revile them or find them irresistible? Why waste our precious time with such distant personalities? When politicians knock, why do we open the door?

In their more self-regarding moments, your authors see this book as a counterpart to one of the finest ever written by an American political scientist: *Political Ideology: Why the American Common Man Believes What He Does* by Robert Lane (1962). There, Lane conducts a series of exhaustive interviews with fifteen ordinary citizens living in the town of "Eastport," teasing out the political spirit of everyday Americans who, he found, were largely allegiant to the nation and tolerant of their fellow citizens. They believed in equal opportunity but not collectivism, in justice but not hand holding. Beliefs like these, says Lane, were reinforced by the men's network of associations in their families, union halls, churches, towns, and villages. Lane found that such beliefs did not simply float about in the ether but were instead the products of everyday dialectic. ?

Lane was interested in Americans' *political ideas*, while we want to understand their *social impressions*. To do so, we could have simply asked people what they felt about a given political leader, using survey instruments to record their reactions. But we chose another approach for several reasons: (1) surveys often ask respondents to reflect on matters they rarely think about, thereby "contaminating" the people they hope to understand; (2) surveys, even the best of them, reduce complex issues such as health care, human rights, and taxing policy to bite-sized questions having little breadth or depth (except, perhaps, when examined in the aggregate); (3) surveyors restrict how subjects can respond to the questions posed ("agree," "strongly agree"), thereby forcing subjects into modes of response not of their choosing. Despite these limitations, survey research has taught us a tremendous amount about political life.

Here, we trace political perceptions to the world of words. When doing so, we try not to be overly determinative because words only do some of life's work. People are also influenced by how they have been raised, by their lifestyle choices, by their friends and associates. Their social understandings also arise from memories and expectations, from sudden life changes, and from pressure groups and media experiences.

Given the power of such forces, it is tempting to overlook words. But if critic Kenneth Burke (1966) is right, it would be folly to do so because words use us even as we use them. So we take words seriously here by examining a large dataset (around 30,000 texts) and tracking how politicians, the press, and ordinary citizens present their thoughts. We also try to get at an especially subtle thing—political tone—by looking for its roots in language behavior. When doing so, we reflect on incidents people have long since forgotten: how a mother's voice told them she was upset; why one high school teacher made them laugh while another made them sit up straight in class; how an interviewer's odd choice of words signaled that they had lost the position halfway through the job interview. By the time people reach maturity, they have become experts on tone. But experts about what?

The Ubiquity of Tone

There are few words in the English lexicon more mysterious than *tone*. Even that haven of wordiness, the *Oxford English Dictionary*, seems undone by the concept, offering eleven definitions of the word grouped into three broad categories, thereby deriving twenty-one separate understandings. Lay lexicographers are no more definitive. Business leaders talk of setting the right tone for the organization and children are admonished for having used the wrong tone of voice. In the 1950s it was considered de rigueur to drive a two-tone sedan; years later their adult children sought out a toned physique. On other fronts, a reviewer writes that a movie's "tone is facile at best and smug at worst" (Puig, 2010, p. 4D), while the snarky judge of *American Idol*, Simon Cowell, enjoyed telling contestants they were tone-deaf.

Tone is an omnipresent if ill-defined concept, but that hardly stops people from using it. Aphorist Mason Cooley declares that "the higher the moral tone, the more suspect the speaker," while Truman Capote hisses that "the quietness of his tone italicized the malice of his reply." Former New York City mayor Ed Koch tells us that "tone can be as important as text" without telling us what that means, while Supreme Court Justice Louis Brandeis speculates that "we are not won by arguments that we can analyze, but by tone and temper." Throaty Broadway star Harvey Fierstein jokes that "the average voice is like 70 percent tone and 30 percent noise [while mine] is 95 percent noise," but suffragette Elizabeth Cady Stanton is deadly serious when declaring that "the whole tone of Church teaching in regard to women is, to the last degree, contemptuous and degrading."[1]

Historically, tone was first mentioned with reference to sound. One of the earliest known uses of the word in the English language was that of the fourteenth century mystic Richard Rolle of Hampole (1863, p. 249), who comforted the righteous with the knowledge that they would hear the "sweet tones of music" in heaven. Present-day musicians continue to talk of tonality and atonality, of tone poems and twelve-tones, and seem to understand what one another are saying. The *Harvard Dictionary of Music* defines tone as "a sound of definite pitch," which seems clear enough until one hears linguists using the word as well. Written words, they declare, become enveloped in a tone language "if the pitch of the word can change the meaning of the word" (Yip, 2007, p. 229). Linguists talk of intonation, the use of pitch to denote shades of meaning, and how words become accented and thereby create entirely new meanings (Yip, 2007).

Despite this ambiguity, one thing remains constant: tone affects people's perceptions of others. Early discussions of this linkage can be traced to two European thinkers—Jean-Jacques Rousseau and Thomas Sheridan. Rousseau, in his 1781 *Essay on the Origin of Language*, made explicit leaps from music to language and thence to persuasion, observing that "a language that has only articulations and voices therefore has only half its riches; it conveys ideas, it is true, but in order to convey feelings, images, it still needs a rhythm and sounds, that is, a melody" (1998, p. 318). Taking the matter a step further, Sheridan argued in his 1762 *Lectures on Elocution* that tone is how people share with one another "the true signs of the passions" (2001, pp. 884, 882).

So tone is both oral and aural, spoken and written, verbal and nonverbal. It is also visual. Artists use the concept to explain shadings, with tone being "created by varying a color in its light and dark qualities." Visual tones, in turn, are alleged to have *value*, the "quality by which we distinguish a light color from a dark one, such as light blue from dark blue" (Krug, 2007, p. 106). In the art world, tone is linked to people's perceptual experiences: "The framework of light and dark areas that makes up any picture—the broad tonal pattern—is often what first attracts the viewer's attention and provides the immediate introduction to the mood and content of that picture" (Jennings, 2006, p. 219). Tone in art. Tone in music. Tone in linguistics. And in sociology too? When discussing the depth of color bias in the United States, Margaret Hunter observes that "systems of discrimination operate on at least two levels in terms of race and color. The first system of discrimination is the level of racial category (i.e., black,

Asian, Indian, etc.). The second system of discrimination is at the level of skin tone—darker skin or lighter skin" (2005, p. 7).

Tone also has psychological properties. It helps create the backbone of a story, say Burroway and Stuckey-French (2007, p. 176), fueling its narrative voice. A "sinister atmosphere," they note, "might be achieved partly by syntax, rhythm, and word choice" although these authors fail to explain how such transformations come about. That is how it is with tone, a thing quickly discussed but hard to explain. Still, tone persists. Dylan Thomas's famous poem written for his dying father, for example, begins with this line: "Do not go gentle into that good night." We are immediately put on alert and then the tone darkens: "Old age should burn and rave at close of day." By the poem's third line, we are aware of the poet's anguish, of his urgency and frustration, and, yes, of his anger: "Rage, rage against the dying of the light." Tone becomes the clue to the poet's *attitude* about things. Poetry, when it is wonderful, draws us into that attitude (Campbell & Burkholder, 1997, p. 38).

Dylan Thomas is one thing—one brilliant thing—but we are concerned with more prosaic matters here. Our focus is on politics, whose tone is often plebian. Writing for *Time* magazine in late 2007, for example, columnist Joe Klein (2007, p. 35) argued that the Democratic candidates were "tone-deaf" on matters of national security. This is not to say the Democrats were completely inept, however, since just a few months later *The New York Times* reported that Hillary Clinton and Barack Obama had struck the right chord for their campaigns: "In a city known for its fierce prizefighters, the political tone was purposefully gentle on stage here at the Cashman Center in downtown Las Vegas" (Zeleny & Healy, 2008, p. A19).

What do such commentators mean? What are they seeing and what are they sensing? What does *The Washington Post*'s reporter Mike Allen mean when noting in the fall of 2002 that George W. Bush's "government events had a political tone" (2002, p. A5)? How could government be anything but political? And what did reporters mean when identifying "political tone shifts" among black church leaders in New England during the 2004 campaign season (Paul, 2004, p. 2) or among Republican campaigners in Iowa four years later (Zeleny, 2011)? What did *USA Today* mean when declaring that Barack Obama had taken "steps to tamp down the often harsh political tone in Washington" during his first ten days in office (Hall, 2009, p. 4A)? Is tone a mere adjunct to politics or its very essence?

Tone vs. Style

We treat tone as a subset of the larger concept of *style*, which, in classical terms, refers to the full complement of devices—syntax, imagery, register, voice, predication, lexicon—that bring ideas to life. Rhetorical scholars have examined style from a variety of perspectives. Edwin Black, for example, identified what he called the "sentimental style" that was popular in the nineteenth century, a kind of over-the-top approach that elevated the grandeur of its arguments. Black (1978, p. 78) says that the sentimental style was "notable not so much for its stately movement or its piling on of adjectives or its tendency to tear passions to tatters" but because of the way those elements were combined in public oratory. In many ways, says Black, this florid style obscured reality even while revealing it, forcing audiences to reach higher, further, for the ideas addressed. Orators like Frederick Douglass and Daniel Webster therefore talked in code. It took a patient people (and an educated people) to follow its serpentine path. Such a style reverenced language for its own sake, a far cry from the hyper-efficiency of twenty first century political discourse.

Karlyn Kohrs Campbell (1989, p. 13) has traced the style of early feminism, an approach that combined "the crafts of housewifery" with the overtones of maternal care. The result, says Campbell, was a highly personal style quite distinct from the formal, masculine approach common at the time. The feminine style relied heavily "on reported experiences, personal anecdotes, and homespun examples." Recounting the approach of the early activist Angelina Grimke, Campbell (1989, p. 13) notes that she combined self-reflexivity with directness—"What came ye out for to see? A reed shaken by the wind?"—a style that befriended her audience and challenged it as well. With these words, says Campbell, Grimke let people know that she was strong but not brazen, personal but not cloying. A new political sensibility was born at that moment, and a new social movement as well.

Walker Gibson's (1966) analysis of mid-twentieth century America is also textured. He describes three forces operating powerfully at the time—a stridency born of the Second World War, a formality arising from an increasingly bureaucratized system, and a solicitousness resulting from the urban "hustle" of a mercantile culture. This resulted, says Gibson, in three rhetorical styles—tough, sweet, and stuffy—each of which produced a different rhetorical "personality" that reached out in different ways. The Tough Style demanded compliance; the Stuffy Style asked for deference; the Sweet Style requested amiability. Each style presented a different social character for inspection and each sent a meta-message about who could be believed and what was important. Operating mostly with his own keen insights rather than any scientific apparatus, Gibson created a kind of "style machine" to measure prose passages. His early work continues to inspire any serious student of verbal tone.

A more recent study by Robert Hariman (1995, p. 2) argues that our political experiences are rife with "relations of control" that are ultimately "negotiated through the artful composition of speech, gesture, ornament, décor, and any other means for modulating perception and shaping response." When seeking power, says Hariman, we inevitably leave behind distinctive markers of our quest, markers that are often rhetorical in nature. The Realistic Style, says Hariman, assumes that scientific measurement will lead us to truth, while the Courtly Style respects only traditional authority. The Republican Style is different still, trying to introduce an audience to some sort of transactional space where give-and-take is possible. Each of these styles, says Hariman (1995, p. 168), "provides 'the 'recipe knowledge' for effective participation in a particular political locale."

Generally, rhetorical studies of language have gone in one of three directions. Studies of *conceptual style* have examined how modes of thought interact with historical trends to change discursive formations. So, for example, Postrel (2003) traces the impact of aesthetic beliefs on modern social trends, while Lanham (2007) looks for their roots in new economic assumptions and Clark (2004) in people's changing relationships to the natural environment.[2] Those who have studied *political style* have looked at how regimes of control become embedded in texts operating in a given polity. Connolly (2008) has examined the "punitive orientations" of the religious Right, while Pfau (2005) has looked at "conspiratorial mindsets" and Stephen Hart (2001) at "progressive identities" to explain patterns of social activism. Finally, students of *cultural style* broaden the object of analysis considerably, looking at how modes of entertainment (Farrell, 2011), popular fashion (Wilkins, 2008), performance routines (Brummett, 2008), and even hair and clothing (Walker, 2007) bespeak a given society.

The foregoing studies are enormously provocative but we are after something humbler here. We focus on **tone**, *a tool people use (sometimes unwittingly) to create distinct social impressions via word choice.* We operate on the assumption that certain words, when drawn upon often enough, leave people with shared but often elusive perceptions of others. Sometimes, even mere function words can tell us a great deal about our fellow human beings (Pennebaker, 2011). Jeanne Fahnestock (2011, p. 77) describes how such processes unfold:

> Like the galaxies in a map of the universe, words in the English lexicon cluster in meaning groups or lexical fields. This simple fact determines the predictability of a rhetor's word choices, delimiting both the subject matter of an argument and any ancillary fields brought into use for their effects. The appearance of predictable words can even predispose audiences to the acceptability of a case.

Those who study tone typically use critical tools, and we will use them as well. But we will also do something else. We will use content analysis to identify specific lexical fields and to assess their relative usage. Operationally, content analysis involves (1) formulating clear ideational or linguistic categories, (2) establishing dependable definitions of those categories, (3) training coders to identify their occurrences in a large number of texts, and then (4) comparing their usage.

Social scientists have used these techniques before when studying political tone. Kaid (2004) has monitored the growth of negative political commercials in the U.S., and Ansolabehere and Iyengar (1995, p. 9) have plowed similar ground, concluding, rather ominously, that "attack advertising actually suppresses voter turnout." Subsequent studies have been less sure about that conclusion, although scholars do agree that campaigns routinely go negative toward the end of the election season (Ridout & Franz, 2008). Other scholars have found that candidates are just as likely to go negative online as when using traditional media (Druckman, Kifer & Parkin, 2010). While useful, such studies often treat tone dichotomously—as either positive or negative—and that can miss the complexity of the texts being studied.

A similar charge can be made of studies examining news bias, one of which concludes that "network news coverage of incumbent presidents is decidedly negative" (Eshbaugh-Soha, 2010, p. 121), a finding that holds for local newspapers as well. Like campaign ads, political journalism can have powerful effects. Too much negative news can produce "agenda-setting effects" (by emphasizing ideas that voters might not have thought of otherwise) as well as "priming effects" (by training voters to be on the lookout for ideas helpful or unhelpful to the party in power). As Tamir

Sheafer (2007, p. 26) explains, the news media "attach an evaluative tone
(i.e., positive, negative, or neutral) to objects or issues" which produces
spillover effects on electoral mood. While many believe they can rise
above the news and look at things objectively, all tones have their consequences—some obvious, some subtle, and some not yet identified.

Studies of tone are often based on *lexical layering*, which trades on
four key assumptions: (1) Families of words have their own distinctive
valence but become mutually implicative when combined; (2) tone becomes more identifiable when word families are commingled; (3) tone becomes more forceful when these families are repeatedly commingled; and
(4) lexical layering explains differences among rhetorical genres—how a
poem can be distinguished from a movie script, for example (Ishizaki &
Kaufer, 2012). As a result of lexical layering, most of us become instinctive
students of tone; we depend on those instincts each day.

Estimating Tone   Using one word to do two much ??

If the foregoing has established one thing it is this: Tone is irrepressible
but often mysterious.[3] People naturally sense its presence but struggle to
explain it. So, for example, a Boston headline recently spotted "A New
Political Tone in Southie" and described it as follows:

> Think of it as South Boston's version of a rare lunar eclipse, something that
> happens only once or twice in a generation. A state rep's seat opens unex-
> pectedly and five young, earnest neophytes (four Democrats, one Republican)
> scramble to fill the void and seize an opportunity. In a place where campaign-
> ing has often been a full contact sport, the spirited quest for the 4th Suffolk
> District has been unusual for its civility. Campaign signs have remained in
> place. Debates have been seriously cordial affairs, which only seems to remind
> everyone that this crop of candidates—born after busing, raised in the Internet
> age, college educated and acutely aware of the change that has swept over the
> neighborhood—is pursuing an ancient tradition in a new way. (Gelzinis, 2010)

Context

What sort of tone is being described here? The list is a long one: ear-
nestness, entrepreneurism, novelty, awareness, respectfulness, cordi-
ality, civility. The story goes on to describe a new crop of pols eager to
serve the people, candidates who reject the pugilism of their forebears.
A reader senses that the reporter has spotted something important here

even though the scribe neither defines his terms nor specifies the norms from which the "new" tone allegedly diverges. Instead, he provides examples—one candidate is said to be committed to "keeping South Boston family friendly" while another tells young people that "anything is possible if you're willing to try." These examples are hopelessly vague but somehow the story makes sense, the kind of mysterious sense that "tone" often makes to everyday news consumers.

We try to remove some of the mystery in this book by examining how political institutions affect a given speaker's tone and how his or her personal circumstances change it as well. When doing so, we make this fundamental assumption: *that tone is the product of (1) individual word choices that (2) cumulatively build up (3) to produce patterned expectations (4) telling an audience something important (5) about the author's outlook on things.*

We operationalize this assumption by using computer-assisted text analysis (CATA), an approach that is now being used to do social-network analysis, relational and cluster modeling, and qualitative data mining. These techniques also have practical uses: to filter spam mail, to manage medical records, to analyze consumers' sentiments, to monitor social conflict, and even to spot incipient terrorism (Zhu, 2010). Other scholars have used these methods to detect emergent policy changes (Benoit, Laver & Mikhaylov, 2009), to classify congressional speeches by topic (Purpura & Hillard, 2006; Quinn et al., 2010), and to examine new political ideologies (Thomas , Pang & Lee, 2006; Diermeier et al., 2007). The blogosphere is also ripe for such techniques. One author, for example, tracked "inbound" and "outbound" links to see if conservative bloggers have become more prominent (Ackland, 2005), while Hargittai, Gallo, and Kane (2008) took the opposite tack to see whether the World Wide Web has increased cross-ideological discussion. One of the more intriguing uses of automated content analysis is Matthew Hindman's *Myth of Digital Democracy* (2008), which identified the existence of a "googlearchy" that permits a small but powerful set of elites to dominate political discussion.

While useful, many of these approaches operate rather remotely from the text itself, concentrating on who said what to whom rather than on how they said it. Here, in contrast, we examine the lexical building blocks of political discourse. We assume that when a speaker chooses one word over another (consciously or unconsciously), both cognitive and affective resources are being drawn upon. And when certain groupings of words are deployed, we further assume, even more complex matters come into play.

Others disagree. Some computational linguists treat word choice as the least consequential decision made during encoding, stressing instead a passage's morphology, syntax, prosody, or psycholinguistic properties. But understanding why some words are preferred over others ("economical" vs. "cheap"), why certain words are never used ("cunctator"), why other words are considered nonpareil (such as "nonpareil"), why some words come ("sexting") and why some words go ("square")—opens up worlds enough for the present authors. Indeed, it is because word choice is so often underestimated that we find it especially intriguing. Feeling superior to someone, after all, reduces our surveillance of that individual and that gives them special advantage over us. Con artists and pickpockets have understood this principle for centuries: becoming dependent on another reduces your autonomy and increases their authority over you as well as your ability to maneuver.

In this connection, we make several assumptions: (1) Speakers rarely monitor their individual lexical decisions, (2) they have no ability at all to monitor lexical *patterns*, (3) speakers think they have considerable control over such matters, and therefore (4) they invite the enterprising researcher to study what they have deemed unworthy. These propositions hold with special force in the political world, where speechwriters, advertising executives, campaign consultants, and politicians see themselves as verbal experts. They pore over the details of a press release on a touchy subject, relying heavily on lay theories of language ("'litigate' sounds better than 'sue'") even though they could not defend their assumptions if asked to do so. While politics is a world of words, it is also a world of poorly understood words, poorly remembered words, and poorly theorized words.[4]

That is where computers come into the picture. Computers remember, ostensibly forever. Computers detect continuities and discontinuities. If properly coached, computers can track associations across semantic space, note situational changes (and changes within those changes), distinguish the characteristic word choices of one person from those of another. Computers can also detect the stabilities in language behavior, the things that never change.

The program being used in this study is DICTION 6.0 (www.diction-software.com) created by the first author and Craig C. Carroll. This is a multiplatform program written in Java that deploys some 10,000 search words in thirty-three word lists or dictionaries and that includes several calculated variables as well. None of the search terms is duplicated in these lists, which gives the user an unusually rich understanding of a text. The program also produces five master variables by combining (after standardization) the subaltern variables. The master variables were chosen intentionally, the assumption being that if only five questions could be asked of a given passage, these five would provide the most robust understanding. Based on an analysis of some 30,000 verbal texts, no statistically significant relationship exists among any of these master variables, meaning that each sheds unique light on the passage being examined.[5]

Figure 1.1 provides DICTION's complete variable structure. Although these particular instantiations are the authors' own, each master variable was stimulated by the work of others, and each is particularly well suited to the study of American politics, as numerous investigations have shown (Lim, 2008; Hamilton, 2003; Patterson, 2002). **Certainty**, for example, derives from the work of the general semanticists, particularly Wendell Johnson (1946), who studied how language becomes rigid and what happens as a result. Definitionally, Certainty indicates resoluteness, inflexibility, and completeness and a tendency to speak ex cathedra. **Optimism**, language endorsing some person, group, concept, or event or highlighting their positive entailments, was inspired by James David Barber's *Presidential Character* (1992). Optimism, for Barber, was a key dimension

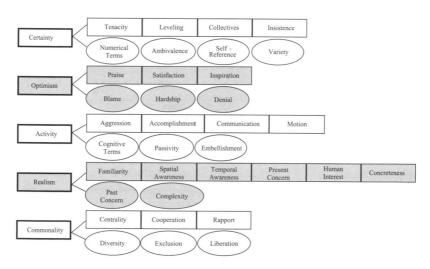

FIGURE 1.1 Constructed variables for DICTION analysis.

for understanding political personality, although Barber himself used the construct more anecdotally than empirically. Barber was also concerned with **Activity**, although DICTION's development on this dimension is more indebted to the work of Osgood, Suci, and Tannenbaum (1957). Active language features movement, change, the implementation of ideas and the avoidance of inertia and helps distinguish reflective from nonreflective texts.

A fourth dimension is **Realism**, language describing tangible, immediate, recognizable matters that affect people's everyday lives. This dimension taps the pragmatism John Dewey (1954) found endemic to Western experience. Finally, **Commonality**, language highlighting the agreed-upon values of a group and rejecting idiosyncratic modes of engagement, draws on the social theorizing of Amitai Etzioni (1993) and Robert Bellah (Bellah et al., 1991), although neither scholar was concerned with verbal behaviors per se.

Other automated content analytic systems exist but DICTION is unique in at least two ways: (1) its dictionaries are unusually exhaustive and (2) it provides norms for all the data it processes, thereby letting a user compare a given passage to some forty genres (e.g., speeches, news coverage, advertisements, citizen commentary, religious sermons, corporate reports, theater scripts, television drama). Perhaps as a result, DICTION has been used in a variety of disciplines, including journalism (Cho et al., 2003), management (Finkelstein, 1997), education (Graddy, 2004), sociology (Huffaker & Calvert, 2005), psychology (Harris & Gresch, 2010), child development (Collins & Vinicius, 2009), composition studies (Sands, 2002), accounting (Sydserff & Weetman, 2002), diplomacy (Bashor, 2004), leadership (Bligh, Kohles & Meindl, 2004; Feste, 2011), readership studies (Collins et al., 2004), religion (Eidenmuller, 2002), law (Allison & Hunter, 2006), and political science (Crew & Lewis, 2011; Collier, 2006).

DICTION also lets scholars build their own dictionaries for specialized purposes. A user may construct up to ten such dictionaries (up to 200 words in length), which DICTION will then use in its search routines. We have used this capacity throughout the book, drawing especially on five custom dictionaries: (1) **Patriotic terms** (*homeland, justice, liberty, pilgrims*, etc.), (2) **Party references** (*Democrats, Republican*, etc.), (3) **Voter references** (*constituents, electorate, citizenry*, etc.), (4) **Leader references** (*Adams, Lincoln, Roosevelt, Perot*, etc.), and (5) **Religious terms** (*doctrine, spiritual, heavenly, Sabbath*, etc.).

DICTION is ultimately no better than its basic premises, one of which is *the assumption of transposition* — that quantifying qualitative phenomena can be meaningful. At first this sounds heretical until one remembers that people constantly use mathematics to make judgments about others. A person who "gushes," for example, is one whose needless dilations are deemed obnoxious. Similarly, when we judge one person voluble and another taciturn we are making arithmetic judgments. Professional wordsmiths also rely on mathematical intuitions: the "arcane expression" is one with too much type for its token; the "common touch" derives from words lying at the center of the normal distribution; "rhetorical range" is exhibited by those who successfully adapt to social situations. In short, programs like DICTION depend on very human understandings of proportionality.

A related postulate is DICTION's *assumption of additivity* — that things increase in importance as they increase in number (e.g., that 10 uses of a term like *death* is twice as worrisome as 5 uses). There is a straightforward linearity to this assumption, even though everyday experience sometimes shows that *infrequent* appearance of a word or phrase is more important. If, for example, the mayor of an American city cursed but once during his monthly remarks to the city council, that fact would be headlined in the local tabloid, even if the good mayor also invoked the deity twenty-seven times. Because they are inherently more attracted to central tendencies than to outliers, that is, programs like DICTION would miss some of the news in the mayor's speech. But it would not miss all the news. It might note, for example, that sin captures the attention of the press at the precise ratio of 27:1.

The foregoing matters apply to all automated content analysis, but DICTION further makes an *assumption of semantic independence* by taking words out of context. Because DICTION breaks a text into its constituent features, it violates the text-as-received. Thus, the program cannot distinguish between a sentence like "the dog bit the man" and "the man bit the dog." For some, this is the program's fatal flaw. But by concentrating on the *similarities* in these two sentences, DICTION would note other things: that people take their dogs to the park rather than their microwave ovens; that dogs are more likely to be bitten by people today than, say, by mountain lions (as they might have a hundred years earlier); that man and dog are equally capable of biting, a token of their common mammalian status. By attending to these matters and not to the forensic aspects of the encounter, DICTION sheds light on domestic ecology, interspecies collaboration, and human compensatory behavior.

DICTION also assumes that context is evanescent, that context at Time 1 is different from context at Time 2. So, for example, the experience of watching a favorite movie at Christmas each year changes as we age: we notice things we hadn't noticed before; we are affected more deeply when watching it with grandchildren than when watching it alone. Each such encounter with the movie is a nonreplicating event; each new text comes nestled within a matrix of other texts.

Context is also deconstructive. When a politician argues that their words have been "taken out of context," they describe the human condition: Context vanishes the moment it comes into existence. From then on, people "infect" a text by the simple act of perceiving it selectively. They are "gist processors," say Brainerd and Reyna (1993), taking what they need and leaving the rest. They are the victims of "spreading activation," argue Boynton and Lodge (1994), inundated by associations suddenly triggered off in their minds. In other words, context is less important to an in-the-moment audience than to an after-the-fact analyst.

DICTION assumes that people listen for context but that they also listen for "lexical weight" when taking in a text, for a certain *amount* of assurance or vitriol. People do their own "dictionary look-ups" to simplify what they hear, to see if they have fallen into a novel or predictable situation. In other words, the right amount of patriotic or religious language can calm people's souls *no matter how those word families are distributed in the text*. This means that words in a text are affected not only by the words surrounding them but also by the "lexical histories" to which they are heirs. So, for example, ethnic slurs are hurtful to people regardless of the context in which they are uttered.

DICTION is also completely transparent; it operationalizes everything it touches. It contains no mysteries; it finds what it searches for, nothing more and nothing less. That makes it somewhat more dependable than human coding. All too often, the human coder constructs a set of categories for a given research task, reports the findings, and then studies a new set of texts with yet another coding instrument, omitting the necessary step of replication. Because it uses invariant categories, a program like DICTION offers conceptual stability across studies, thereby providing a wide range of benefits to the student of verbal tone.

Some observers will criticize a program like DICTION because it stands so far away from a message, ignoring its nuances. But getting too close to a text can also be problematic. The "demand characteristics" of a powerful utterance can seduce the analyst as well as the audience. Who in 2012, for example, could inspect remarks by Fox's Bill O'Reilly without having their blood stirred (either positively or negatively)? A program like DICTION interrupts these natural forms of social identification by pushing *its* questions to the fore, by insisting that *its* verbal categories receive special consideration (versus those Mr. O'Reilly might prefer). By disrupting a text in these ways, DICTION can override its demand characteristics.

There are two great research traditions in textual analysis: (a) individual case studies and (b) cross-textual studies. DICTION research falls in the latter domain. It assumes that people's sensitivities to tone are shaped by their experiences with previous texts and that these discursive memories help them recontextualize all incoming messages. For these reasons, studies using DICTION depend heavily on normative data. When a contemporary American listens to Barack Obama, that is, he or she may be simultaneously relistening to Martin Luther King (because of Obama's inspirational capacity) or Jimmy Carter (because of Obama's occasional pedantry). This means that people use all they have to use when decoding a message, applying their personal histories-of-consumption to each new text/DICTION assumes that knowing one thing requires knowing another thing as well./

The data reported in this book depend heavily on this latter assumption. They derive from the Campaign Mapping Project conducted at the Annette Strauss Institute for Civic Life at the University of Texas at Austin since 1996. The project's goal has been to analyze campaign materials produced during U.S. presidential elections from 1948 to the present in a steady and consistent way. The project has three purposes: (1) to produce a comprehensive view of campaigns by bringing together many different political voices—the people, the candidates, and the press; (2) to develop an objective view of campaigns by producing results that can be verified by others; and (3) to develop a normative view of campaigns so that each campaign can be viewed in light of those that preceded and followed it.

Thus far, the project has collected and analyzed the following materials (in 500-word segments): (1) **campaign speeches** (*n* = 4,335 segments): formal remarks given by the major candidates between late July and early November of the campaign year, including nationally televised addresses as well as local stump speeches; (2) **policy speeches** (*n* = 2,174): remarks delivered from the Oval Office or in international settings, with a heavy oversampling from the presidency of George W. Bush; (3) **cam-**

paign debates (n = 907): all presidential debates between 1960 and the present, with each debate being segregated by speaker prior to analysis; (4) **political advertising** (n = 719): a sampling of major party and independent party ads broadcast over television; years include 1960 and 1976–2008; (5) **print coverage** (n = 11,037): feature and nonfeature stories from *The New York Times*, *The Washington Post*, *The Christian Science Monitor*, *Atlanta Constitution*, *Chicago Tribune*, *Los Angeles Times*, as well as AP and UPI syndicate stories; (6) **broadcast coverage** (n = 2,370): a sample of nightly newscasts produced during the 1980, 1988–2008 campaigns by the news bureaus of ABC, CBS, NBC, CNN, and PBS; (7) **letters to the editor** (n = 8,125): letters written to the editors of twelve small-city newspapers between 1948 and 2008;[6] (8) **contrasting genre** (n = 3,296): a variety of oral and written, fictional and nonfictional texts (e.g., religious sermons, business reports, social movement speeches, Internet documents, novels and short-stories).

This book continues a fifteen-year project designed to capture the tonalities of American politics. While the project is ambitious, it has its limitations: it focuses on national rather than regional leaders and only on U.S. leaders at that; it ignores the visual aspects of contemporary political persuasion; it concentrates on "legacy" media (newspapers, television) rather than Web-based modalities like Facebook and Twitter; it ignores the day-to-day, interpersonal channels that determine so much in political life. Despite these shortcomings, constancy has been our ally. All of the data reported here are replicable, depend on the same operationalizations, and have been subjected to tests of statistical significance. Because verbal tone is such a complicated thing, we will take pains in the book not to overstate our findings, a special obligation when dealing with such a large dataset.

Without doubt, then, we walk a tightrope here when trying to bring scientific precision to a subtle phenomenon like tone. Is such an enterprise doomed from the start? Does the very concept of tone force us to stumble through the graveyard of vagueness? While tone is a formidable enemy, it is not impregnable. We are buoyed up by three unquestionable facts: (1) politicians use words to do things, (2) they use them in varying proportions, and (3) their audiences react to these deployments cognitively and socially.

But is counting things enough? No. We will not rely on numbers alone here but will give readers a feeling for the texts we have processed to show how powerful words can become when used collectively, seri-

What does counting have
to do w/ audience reaction ?
reception

ally. We will avoid divorcing ideas from language since a reified understanding of politics is no understanding at all. Above all, we will work
hard to uncover the social impressions created by the rhetorical patterns
identified.

Most important, we will remember that using a computer to do textual analysis has both strengths and weaknesses. Consider an analogy: the
case of two police officers in a midsized American city. Under the logic
of community policing, Officer Madrano has been assigned to jiggling
door handles and has gotten to know the shopkeepers on his beat over
the years. He knows when to be concerned that a light is still burning in
D'Ambrosio's meat market (a burglary? a late delivery?) or when an un-
latched door at Krasawski's repair shop means carelessness or trouble.
Madrano know his clients like the back of his hand.

Officer Harrigan knows few such people. He works the helicopter unit
and sees only rooftops and highways from above. The people on Madrano's beat are but specks to Harrigan—ants driving automobiles. But the
reverse is also true: Cast as he is in the middle of things, Madrano cannot
see how the interstate highway bisects the downtown corridor and thus
concentrates crime in one sector of the city. Unlike Harrigan, Madrano
cannot see how differential lighting patterns (easily seen from the air)
make some areas ripe for crime or why police chases wind up on the east
side of town because of its proximity to the warehouse district. Harrigan
knows his city only from a distance but that very distance lets him see *relationships*.

DICTION is Harrigan's program. It does not know Madrano's city as
Harrigan knows it; it only knows the city as Madrano does *not* know it.
Because computer-aided text analysis cannot be dazzled by context, by
close-up observations, it sees what nearsightedness occludes. DICTION
reveals things in the large and therefore highlights structural regularities.
In hovering above a text as it does, DICTION makes the text "strange"
(as the phenomenologists might say), shaking an observer out of the false
comfort afforded by premature familiarity with a text. DICTION quanti-
fies what others do not think to quantify and therefore points up the true-
but-not-noticed.

The assumption here is that, for too many years, we have known
American politics only from Madrano's point of view—up close and
personal. But knowledge must be arrived at pluralistically. For progress
to be made, old categories must be reexamined, old orthodoxies questioned, and new ways of seeing things imagined. We will count words in

this book because words are sent to voters in specific quantities and that must mean something. It is time, we feel, to become acquainted with Harrigan's city.

Tone at Work

A remarkable thing happened at 11 p.m. on Wednesday, April 6, 2011. Two men walked in tandem to a microphone stationed outside the White House and said nothing. Their nothing became news. The two men, Senate majority leader Harry Reid and House speaker John Boehner, had been trying all day to hash out a budget agreement to avert a government shutdown. It took them roughly thirty seconds to tell the Washington scribes that a deal had not been reached; then the press supplied the news: "I hear they actually get along well in private," observed one reporter. "One senses they really want to make this work," said another. "They seemed incredibly earnest," chimed in a third. When hard news becomes scarce, that is, tone was relied on for soft news. Tone—Harry Reid's shy demurrals, John Boehner's measured words, the two leaders' presumed mutuality—was the only news available on that April evening, but that was news enough for many anxious Americans.

Our book's thesis is this: *Political tone addresses problems that cannot be addressed by other means.* No deal brokered yet? Tell reporters that ... affably. No deal brokered yet? Use the future rather than the present tense. No deal brokered yet? Issue a statement featuring possibilities. An old truism in politics is that there is never enough money or votes to go around. Language, in contrast, is inexhaustible, so this book makes a three-part argument: (1) political tone provides a handy barometer of how politicians cope with changing circumstances; (2) political tone is a subtle yet tangible force that can be assessed scientifically and heuristically; and (3) political tone helps explain voters' intuitive, often inchoate, reactions to political events. We will treat tone as that which mysteriously "leaks out" of a text to reflect a speaker's take on things. We believe that word choice—singly, collectively—is partly responsible for this leakage.

We operate here much as Sherlock Holmes did when studying the shoes people wore. Holmes noticed that personality was often revealed in an individual's footwear—unpolished shoes meant a depressed person, scuffed shoes revealed a man in a perpetual hurry, shoes worn at the heel betrayed a woman down on her luck. Holmes knew that attending to just *one* thing is helpful since attending to a great many things can confuse or mislead. By attending to word choice and nothing else—not syntax, not intonation, not periodicity—we therefore shut our eyes to the "full behavioral display" of human interaction, steeling ourselves against the forces that bedazzled Dr. Watson but that Holmes cleverly ignored. The hedgehog, not the fox, will be our guide here.

This book acknowledges that people sense they know others but often cannot say how or why. "Trust but verify your impressions" will be our motto as we treat people's everyday perceptions *as data* and then look for ways of explaining those perceptions. This is a hazardous business but no more hazardous than, say, imagining that a public opinion poll tells us what lies in the human heart or that a laboratory experiment predicts real world events perfectly. Tone is a slippery concept but no slipperier than "cognitive dissonance" or "regime realignment" or the other "thick constructs" that scholars use to understand political life.

Political Tone follows a problem-solution format. We concentrate here on eight forces that operate in the political world—ambition, ideology, institutions, and the like—forces that challenge the nation's leaders and that affect their rhetoric. If it were not for these forces, all political discourse would sound identical and all politicians would steer to the same safe harbors. But circumstances determine everything in politics. New tensions break out, stubborn problems reappear, fresh political personalities demand attention. Politicians react to these developments, and this book describes what happens as a result.

Chapter 2, for example, asks a basic question: what distinguishes establishment politics in the United States? Our answer is that the sheer diversity of the United States becomes impressed on its leaders' rhetoric, causing it to be vague at times, indistinct at other times, but "elevated" at all times. American politicians also seek the middle ground of language, not because they are afraid to take strong stands (although many are), but because linguistic boldness can unseat traditional power relations. As a result, the standard rhetorical formula in the U.S. is often this: Let us come together but remain slightly invisible to one another as well.

The American story of partisanship has been odd from the beginning. On the basis of size and diversity alone, the U.S. could have become a nation that made Italian politics seem monolithic. But it did not. Only two major parties resulted and that is a curious thing, perhaps even a miraculous thing. While American voters are habitually willing to explain their worldviews in considerable detail, politicians often trim the edges off their partisanship. Chapter 3 acknowledges the importance of party politics but complicates the picture by showing how partisanship is as much a cultural as a political story in the United States.

Chapter 4 identifies the impress of modernity on American culture, showing what can be learned by paying attention to "time" and "space" words. That may seem like a trivial thing to do but, we shall argue, the mature presidency of George W. Bush and the jejune presidency of Barack Obama differed dramatically on the space-time continuum, thereby revealing a contrasting physics. Bush clung to an older "spatial imaginary" where certain stabilities were instantiated from the beginning and that became the backdrop for all later discussions. Obama's world is a more dynamic place where ideas, and allegiances, move with warp speed. In struggling with modernity as they do, Messrs. Bush and Obama tell a story that is larger than both of them.

Human institutions also affect what happens in politics. During the last two hundred years, for example, the presidency became increasingly formalized even as other institutions came on line, including the judiciary, Congress, the federal bureaucracy, the business sector, and the mass media, all of which sought political advantage. Chapter 5 shows how recent American presidents have dealt with these competing forces, not by confronting them directly but by circumnavigating them rhetorically. Thus, while Ronald Reagan knew that few Americans wanted to hear about politics on Saturday mornings, he sought them out nonetheless. His "end-run" on weekends have since become a political staple, and chapter 5 explains why.

While part 2 looks at broad-based societal forces, part 3 examines idiosyncratic factors, analyzing how four contemporary politicians played the hands dealt to them. Nobody dealt himself a worse hand than Bill Clinton when pursuing a dalliance with a certain young woman partial to berets. Many thought that the Monica Lewinsky scandal would mean the end of the Clinton presidency but, as we show in chapter 6, the president took his lumps and then, through the magic of persuasion, turned that scandal into just another road marker on a spirited political journey.

George W. Bush and Bill Clinton could not have been more different, and their political circumstances differed as well. We show in chapter 7 how President Bush gave the lie to one of the most popular stereotypes about him—that he was an unthinking ideologue—and we show across an enormous database just how wrong that perception was. How was it possible, we ask, for Bush to be so ideological and yet never fully trusted

by the American Right? It was Bush's rhetoric that created those perceptions, revealing him to be a far more nuanced politician than traditionally assumed. His rhetoric emerged from a cauldron of turmoil and yet
his appearance suggested an equanimity of spirit, a finding that will surprise many.

Chapters 8 and 9 focus on the very different problems confronted by
Barack Obama and Sarah Palin, a political odd couple. Obama, we will
show, ran a campaign in 2008 distinguished by a revolutionary political
tone—he was forthcoming about the difficulties confronting the American
people but embraced them in starkly communal ways. In essence, he took
his greatest liability—his inexperience in national politics—and combined it with his signal strength—that of a talented community activist—
and produced a confection suitable to the nation's electorate. He somewhat forsook that tone when taking office, however, and we show what
that cost him in the eyes of the American voter.

Sarah Palin had neither Barack Obama's intellectual sophistication
nor his broad political vision. But she had one thing that all politicians
have and she had it in spades: overweening ambition. She also had an un-
disciplined mind and that would normally sink one's ship. But not Palin's.
She had no political compass, but she had derring-do and an infectious
personality. Her political trajectory may have been unsteady but people
found in her a bold accessibility rarely found in political circles. No less an
authority than Elvis Presley once declared ambition to be "a dream with
a V8 engine." The former governor of Alaska epitomizes that dream, that
engine.

Overall, then, this book constitutes basic research. We present no overarching theory of discourse and we do no model building. Our work is
descriptive and we operate in a space somewhere between rigorous hypothesis testing and textual description. We turn words into numbers but
we use rich textual examples throughout. In doing so, we concentrate not
on the substance of politics—on what was said, on the stated arguments—
but on the tone of politics—on how what was said was said.

Conclusion

Many social scientists would willingly cede all discussions of tone to the
literary critics. But politics will not allow such a retreat: The Tea Party is
formed. Donald Trump attracts attention. Smart phones start a rebellion

in the Middle East. A half-dozen rebellions. Bobby Jindal, the young governor of Louisiana, is declared a savant today, a has-been tomorrow. Jesse Ventura wrestles; Jesse Ventura governs; Jesse Ventura shills for a sports book. And there is more: consultant Frank Luntz is declared brilliant for coining the term "death taxes," female candidates are told to "man up" on the campaign trail, Joe Biden whispers that a new law is a "big fucking deal" on national television. Politicians, words, politicians who make words, words that make news. An endless cycle.

From one point of view, language is irrelevant to governance. Pure politics, raw politics, admits to nothing but power: military power, financial power, technological power. Compared to these forces, language seems but an afterthought, an empty shell. But if that were true, why would scholars estimate that 80% of the growth in the White House staff over the years has produced not more policy experts but the most sophisticated message machine in human history? Political language now attends power and, sometimes, as with threats or promises or diplomacy, it becomes power. Words can also become a miracle, a healing, as when the Twin Towers fell or when the tsunami hits. This book takes all of these words seriously because, in the short run and in the long run, words are us.

PART II
Societal Forces

CHAPTER TWO

Diversity and the Accommodating Tone

Hating politics is a storied American pastime. This is really quite re-markable, given the nation's standing as the first mass democracy and its durability as a functioning political state. And yet denouncing politicians is a perennial. Here are but a few examples:

- "Frankly, I'm fed up with politicians in Washington lecturing the rest of us about 'family values.' Our families have values but our Government doesn't."
- "We feel we have lost control of our own government, that it has become our master instead of our servant, that we are being ruled by special interests, and by politicians who don't care about us."
- "Social Security has been exploited by politicians long enough. It is time to stop frightening seniors."
- "Every day, the American people are being deceived by politicians who want their votes and nothing more."
- "Is it any wonder that the American people are losing faith in their politicians?"[1]

Harsh words. But most remarkably, the foregoing statements were uttered by men running for the highest office in the land: Bill Clinton, Jimmy Carter, George W. Bush, Barry Goldwater, and John Anderson. Like Groucho Marx, they seem aghast at the thought of joining any club that would have them. Despite their misgivings, three of their applications were accepted. So why the denunciations? What made them think that doling out such opprobrium would get them elected? Do teachers, law-yers, or architects savage their own kind as a matter of course? Mugging an institution in order to save it? Only in politics.

Several things are interesting about these attacks: (1) they constitute a trope deeply rooted in American culture; (2) they now serve as a kind of lingua franca, a way for ordinary voters to make connections with one another; (3) the press—the only profession protected by a Constitutional amendment—routinely leads these attacks; (4) these attacks have become a hardy form of popular entertainment; (5) nobody seems to worry much about the cultural costs of these denunciations.[2]

Wags of all stripes have lambasted politics throughout Western history, and reading these deconstructions can be instructive. Almost always, they reveal a mournful idealist whose basic claim is that "politics is too." Too powerful, too impotent. Too doctrinaire, too tractable. Too inclusive, too exclusionary. As we see in table 2.1, the criticisms made of politics reveal what people aspire to in a civil society but also what frustrates them about living there. Politics is derided in Table 2.1 for being too slow or too fast (Utility), too self-serving or banal (Virtue), or for being irresponsibly transactional (Reciprocity). Although politics is an economic enterprise—a mechanism for deciding who gets what from whom at what cost—it also depends on collective agreements about some larger good (Affect). Most frustrating of all, politics takes on work that can never be finished (highways, health care, national security). Thus, its most indis-

TABLE 2.1 **Popular laments about politics.**

Dimension	Excessive	Insufficient
Utility	*Dominant*: "Politics is the skilled use of blunt objects." *(Lester B. Pearson, 1897–1972)*	*Dilatory*: "Politics is a strong and slow boring of hard boards." *(Max Weber, 1864–1920)*
Virtue	*Pretentious*: "The end move in politics is always to pick up a gun." *(R. Buckminster Fuller, 1896–1983)*	*Devious*: "Politics—a strife of interests masquerading as a contest of principles." *(Ambrose Bierce, 1842–1913)*
Reciprocity	*Vulgar*: "It has been said that politics is the second oldest profession. I have learned that it bears a striking resemblance to the first." *(Ronald Reagan, 1911–2004)*	*Arrogant*: "Politics are now nothing more than a means of rising in the world." *(Samuel Johnson, 1709–1784)*
Affect	*Glib*: "Politics is the entertainment branch of industry." *(Frank Zappa, 1940–1993)*	*Hostile*: "Politics, as a practice, whatever its professions, has always been the systematic organization of hatreds." *(Henry Adams, 1838–1918)*
Flexibility	*Flaccid*: "The choice in politics isn't usually between black and white. It's between two horrible shades of gray." *(Peter [Lord] Thorneycroft, 1909–1994)*	*Rigid*: "Politics is the art of preventing people from taking part in affairs which properly concern them." *(Paul Valéry, 1871–1945)*

or "government"

pensable features—Adaptation, Negotiation, Diplomacy—leave a bad taste in the mouth.

These critiques tell us something even more important—that people recognize politics when they hear it. But *how* do they distinguish politics from literature, religion, biology, or football? To laugh shrewdly at something, after all, requires that we know it in an intimate, recoverable way. But what is it that we know? Do political leaders give off cues that distinguish them from other social actors? Does establishment politics produce unique discursive markers that set it apart from other occupations or lifestyles? If so, do these markers help explain why politics upsets so many of us and why even politicians feel obliged to denounce their own profession?

Most Americans can intuitively explain what makes politics "political." They can tell you that politics addresses matters obliquely rather than head-on. They can tell you that politicians circumlocute, that they talk around a topic rather than confront it head-on. And they can tell you that politicians constantly claim what Walker Gibson (1966) calls "unearned familiarity," a coziness not warranted by their existing relationships with voters. But while most Americans can tell you such things, they cannot tell you how they know what they know. Heretofore, scholars have only done a bit better.

We try to improve on those conditions here by comparing the essential features of political messages to a variety of other texts, a project begun some years ago with a more modest dataset (Hart, 2000). Based on DICTION analyses of some 30,000 passages, we will show how political messages distinguish themselves from other texts—press reports, social activism, citizens' communications, entertainment fora, etc. We report that politics is a proletarian activity, constantly in search of the average voter. We find further that politics constantly denies itself, transcending quotidian matters in a search for grander purposes. We also find that politics produces a restless text, one that resists narrow agendas to motivate a complex polity. The geometry of politics has many angles and that makes it easy to satirize. But it also deals with life and death, and that makes it what it is—charming, irritating, inspiring, frustrating, and all the other present participles in the English language.

Our overall argument is this: establishment politics in the U.S. is especially accommodating because the nation is haunted by its diversity. How could it be otherwise in a country with 330 million people, a land mass

US — exclusionary —

forty times that of the United Kingdom, a once-Christian nation gone increasingly Muslim, a place where 90% of the people have only 30% of
the wealth, a country getting older and younger at the same time, more
Asian and Hispanic as well? "We Americans were not what we were," observes Samuel P. Huntington (2004, p. 11). Our "imagined collectivities"
have shrunk and our "notions of structure and power" have thinned out
as well, says Daniel Rodgers (2011, p. 3). Americans increasingly "belittle
unum" and "glorify *pluribus*," says Arthur Schlesinger (1998, p. 21), and
then there is the raw politics itself: "On the right and the left, mulling bitter struggles over abortion, politics, and race, people voiced concern that a
certain testiness, and beyond, even fragmentation, had come to afflict our
national life" (Rieder, 2003, p. 1). Out of all this can a functioning polity
arise? Only with rhetoric, we argue here.

Reducing Distance

Politics is a natural thing but it is rarely treated as such. More often, it is
seen as an alien thing, an intrusion into the ordinary world of ordinary
Americans. For most people, politics comes from another place and those
who speak it speak a foreign tongue. Seated at a bar, in a blue-collar section of town, a fellow would be taking his life in his hands to speak of a
"great and good city," of a people "mourned but not forgotten," of jobs
"beckoning for the willing and the committed." This is language spoken
from a perch, language that sees far and wide but that is removed from
the workaday world.

Anyone who speaks in public, of course, must go beyond the vernac-
ular. Public words must suffice for all and, once spoken, they cannot be
recalled. Once spoken, they also admit to a gaggle of interpretations
and counterinterpretations. For its part, politics must address the present moment as well as many moments to come, only some of which can
be anticipated. Politics becomes orotund as a result—language in the
large—which is not to say that it becomes poetic. It is, instead, eminently
ordinary. As we have said earlier: "Even being born is a proto-political
act: We are named and foot-printed and then registered in City Hall.
Eating is a political act, and so we have a Department of Agriculture to
feed us and a Food and Drug Administration to feed us safely. Breathing
is a political act, and so the Environmental Protection Agency watches
over us. Dying is a political act, and so our town mortuaries are in-

spected annually. Politics envelops us from cradle to grave" (Hart et al., 2005, p. 22).

And yet . . . there is distance. There is distance between leader and followers, between now and then, between here and there, between haves and have-nots. There is psychic distance as well: Politics is ultimately a place of mystery. Even with stringent rules governing transparency and with open-records laws, everything cannot be known by everyone in a large and heterogeneous society. Not surprisingly, such distance breeds distrust. "Whenever a man has cast a longing eye on" public office, Thomas Jefferson once declared (2009, p. 70), "a rottenness begins in his conduct." Abraham Lincoln, too, warned of "men who have interests aside from the interests of the people" and who are, as a result, "at least one long step removed from honest men" (Sandburg, 1954, p. 51). For Jefferson, political distance was an ocular thing and, for Lincoln, a horizontal thing. For Mark Twain, its vertical qualities foretold its downfall: "History has tried hard to teach us that we can't have good government under politicians. Now, to go and stick one at the very head of the government couldn't be wise" (Scharnhorst, 2006, p. 6).

Because of its extraordinary land mass, these issues of distance have been especially important in the United States and have been exacerbated in recent years by a nation gone digital, by an increasingly "managed" citizenry (Howard, 2005). While some scholars (Owen & Davis, 1998) see possibilities of bridging the divide between leader and led via the new social media, little evidence of that result has appeared to date (Pew Research Center, 2010). As Russell Dalton (2004, p. 27) has argued, "The mass of evidence thus demonstrates that the American public has become increasingly skeptical and distrustful of the politicians who lead them." A Gallup poll only adds to those concerns, concluding that "Americans continue to have more trust in themselves to make judgments under the country's democratic system than they do in the men and women who are in political life, with 69% of Americans expressing 'a great deal' or 'a fair amount' of trust in the former, and 47% in the latter" (Newport, 2010).

In many ways, these results were foreordained because the United States has always been what Benedict Anderson calls an "imagined nation." As Anderson (1983, p. 6) notes, "Members of even the smallest nation will never know most of their fellow members, meet them, or even hear of them, yet in the minds of each lives the image of their communion," and that effect has been magnified a thousand times since 1776. As a result, the U.S. is now one of the most imagined of all nations.

Deprived of a shared religion or ethnicity, it had to confront its own im-
possibility right from the start. As the nation grew, it lost its land-based
contiguities and came to depend on ideas to keep it together. "The
rhetoric of American identity," says Beasley (2004, p. 28), was ultimately
grounded in "a shared way of thinking" and not in the geo-centricity that
had let its European counterparts thrive. Distance. A hobgoblin in the
U.S. right from the start.

The solution? To speak the American people into being and to do so
constantly, fervently. A government of the people. The hope of the free
world. One nation under God. These are trite phrases, which is to say they
are oft repeated, which is to say they no doubt serve some great purpose.
But what? Political consultant Robert Shrum once warned John McCain
against "politicizing" Hurricane Gustav in 2008, and to put the "political
rhetoric aside" (Baker, 2008, para. 15), but that was like asking a fish to
fly. Given Americans' distances from one another, a natural disaster helps
them come together, to reinforce a sense of fellow-feeling. Americans depend on politicians for a sense of shared identity, says Stanley Renshon
(2001), because things—iPads, the New York Yankees—cannot alone suffice. A large population with vast economic gradations and with theolo-
gies that often mix poorly presents an unending sociological challenge. It
takes a politician to help a first-generation Cuban-American feel kinship
with a Methodist farmer in Kansas. Distance. Still a hobgoblin, two hundred years later.

One way of bridging these distances is quite plain: Politicians try to
"flatten the hierarchy" between them and the American people. There is
more than one irony here since American politicians are almost always
white (Terkildsen, 1993), male (Sanbonmatsu, 2002), wealthy (Borchert &
Zeiss, 2004; Mitchell, 1959) and better educated than the electorate they
serve (Emler & Frazer, 1999). These demographic differences cannot be
easily eradicated (except, perhaps, via patient political recruitment), so
American politicians turn to discursive strategies: *They become average.*
At first this sounds heretical since Americans hate to think of themselves
as average. Indeed, they think of themselves as special, which is why one
newsmagazine found it newsworthy to report in 2011 that Barack Obama
had referred to "American exceptionalism" more often than that noted
exceptionalist, George W. Bush (Schlesinger, 2011).

But the American people are also attracted to averageness. As Anna
Creadick (2010) reports in her fascinating book, *Perfectly Average*, Americans often yearn for normality; this was especially the case during the tu-

mult following World War II. "Between 1943 and 1963," says Creadick (p. 143), normality "functioned as a powerful epistemological category through which to measure and define American life." The author traces this search for averageness from notions about the human body to citizen character itself, from raw economic desires to sociological affinities. But she also reports profound philosophical questions about this quest for the middle way: "The painful irony was that for all Americans normality proved to be not only highly desirable but also completely beyond reach, no matter how close they seemed. Normality presented an impossible combination of the typical and the ideal: to achieve it, one would have to become perfectly average" (p. 2).

Being normal was a key cultural concept in mid-twentieth century America, but the nation also had other flirtations. The countercultural movements of the 1960s and 70s pointed up alternatives, as did the civil rights movement and the women's movement, not to mention a steady barrage of edgy social fashions, televised awards shows, and an ample supply of showboating athletes. But all of these alternatives have been met with sharp, often loud, criticisms from the hoi polloi. And when change did come, as it inevitably must in a dynamic, hard-charging economy like the United States, Americans quickly declared their new inventions (the radio, the television, the smart phone) to be the new normal, so powerful was their need to domesticate the exotic.

U.S. politicians have long understood such matters. We noticed that tendency in earlier research when discovering that winning presidential candidates were significantly more likely to approach the linguistic mean than were losing candidates, a rule to which there were few exceptions (Hart, 2000). What might this mean for politics writ large? Research by Schutz (1995) reports that politicians seek a linguistic midpoint between entertainers and policy experts in order to balance their needs for visibility and sociality. Similarly, Doerfel and Connaughton (2009) find that politicians hover near the center of their "semantic networks," with "peripheral" matters almost always being abandoned by winning candidates. In a study covering a wide array of nations, Anderson (2007, p. 21) concludes that using "discourse that is ordinary at least to a large number of citizens" is crucial to achieving political harmony, even in societies harboring great ethnic and religious diversity.

To test this "man of the people" hypothesis, we developed a Normality Index by rewarding scores lying closest to the mean and penalizing scores as they successively departed from the mean. We performed these calcu-

lations for all forty one of DICTION's variables, including its thirty-three dictionaries, its two calculated scores (Variety and Complexity), and its five customized dictionaries (Patriotic Terms, Party References, Voter References, Leader References, Religious Terms). For each variable, we assigned an integer value of 5 to any score lying within ±½ standard deviation from the mean, of 4 to a score lying within the next ½ standard deviation, and so forth until an integer of 1 was recorded for any score departing from the mean by two standard deviations or more. This resulted in a mean Normality score of 150, with a standard deviation of 10.9 and a range from 41 to 205 (for the 21,968 passages examined in this phase of the study, 25% of which were political texts). While this is a rough-hewn measure, it proved a handy way of identifying textual idiosyncrasies.

For what it is worth, John Anderson delivered the most "normal" speech in our sample (with a Normality score of 185) during the last sixty years. His remarks were, as one might expect, unremarkable. They sounded perfectly average, which is to say they sounded perfectly political:

> In recent years some Americans have concluded that our greatest days are behind us and that we must reconcile ourselves to diplomatic and economic decline. I disagree, and so do most of the Americans I have met during the year I have spent campaigning for President. To be sure, they are weary of bad government, but they are filled with ideas, with energy, and with the hope for a better future. They are willing to sacrifice to gain that future. All they want is a government that presents them with a clear, believable program for the future, that enables them to save and to plan with confidence, that encourages innovation and risk-taking, that reduces regulation, and liberates their energies. This is the kind of government my administration will endeavor to give them. (Anderson, 1980, September 11)

Nothing about Anderson's remarks calls attention to itself. No flights of fancy here, no extended metaphors. His speech crawls to its conclusions. It is banal, devoid of personality. That was not Bob Dole's tone. Dole produced the lowest score in our sample (112) during a speech he gave in Grand Blanc, Michigan, on October 22, 1996. Dole was not one to beat around the bush, a trait made amply apparent in his introduction:

> And the road to the White House runs through Michigan. We're going to carry this state on November 5th. You wait and see. And I want to welcome all of you here today to the Bill Clinton retirement party. Thanks for coming out.

And obviously I'd be proud to be in the home of the Bobcats. Bobcat, keep that in mind. We've never had a Bob—uh, oh, must be another precinct. We've never had a Bob in the White House. Don't you think it's time. Yes, right. We do have a cat in the White House, Socks. But we don't have a Bob in the White House.

When getting into the meat of his speech, Dole sounded consummately Republican—less regulation, more free enterprise—but always with his own, syncopated Doleisms. His tone calls attention to itself—pleasantly, to be sure—which is why he was beloved in many circles. During the conclusion of his speech, Dole works against the grain once more, making policy issues deeply personal:

> We had cut drug use in half when [Clinton] became president. Now it's doubled in the last 45 months. I promise you that in the first four years of our administration, we will cut drug use in half and protect some of the young people you see up here on the stand with me up here on the podium.
>
> And I would say to them—please don't start. If you've started, stop—whether it's drugs or alcohol or cigarettes or whatever. This is an opportunity for young people. You know, it's your life. It's your future. You're going to be the future of America. One of these days, somebody will be standing here running for public office—maybe right in the group up here. And they want to be able to look you in the eye and say I didn't do it. Just don't do it. Just don't do it. Just don't do it. And then we'll have a better future. (Dole, 1996, October 22)

Our data show that John Anderson, not Bob Dole, was the norm. We discovered that by comparing the Normality Indices of political texts to a variety of other genres. We were agnostic when launching this inquiry, treating political discourse as something of a "black box," so we threw our nets wide across diverse cultural offerings. The genres we examined included: (1) **Public Dialogue** ($n = 963$): interchanges found in political debates, theatre scripts, phone conversations, multi-authored internet chat, and problem-solving group discussions; (2) **Formal Speechmaking** ($n = 3,442$): segments from speeches delivered by political candidates, sitting presidents, social movement leaders, corporate executives, and mainstream religious leaders; (3) **Print News** ($n = 7,657$): news reports on a variety of topics including politics, technology, finance, science, and health; (4) **Television Fare** ($n = 1,550$): segments from nightly news shows during campaigns, popular product advertisements, as well as primetime come-

dies and dramas; (5) **Personal Expression** (6,403): letters to the editor in
twelve small-city newspapers, email correspondence produced in various
work settings, popular music lyrics, and wide-ranging poetry and verse;
(6) **Professional Commentary** (n = 424): newspaper editorials, philosophical essays, legal documents, and corporate reports; (7) **Blogs** (n =
370): single-author extracts from web logs focused on politics, entertainment, business, technology, or people's personal lives.

As we see in figure 2.1, whenever politics is contrasted to any of its discursive neighbors, something remarkable happens: Nothing remarkable.
Political speakers constantly look for everyday words to grapple with
everyday concerns.[3] Technical words, colorful words, convoluted words,
words with a wide sociolinguistic arc, are typically eschewed. Gone too
are introspective examinations, great gobs of breast-beating, experimental thoughts, ad hoc philosophizing, as well as facile words and things that
go bump in the night. In their place one finds distance-bridging words that
argue "I'm more like you than you think. I live in your world and you in
mine. Trust me, I'm no stranger."

In other words, we find that the popular stereotype of the politician-
as-alien is wrong. Figure 2.1 shows that it is not state actors alone who
tend toward the middle. Reporters reporting on politics (vs. science, finance, or technology) do so as well. So too do ordinary citizens when
writing their letters to the editor. So too do TV reporters and political
bloggers. *There is something about The Political that draws people to unadorned speech, to speech that accommodates others.* While some of the
differences seen in figure 2.1 are greater than others, the overall pattern
remains a pattern.

Our Normality Index is admittedly a blunt instrument. It is embarrassingly devoid of "content," attending only to who picks everyday words
and who does not. The great political orators of the past—the Lincolns,
Churchills, and Roosevelts—would be disadvantaged by our measure.
They were poets-of-the-public. Their words were meant to surprise an audience, especially when speaking on great occasions of state. But there are
many more moments in politics when sewer lines, health care, banking reform, and immigration laws are being discussed. Hence the normality. Reporters, being the wordsmiths they are, are dismayed by such stuff. They
instinctively tilt their ears toward the uncommon expression and hence
are drawn to the high art of a Winston Churchill and even the low art of
a Bob Dole. Because he so detested working from a script, Dole always
stood out on the campaign trail.

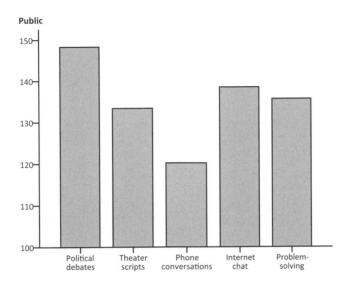

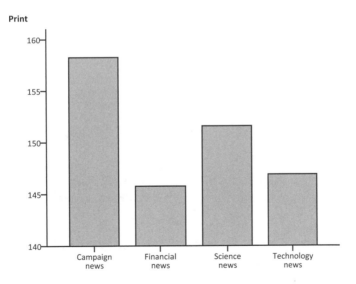

FIGURE 2.1 Normality scores for political texts vs. other genres.

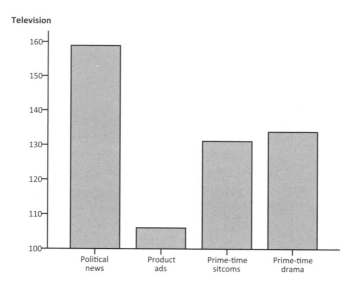

Television

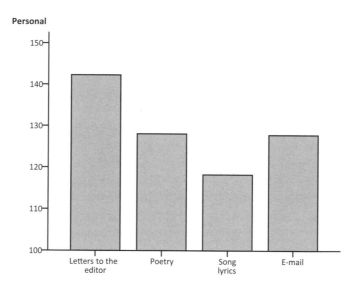

Personal

FIGURE 2.1 (continued)

Professional

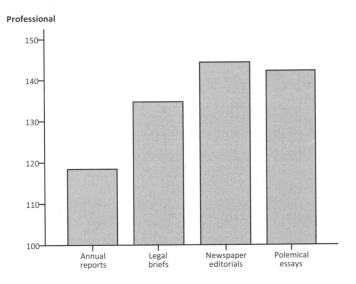

Online

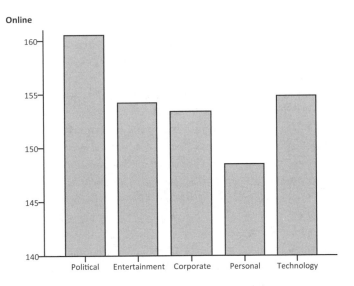

FIGURE 2.1 (continued)

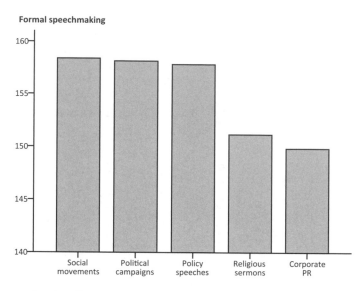

Formal speechmaking

FIGURE 2.1 (continued)

"plain" style

Dwight Eisenhower, another earnest Midwesterner, did not stand out. Although he was a writer of some repute, Ike's speeches rarely smelled of the lamp. They were workmanlike instead, unadorned and folksy. Over his eight years as president, Eisenhower spoke on countless occasions but, with the exception of his famed address on the military-industrial complex, none of his speeches haunts the national mind. It is hard for your authors to illustrate averageness because it is, well, average. One of Ike's campaign presentations when running for reelection in 1956 (Normality Index = 180) might suffice:

> It is really a great privilege to welcome you here tonight. I have looked forward for a long time to a chance to talk to a sort of a cross section of America and talk about the things that are on their minds, except those that are on mine, thinking that I know what you are thinking. Now, I know that among you there are Republicans and Democrats and Independents, and first voters, everything. And I am not going to ask you to vote for anyone, except this I will ask you, the only request: please vote, that is all, please vote.

We see here that Ike has looked forward to the event not "with unbridled anticipation" but "for a long time." He is interested in what people "have on their minds" and, curiously enough, what he has on his own mind. He is also fully committed to voting. Thus far his remarks have not caused a Washington reporter to reach for her notebook. He then goes on:

> I said a little while ago something of my own background. How I could ever forget this: people make up America! If you say you are patriotic it means this: you are not just thinking of the land from Florida to Oregon or from San Diego to Portland, Maine; you are thinking of the people that populate this country. They have something in common with you, pride in their citizenship. That is the most precious thing that anyone can have. Therefore, you or anybody else is just as important to me as any millionaire that ever walked the earth.

We learn here that Americans are people and we learn it thrice more. We learn that "pride in citizenship" is a vaunted trait but Ike issues no halcyon calls in its behalf. He is, instead, conversational, which is to say that he picks words easily understood, the kind of words that give listeners a sense of orientation. He then goes on to praise those from the corporate sector who have become part of his administration:

> Now, I have three or four very successful businessmen in the Cabinet. My friend, the Defense Department is spending something like forty billion dollars a year of our money. Most of that goes into, or a great deal of it, into procurement of things—tanks and planes and guns and ammunition and all of these modern weapons. Who would you rather have in charge of that, some failure that never did anything or a successful businessman? I got the head of the biggest company I could go to, General Motors, and said, "Will you come in and do this for us?" I think he has been doing a good job.
>
> I have got another businessman of that same kind in charge of the Treasury, because he is the kind of man that doesn't just hoard money, he uses money for the good of America, to build jobs. Why shouldn't he be a businessman? There is a businessman in the Commerce Department, a very successful small-business man, jewelry and that kind of thing, a very excellent man. But I have got Jim Mitchell in the Department of Labor, and he is the best Department of Labor man that we have ever had in the history of the whole office. (Eisenhower, 1956, October 12).

There is no adjectival excess here: businessmen are "successful," their companies "big," their work as public servants "good." Ike's questions are devoid of rhetorical flourish, his verbs invariant: "got the head," "got another businessman," "got Jim Mitchell." His referents are indistinct ("same kind," "that kind," "kind of man") and, while he consistently gives praise, he is largely atonal. Ike speaks American and he speaks it fluently. He is, in that sense, what Richard Sennett (1978) would call a "public man" who, upon entering the arena, has left his private self behind.

Robert Frost once noted that "poetry is about grief and politics is about grievance" (Monteiro, 1998, p. 104). We detected precious little poetry in the political texts we examined. We found an effervescence at times but, more often, language intended to ferry ideas along quickly. Literature, in contrast, wants to be savored, sermons contemplated, advertising remembered. Lawyers and accountants use language protectively, erecting signage to fend off the casual passerby. Entertainers draw one in with passionate language if they can find some, silly language if they cannot. Politicians, in contrast, stand on the sidewalk wearing brown tie-shoes.

The data reported here will not please long-time reporter Joe Klein. In *Politics Lost*, Klein asks more of rhetoric. Recounting the speech Robert Kennedy gave in Indianapolis on the evening of Martin Luther King Jr.'s assassination, Klein praises a courageous speech, one filled with genuine emotion. Klein reports few "Kennedy-like moments" today, when a politician will "tell their supporters an inconvenient truth, or force their detractors to think in a different way; moments when they stumble across a new and gorgeous locution, when they inspire with high-flown or overblown or untested words" (2006, pp. 8–9). With politicians now uttering phrases carefully warranted by focus groups, the results are obvious, says Klein: "American politics has become overly cautious, cynical, mechanistic, and bland" (2006, p. 13).

But then there is the matter of diversity, and hence, the matter of distance, and hence again, the need to accommodate others. Politicians talk as they do because they are, really, artisans and not artists. They build bridges between people and ideas, between people and people. Joe Klein is right to seek out language that calls attention to itself, and there are surely moments for this—when great challenges confront us and thus when grand opportunities await. There are travails, too (1968 comes to mind), but it ultimately takes a conjoined people to accept those challenges and to seize those opportunities. In a nation as diverse as the United States, estrangements abound and they abound constantly. Our data show that it takes a plebian rhetoric, a rhetoric of accommodation, to connect people to their government and to drive them to the public square. Grand occasions demand grand rhetoric but, in the everyday world of politics, ordinary words will do.

Managing Relationships

In many ways, the life of an American president is a grand and impossible thing. He jets about the globe visiting with powerful business and governmental leaders, not to mention a gaggle of sports and entertainment celebrities as well as the world's best thinkers and artists. Then, wrenchingly, he must meet the American people on their own terms, speaking a common patois to keep the flame of participatory democracy alive. Because theirs is a limited franchise, presidents are reminded on a daily basis—through press reports, through public opinion polls—that power goes to those who relate best to others, which is why leaders often resort to the middle ground of language.

An American president must manage many relationships, including foreign heads of state, members of the business community, leaders on Capitol Hill, high-ranking officers at the Pentagon, hundreds of state and local officials, and thousands of federal bureaucrats. But the president has a special relationship with those who give him his franchise—the American people—and with those who hector him each day—the Fourth Estate. Understanding those two relationships is crucial to understanding how presidents make decisions and what gives American politics its special tone.

To achieve such understandings, we examined the language habits of all three actors. To capture the **Citizen's Voice**, we looked at letters to the editor (n = 8,125) written to local newspapers in twelve small cities around the country between 1948 to 2008. For the **Press's Voice**, we examined print articles (n = 11,037) from the AP, the UPI, *The New York Times*, *The Washington Post*, *The Christian Science Monitor*, *The Atlanta Journal-Constitution*, the *Chicago Tribune*, and the *Los Angeles Times* between 1948 to 2008. The **Political Voice** was restricted to campaign speeches (n = 3,903) given during presidential campaigns between 1948 and 2008.

Overall, our data point up the endemic aspects of politics and caution against an overly liberal understanding of the political, an understanding that has become popular in the academy in recent years. Stanley Fish (2002) lays out the premises of this approach: "Any action we take or decision we make or conclusion we reach rests on assumptions, norms, and values not everyone would affirm. That is, everything we do is rooted in a contestable point of origin; and since the realm of the contestable is the realm of politics, everything is political." Fish may be right, but *establishment* politics is a much narrower thing; that becomes especially clear when elected leaders are compared to those addressing political matters in lay or press venues.[4]

As we see in figure 2.2, elected politicians are dramatically higher on Realism than either of the other social actors.[5] That Americans are a bottom-line, unphilosophical people is by now cultural lore. As Louis Menand (2001) observes, post–Civil War intellectuals first identified Americans' tendencies to think about ideas as being rooted in the lived experiences of people and not as abstract concepts. "Ideas are not 'out there' waiting to be discovered," says Menand (p. xi), but are instead "tools—like forks and knives and microchips—that people devise to cope with the world in which they find themselves." American politicians implicitly understand these cultural assumptions and they understand too that abstract ideas have a short shelf life in the United States. That keeps them constantly looking for instantiated ideas, for ways of tapping into voters' immediate felt needs. Their high Realism scores show their tendencies in this regard.

Politicians also project a greater air of confidence (higher Optimism, higher Certainty) than reporters or citizens.[6] Collectively, these quali-

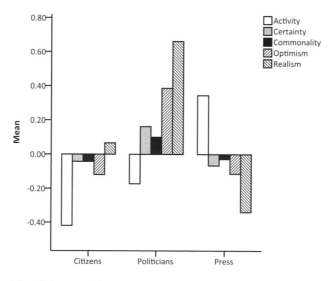

FIGURE 2.2 Establishment politics: confidently pragmatic.

ties suggest storied American resolve: "We are on the job; nothing will vanquish us; we'll fix that nuclear waste dump next week." Many Americans grow tired of these endless promises and all the cheeriness. And yet. And yet. And yet, quadrennially, tens of thousands of the nation's citizens troop through the snows of Iowa and New Hampshire to find a new version of The American Plan. "Throw the bums out" competes with "four more years," and $16 million is spent in the bargain. This is all mere rhetoric, of course, but it continues to intoxicate enough people enough of the time. Mere indeed.

But there is also another way of looking at these data—to imagine living in a place where politicians refuse to address the issues of the day, to be resolutely irresolute, or to paint their pictures in umber. "Then you'd miss us" the politicians sing in chorus. "Who would be there to give you that stiff upper lip, to help you get through the torments of a plunging Dow? Who would tell you that just a bit more microelectronics will fix what ails you? Yes, you don't like our pontifications and our overstatements and you certainly don't like our preening. But, then, why do you gather 'round whenever we hail you? And tell us one more thing: Why do scholars continually show that the most optimistic candidate usually wins elections? Be honest, now: Can you live without us?"[7]

Our data show the essential pluckiness of American politics but there is some element of whistling through the graveyard here since the essential *relationship* between the president and the people is fraught, endlessly fraught. Public opinions scholars continue to show undulating sentiment during a chief executive's tenure—even for the popular presidents—which requires an almost constant outpouring of Realism, Certainty, and Optimism (Gronke & Newman, 2003). The American people love their presidents except when they do not, which leads to a nonstop Rhetoric Machine. Whether or not this machine has functioned optimally is a source of debate among scholars (Edwards, 2003; Lim, 2008; Druckman & Holmes, 2004), but no American president has dared test those hypotheses by being endlessly snarky . . . or quiet. And so the machine continues to hum:

> My focus is on working families—people trying to make house payments and car payments, working overtime to save for college and do right by their kids . . . Whether you're in a suburb, or an inner-city . . . Whether you raise crops or drive hogs and cattle on a farm, drive a big rig on the Interstate, or drive e-commerce on the Internet . . . Whether you're starting out to raise your own family, or getting ready to retire after a lifetime of hard work. So often, powerful forces and powerful interests stand in your way, and the odds seemed

stacked against you—even as you do what's right for you and your family. How and what we do for all of you—the people who pay the taxes, bear the burdens, and live the American dream—that is the standard by which we should be judged. And for all of our good times, I am not satisfied. To all the families in America who have to struggle to afford the right education and the skyrocketing cost of prescription drugs—I want you to know this: I've taken on the powerful forces. And as President, I'll stand up to them, and I'll stand up for you. (Gore, 2000, August 17)

These happen to be the remarks of Al Gore at the 2000 Democratic National Convention, but they also typify the American politician writ large. Gore introduces all the characters in the American pantheon here—The Working Stiff, The Family Man, The Wronged Individual, The Scared Senior, The Fearless Leader, The Decent Citizen. Gore cites a litany of problems but leaves little doubt that solutions can be found and that he knows just where they are. His remarks score high on our Normality Index, which is to say that there is nothing terribly stylish about them. Instead, he is resolute and businesslike and leaves little doubt that a better future beckons.

But not for M.G. in Trenton, New Jersey, who opined a bit later in this way:

Vice President Al Gore is dead wrong about pharmaceuticals. At the recent Democratic National Convention, Mr. Gore saw fit to put the pharmaceutical industry in the same category as "Big Tobacco" and "polluters." I am personally offended at this vicious and unwarranted attack. I've worked in the pharmaceutical industry for more than 15 years. I've been fortunate to work on projects that have placed significant treatments for hepatitis-C, HIV (AIDS), and life threatening asthma on the market.

Like many of my colleagues, I went into pharmaceutical research for the express purpose of making a real and tangible impact on the betterment of the human condition. For me, it was an excellent marriage between my life purpose and my career interests. Apparently, this makes me an evil person in Mr. Gore's eyes. Although I, too, am a "working person" supporting a "working family," I am not deluding myself into thinking Mr. Gore is fighting for me. It looks like this guy will say and do anything to get elected regardless of what damage he causes to the political or social fabric of this country. (M.G., 2000)

M.G. stands in here for many of his brethren depicted in figure 2.2. He waxes philosophical (low Realism), is considerably more dour than Gore (low Optimism), and while he makes himself clear (Gore is "-dead wrong"), he is too self-referential and dilatory to score high on Certainty. M.G. makes his case articulately and probably spoke for many of his coworkers when defending the pharmaceutical industry. In doing so, he demonstrates why the relationship between leader and led needs so much tending in the U.S., a nation where almost all citizens describe themselves as middle-class regardless of their income (Wolfe, 1998). Although it is unclear from this passage whether M.G. had read much Tocqueville, he epitomizes the folks the French traveler met when traversing the young United States in 1835: "In democracy, plain citizens see a man who issues from their ranks, and who in a few years achieves wealth and power; the spectacle excites their surprise and their envy; they inquire how he who was their equal yesterday is vested today with the right to direct them" (2000, p. 212). The fear of government, says historian Garry Wills (1999, p. 19), is so long-standing that it is "a constant in American history." Wills adds that this fear is sometimes sensible, sometimes hysterical, but almost always present.

What is a politician to do? At least three things, as we see in figure 2.3: (1) he or she can emphasize their warmth and humanity (high Self-references), (2) share their understanding of the average Joe (modestly high Voter References and, as we saw in figure 2.2, Commonality scores), and, most important, (3) completely ignore what they do for a living (low Leader References, low Party References).[8] This latter trait is particularly interesting because it betrays a kind of misofamilia (hatred of one's own family) in an attempt to find common ground with an often skeptical electorate. All politicians stand "above politics" as a result, a fact that even a young John F. Kennedy (1956, p. 2) understood implicitly: "Mothers all still want their favorite sons to grow up to be president, but according to a famous Gallup poll of some years ago, they don't want them to become politicians in the process."

One can again turn to Al Gore's speech to the assembled Democrats in 2000 to see how these themes play-out:

> I stand here tonight as my own man, and I want you to know me for who I truly am. I grew up in a wonderful family. I have a lot to be thankful for. And the greatest gift my parents gave me was love. When I was a child, it never once occurred to me that the foundation upon which my security depended would ever shake. And of all the lessons my parents taught me, the most powerful one was unspoken—the way they loved one another.
>
> My father respected my mother as an equal, if not more. She was his best friend, and in many ways, his conscience. And I learned from them the value of

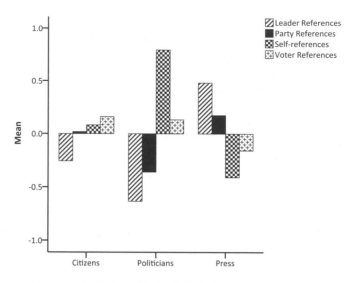

FIGURE 2.3 Establishment politics: ambivalently disclosive.

a true, loving partnership that lasts for life. They simply couldn't imagine being without each other. And for 61 years, they were by each other's side. My parents taught me that the real values in life aren't material but spiritual. They include faith and family, duty and honor, and trying to make the world a better place. (Gore, 2000, August 17)

Gore's remarks here are lovely—thoughtful, personal, and heartfelt. But notice how he fails to mention that his father, Al Gore Sr., served honorably in the U.S. House of Representatives and later in the U.S. Senate. Senator Gore Sr., that is, was a career politician as well as the loving husband of Al Gore Jr.'s mother. The younger Gore could have used the occasion of his acceptance to link his political values to those of his father but he did not. To do so would have been to become partisan (at a political convention!) and to miss a chance for introspection. So Gore did what most politicians do: he went plebian.

If it is hard for politicians to reach the average voter, trading wits with reporters is even harder. Discursively, the two entities could not be more different: Newspapers constantly remind readers which party a politician belongs to, who he or she consorts with, and, as we see in figure 2.2, press reports have two additional features: (1) they are high on Activity (constantly detailing who is doing what to whom) and (2) they theorize about events with little regard to tangible matters (low Realism).[9] News coverage is therefore a hermeneutic enterprise, an attempt to find deep implications in everyday affairs. The press is convinced that there is always more story to the story and the news text becomes inflected with this meta-story as a result.

Not surprisingly, volcanoes of contempt erupt constantly between politicians and the press, a condition foreordained, perhaps, in December 1791, when the First Amendment became the law of the land. Interestingly, the charges that these two institutions hurl at one another are deeply philosophical in nature. Even more surprisingly, the charges often tilt on the very same axes, as we see in table 2.2.

TABLE 2.2 **Mutual distrust of politicians and the press.**

Charge	Politicians on Reporters	Reporters on Politicians
Enmity	"You have to give the press confrontations. When you give them confrontations, you get attention; when you get attention, you can educate." (*Newt Gingrich*)	"The American politics industry fills the airwaves with the most virulent, scurrilous, wall-to-wall character assassination of nearly every political practitioner in the country—and then declares itself puzzled that America has lost trust in its politicians." (*Charles Krauthammer*)
Accuracy	"I won't say that the papers misquote me, but I sometimes wonder where Christianity would be today if some of those reporters had been Matthew, Mark, Luke and John." (*Barry Goldwater*)	"History is a tool used by politicians to justify their intentions." (*Ted Koppel*)
Transparency	"The American people are entitled to see the president and to hear his views directly, and not to see him only through the press." (*Richard M. Nixon*)	"It is kind of tedious after a while, to parse politicians doing the same thing over and over again. The facts change from week to week, but the sort of masquerade doesn't." (*Frank Rich*)
Responsibility	"Another very strong image from the first day was giving my initial press conference in the morning—going down and finding out that everything I had said, the essence of what I had said, was wrong." (*William Scranton*)	"Politicians fascinate because they constitute such a paradox; they are an elite that accomplishes mediocrity for the public good." (*George Will*)
Morality	"I have newspapers coming to me and saying, 'Can we get in on the TARP?'" (*Nancy Pelosi*)	"Politicians have limited power. They can't impose morality on themselves. How can they impose it on the country?" (*Cal Thomas*)
Civility	"I look forward to these confrontations with the press to kind of balance up the nice and pleasant things that come to me as president." (*Jimmy Carter*)	"The only people who say worse things about politicians than reporters do are other politicians." (*Andy Rooney*)

Why, then, does politics sound as it does? Because it must. The broad sweep of data we have reviewed here is highly consistent across time and, when viewed in the large, makes considerable sense. We want our politicians to be sunny, a lesson Jimmy Carter learned in 1979 when he declared a national malaise. We want our politicians to be chummy, but not with White House interns (just ask Bill Clinton) or with Nicaraguan rebels (just ask Ronald Reagan). We also want them to be disclosive (just ask Bill Clinton) and to soar above partisan squabbling (again, ask Ronald Reagan). Above all, we want them to deal with the very real problems the American people face each day. We want them to know how to check out items in a grocery store (just ask George H. W. Bush) and to show up on time when hurricanes hit Louisiana (just ask Mr. Bush's son). This is a lot to ask of anyone, but American politicians try to oblige, thereby echoing what Ruth Benedict (1989, p. 2) has said of us all: "The life history of the individual is first and foremost an accommodation to the patterns and standards traditionally handed down in his community."

Achieving Altitude

Any reasonably complete list of argumentative fallacies contains examples drawn from politics. Politicians routinely use *weasel words* ("we shall make every effort to ... ") and *argument by slogan* ("one problem, one solution, one party ... "). They make a living with *ad hominems* ("you can't trust legislation authored by a man who ... "). They combine *appeals to pity* ("dare we turn our backs on ... ?") with *glittering generalities* ("all real Americans believe that ... ") and *begging the question* ("you can trust me on this ... "). Find a political text and you will find *false dichotomies*, *euphemisms*, and *clichés* galore. Politics, a treasure trove of the illogical.

And the emotional. Politics involves a constant search for ways of overcoming difference. Politicians look for "room to maneuver," a metaphor suggesting a need to glide around intruding objects (existing laws, public opinion, party politics, etc.) when moving toward some important goal. Politicians use high levels of Realism to keep themselves grounded, but the ground is an unpretty place and so they constantly overreach, blending *pathos* with *logos*. Hence the fallacies. Hence the grandiloquence. Hence the metaphors sailing aloft.

And hence the high scores for Patriotic Terms and Religious References and the low Insistence score for politicians, as we see in figure

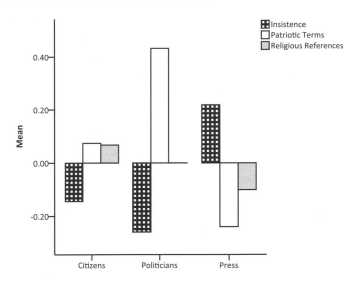

FIGURE 2.4 Establishment politics: roving jingoism.

2.4.[10] Samuel Johnson might opine that patriotism is the last refuge of the scoundrel, but Johnson was an essayist and never had to bring back the bacon to Staffordshire. Similarly, atheists and agnostics may decry the "civic piety" practiced along the banks of the Potomac, but in doing so they overlook the genius of the compromise between church and state in the U.S. Because of the nation's cross-cutting cleavages, it cannot depend on a continuing consensus. It takes "public relations work," says Habermas (1989, p. 141), to turn a social structure (families, localities, economic relations) into a viable "public sphere," a goal that can be achieved in part via "arduous" rhetorical constructions. As Norton (1988, p. 48), points out, "The State has authority over [its subjects] only insofar as it is their author." A vibrant civil society can help to establish social and political bonds, says Beem (1999), but a highly *diverse* society like the U.S. constantly calls those bonds into question. It takes something more, something larger, to bring people together. It takes a transcendent set of beliefs and a way of vivifying those beliefs for an often-distracted polity. That is, it takes rhetoric.

In defending the "democratic vistas" of the *Seinfeld* show, Stephen Olbrys (2005, p. 406) argues that the show "reminds us it is the commonality of our vices that unites us, not the ratification of our virtues." Such a cynical view flies in the face of institutional politics, an enterprise charged with heralding the emotional ties that bind the nation together. This is not easy work since the American people are a true contradiction—a pragmatic people in search of a useful transcendence. "Do I contradict myself?" asks the nation's greatest poet, writing as America. "Very well then I contradict myself," he replies, for "I am large, I contain multitudes" (Whitman, 1986, p. 84). Multitudes indeed, which is why identity politics has long waged an intense battle in the United States with a Rhetoric of All (Gitlin, 1993).

Historically, this search for inclusiveness has often led to discursive excess—"a chosen people," "a shining city on a hill," and all that. Robert Bellah (1992) argues, more positively, that this "civil religion" has also produced a guiding set of beliefs about what the nation might become. In a sense, then, the United States is built as much on a *constituting rhetoric* as on a body of laws. Because of their legion diversities, the American people have "worried constantly about religion," argue Hart and Pauley (2004, p. 3), "and their worrying has been their salvation, perhaps even their glory, as a people." Sometimes their religiosity gets the better of them, argue Domke and Coe (2007), but the long view of American history finds much waxing and waning—the "Mad Men" of the 1950s needed God but the hippies of the 1960s did not. Jimmy Carter, a person of deep religious faith, generally circumnavigated religious matters as president while his successor, Ronald Reagan, pressed them constantly. George H. W. Bush rarely entertained preachers in the White House, while the second President Bush saw them regularly (Domke, 2004). Politics in a diverse society must create an "economy of violence," says Sheldon Wolin (1960, p. 221), so rhetoric is used to regulate the market.

Even George McGovern, the former preacher who, when running for office, tried to destroy all existing pictures of himself in clerical garb, drank from the cup of civil religion. Speaking at Illinois' Wheaton College on October 11, 1972, McGovern (1972, p. 212) called for a recommitment to the nation's core values. "We must have a fundamental stirring of our moral and spiritual values," said McGovern, "if we are to reclaim our true destiny." "That kind of awakening," he continued, "can free us from a relentless devotion to material affluence, with too much for some citizens and too little for others. We must look into our souls to find the way out of the crisis of our society." Stuff this heady is by now common in the U.S., and it draws on old religious themes: a people lost, a people found; a God forsaken, a God embraced. The blessings of liberty, a New Covenant, will surely heal us, the politicians declare. How else can they rally people living in 25,000 different cities stretched across a land mass of some 3,000 miles and a political kaleidoscope ranging from birthers to unreconstructed socialists? God, country, salvation for all.

Figure 2.4 also shows a dramatic difference in Insistence scores between politicians and reporters (as well as the press's avoidance of civil religious themes). Insistence is calculated by counting the use of repeated words and phrases, thereby measuring the extent to which a text stays on topic. Highly "insistent" passages can be found in college textbooks, scientific reports, and legal and accounting statements. Poetry and novels, plays and TV dramas, in contrast, reach far and wide, follow their own serpentine routes to keep us engaged, constantly guessing. Politicians and the press are opposites in this regard, with the former looking for room to maneuver and the latter constantly trying to corral the issues (and the politicians). Press conferences become a field day for these contrasting tones. Ironically, on the very day he signed the Press Freedom Act in the Oval Office (May 19, 2010), Barack Obama refused to take questions from the press. The press is not to be trifled with:

- "Obama is Snubbing the White House Press Corps" (*U.S. News & World Report*)
- "No Questions: Palin Won't Talk To Press" (*Huffington Post*)
- "Sharron Angle may talk to the media (after Election Day)" (*Yahoo News*)
- "If Hillary Clinton continues to duck hypothetical questions, does she deserve your vote?" (*Chicago Tribune*)

Any randomly chosen press conference will reveal this clash in Insistence scores. Consider, for example, the clear and pointed question asked of Barack Obama by NBC correspondent Chuck Todd in July of 2009:

Thank you, sir. You were just talking in that question about reducing health care inflation, reducing costs. Can you explain how you're going to expand coverage? Is it fair to say—is this bill going to cover all 47 million Americans that are uninsured, or is this going to be something—is it going to take a mandate, or is this something that isn't—your bill is probably not going to get it all the way there? And if it's not going to get all the way there, can you say how far is enough—you know, okay, 20 million more, I can sign that; 10 million more, I can't? (Obama, 2009, July 22)

Although Barack Obama—the former law professor and brilliant dialectician—was more than capable of answering a direct question, he began at the broadest level possible: "I want to cover everybody." He then goes on to talk about a single-payer insurance system but quickly digresses to worry about "somebody out there who thinks they're indestructible," doesn't get health care, and then "they get hit by a bus, end up in the emergency room." He then calls the roll: Congressional intransigence; insurance subsidies; hardship exemptions; waste in the system; short term vs. long term options; the average American family; uncompensated care; the duties of the primary care physician; advanced diabetes; the sagacity of dieticians. Throughout, Mr. Obama's answer is thoughtful and reasonably precise, a credit to him since he is admittedly dealing with a complex topic (as are all the topics a president confronts). But does he answer the questions asked? Does he say how he is going to expand health care? Does he specify whether he will cover all 47 million uninsured Americans? He does not, he does not, he does not.

In contrast, when examining a news text carefully, one quickly finds the routines undergirding it: an opening exemplar; the problem-solution exposition; the clash of good and evil; the if-but structure; the ominous conclusion. Each night on CNN, Anderson Cooper employs these formulas. Unable—by dint of his profession—to shake his fist at God for the Japan tsunami in 2011, he finds villainy instead in the nuclear power companies' inefficiencies and in the Japanese government's refusals to disclose what they knew, the same villains he found earlier, halfway around the world, in New Orleans after Katrina.

In operating this way, Anderson Cooper is doing what he should do, using the overdetermined tropes of reportage to examine the innards of an issue. Politicians, in contrast, look away from an issue. They look upward in an attempt to expand the conversation so that more people will feel included. Reporters love specificities but politicians shrink from them reflexively. As public people doing public business, politicians must trade the particular for the general, the electorate for the individual voter. To do their best work, politicians need altitude.

Conclusion

Accommodation is an ugly term, an approach-avoidance word that calls forth and that banishes simultaneously. To be accommodated is to be acknowledged and to be given a half-measure from time to time. But being accommodated is rarely exhilarating and it does not build long-term trust. We accommodate others so they will feel included but we often resent having to make the effort. As Jean Piaget (1954, p. 398) says, "Every acquisition of accommodation becomes material for assimilation, but assimilation always resists new accommodations." Is that any way to live a life?

Only in politics, perhaps. Why does establishment politics sound like it does? Because it must. Do politicians bloviate? They do indeed, a fact evidenced by their high Patriotic and Religious references. Are they often disingenuous? They are, rarely discussing their partisan affiliations or professional associates. Do they pander to the electorate? They do, which explains their frequent Voter References and high Normality scores? Do they circumlocute? They do, as evidenced by their low Insistence scores. Are they egocentric? They are, talking frequently about their dogs, their cats, their kids, their worries, their dreams.

Why these speech patterns? Politicians' high Realism scores suggest an answer: What they do for a living determines who will live and how well and who will die and how quickly. Politicians intervene in human affairs and they do so with special force (hence the high Self-references). Politicians *act* and, by acting, they change what happens in the world. Their high Normality scores grow out of the Mythos of the Commonweal and give testimony to the impossible idea that a democratically chosen leader can make a difference in a large and heterogeneous nation. Politicians' high Patriotic and Religious scores are yet another kind of prayer, a way of saying "all this is perhaps more than we can handle but, with luck, we will prevail." One can disparage such prayers, but then what would one have left?

Disparaging politicians has proven to be great fun throughout American history. According to Boskin (1997), it is a way of being subversive without being radical, a way of keeping political institutions intact. The protagonist in Henry Adams's novel, *Democracy*, adopts that tone, reporting that she had finally learned the ropes in Washington: "I have got so far as to lose the distinction between right and wrong. Isn't that the first step in politics?" (Adams, 1952, p. 133). Yes, but that is because right and wrong are never really the point of politics. Right and wrong are metaphysical concepts and politics rarely deals with them in their absolute forms. Instead, it deals with better and worse, more and less, now and then, fast and slow. It is the relativity of such matters, their incom-

mensurability too, that makes politics politics. As we have observed elsewhere, "Politics is, after all, a great impertinence: It intrudes where it is
not wanted and enforces compromises between opposing forces. It makes
private matters public, balances morality with expediency, and often declares a half-loaf of bread sufficient" (Hart et al., 2005, p. 55).

Harry Truman once quipped, "My choice early in life was either to be a
piano-player in a whorehouse or a politician. And to tell the truth, there's
hardly any difference" (Gosnell, 1980, p. 9). Surely he was right. There is a
pliancy in politics, a solicitousness, that makes it inevitably transactional.
Favors are traded, money exchanges hands, and that creates tensions. But
there are also strictures to be observed: a respect for house rules and
some measure of civility and discretion. American politics sounds the way
it does because it must respond—inevitably and constantly—to a bewildering kind of social diversity. As a result, it adopts a certain tone, the
tone described here.

Partisanship and the Balanced Tone

A political party is many things: an assembly of true believers, a social organization, a magnet for policy wonks, a legal and financial entity, a cadre of hard-working campaigners, a gaggle of people in funny hats.[1] In the United States, political parties have largely come in two varieties—Republicans and Democrats—although it took almost a hundred years for that particular pairing to get settled. But even as the parties were forming, many Americans began looking for a third or fourth alternative, a search that continues to the present (roughly a quarter to a third of contemporary Americans see themselves as "independents"). Over the years, both major parties have given birth to, expunged, and later reabsorbed a variety of splinter groups, a factionalizing process that James Madison worried would undo the young republic he helped establish.

Madison's worries continue to the present, with the Tea Partyers being the latest object of concern. The last thirty years have seen a particularly sharp rise in partisanship in the U.S., with party-line voting having increased and split-ticket voting having declined (Brewer 2009; Yu, Kaufmann & Diermeier 2008). As a result, the parties have adopted a "base mobilization" strategy during campaigns (Levendusky, 2009, p. 128), with the 2004 presidential election being an especially good example. While strategically efficient, this kind of "sorting" among voters is worrisome, with "elite polarization" now making it harder to find a workable middle ground. Worse, says Woodson (2010), extreme partisanship encourages voters to huddle together and dismiss the other side, letting the instinct for compromise shrivel up within them. This problem is further exacerbated by the mass media, say Carson and his colleagues (2010), as "party unity voters" are given more air time than middle-of-the-roaders. During the last thirty years, say Layman, Carsey,

How its meaning has been marginalized

lem so far Domr--

and Horowitz (2006, p. 103), the Democratic and Republican Parties have become both "ideologically cohesive and highly polarized," a troubling confection indeed.

Many voters are worried about these trends. Political scientist Matthew Levendusky (2009, p. 71), for example, finds "far more respondents in the center of the distribution than on the extremes," while other researchers note that excessive partisanship can actually *decrease* a candidate's attractiveness. Thus, while voters know that Democrats are "liberal and inclusive," Republicans "business-oriented and conservative"—partisan stereotypes are fairly robust (Rahn, 1993; Koger, Masket & Noel, 2010; Baumer & Gold, 1995)—they are uncomfortable with what they know. The parties used to "stand for nothing," say Brewer and Stonecash (2009, pp. 208–9), but now they "stand for too much." With the two major parties being "as coherent and polarized as they have been in perhaps a century," says Brewer (2009, p. 3), with ideology now threatening to overtake issue- and performance-based judgments (Woodson, 2010, p. 6), and with voters even having partisan expectations about candidates' personalities (Hayes, 2005), we may now have finally reached the end of Madison's road, a place where everyone knows all they can possibly know.

While these issues are important, we ask another set of questions here. We want to know what it *sounds like* to be a Democrat or a Republican. At first the answer seems obvious—just listen for the policies they endorse. But politics is a nuanced business. We know, for example, that both Al Gore and Bill Clinton were southerners, contemporaries, and neo-Democrats. Did that make them sound the same on the stump? Similarly, both John Kennedy and Richard Nixon were Cold Warriors. Did their shared moment in time override their different political axes? Was Ronald Reagan the son of Barry Goldwater? Was George W. Bush the rhetorical son of his own father? Are Democrats more "democratic" when talking about social welfare? Are Fox News commentators more "republican" than our elected representatives in Washington? Is being able to speak "party tone" an inherent or an acquired trait?

Given the diverse candidates who have campaigned for the presidency during the last sixty years, given the twists and turns of political history, and given the panoply of beliefs now mucking about—New Dealers, supply siders, Reagan Democrats, neocons, paleoliberals—is it even meaningful to uses phrases like *Democrat* or *Republican* anymore? If there are differences between the parties, are these differences tangible, hearable? If heard, are they influential? Are "rhetorical templates" being thrust upon candidates without their knowledge, as part of their cultural upbringing? Does the citizenry—wittingly or unwittingly—listen for these signals when making its political judgments? If so, can computers track these cues, thereby opening up American political history in new and interesting ways? We believe that the answer to all of these questions is yes.

Why might these things be true? In *The Right Talk*, Mark Smith notes that rhetoric "represents the currency of politics in that everything important passes through it" (2007, p. 28). While issues are important, Smith argues, rhetoric provides the elasticity that lets politicians as different as Mitt Romney and Sarah Palin call themselves Republicans. "Like clay not fully molded into shape," says Smith (2007, pp. 22, 23), "interests need assistance to acquire their structure and form" so that "the size of the supporting coalition" can be expanded. While parties obviously must pay attention to the issues they endorse, they must also monitor the "accent" they use (Brewer & Stonecash, 2009, p. 12). Also, with elites becoming more partisan but with a growing number of independent voters, candidates now need rhetoric to mediate these differences. The increasing professionalization of campaigns, say Gibson and Rommele (2001, p. 40), makes "market" more important than ideology and that, of course, introduces rhetoric to the scene.

John McCain learned these lessons in 2008. Somehow, says *The New York Times*'s Adam Nagourney (2009), McCain "lost the 'Happy Warrior' image that had defined his political persona for so long" when, in desperation, he went on the attack. "Tone is important," says Nagourney, because ultimately "the message has to be about big things but tone is how you wrap it." Fine, but what does that really mean? How could something as effluvial as tone determine who becomes the leader of the free world? Is not politics supposed to be about grander things—intellectual vision, performance on the job, human values, a nation's core beliefs? Yes, but it also takes a kind of human physics to give these forces the energy needed to penetrate the national mind set. It takes a physics of words.

Assessing Party Tone

There are at least two potential ways of measuring partisan language. One could operate inductively, throwing a large number of linguistic variables against a known set of texts and then using clustering or factor-analytic

methods to gauge the results. While conventional, such an approach is, we
believe, too atheoretical. So we have operated deductively instead, scan-
ning the scholarly literature for the key philosophical differences between
the parties, identifying their likely semantic correlates, and then passing
over a large text base to see what patterns developed. This approach met
the most important test of any content-analytic scheme—face validity—
and it let us place our bets in clear, phenomenologically defensible ways.

But where to start? We began with a classic statement on these matters—Richard Weaver's penetrating *The Ethics of Rhetoric* (1953). There,
Weaver famously contrasted the liberal and conservative mind sets and
found them embedded in the interstices of language. "Both Republicans
and Democrats have unique political vocabularies," Weaver (1953, p. 166)
observed, "although it remains to be seen whether their styles will survive
the increasing pressures of the mass media or the changing ideological
tastes of the American voter." Typically, said Weaver (pp. 57–58), liberals deploy the *argument from circumstance*, which he called "the near-
est of all arguments to pure expediency." They deploy "the facts standing
around" to validate their claims, thereby producing an un-philosophical,
or even anti-philosophical, mode of discourse, one that "stops at the
level . . . of fact."

So, for example, a Democrat might argue that federal funding should
pour into New Orleans because of its devastating floods and its cultural
and ethnic richness. "Why New Orleans and not Omaha?" a Republican might ask; "good people live in Omaha too and tornadoes have been
known to stalk that city over the years." Republicans habitually use the
argument from definition, said Weaver (1953, pp. 80, 112), grabbing hold
of some "ideal objective" and viewing the universe "as a paradigm of es-
sences." This makes them "conservatives in the legitimate sense of the
word," he argues, because they operate in a noumenal rather than a con-
tingent universe. So, for example, with Democrats standing around impa-
tiently, ready to provide aid, Republicans might ask what principle—what
case-transcendent rule—should guide federal assistance to a devastated
area. What inherent quality, they might ask, does New Orleans possess
that is missing in Omaha—geographical size, financial scale, regional cen-
trality, sociological deservingness? In other words, arguments from circumstance propel one to *act* while arguments from definition make one
reflect. And reflection, of course, slows down the wheels of government.
Impulsive Democrats, thinking Republicans. That was the world according to Richard Weaver at midcentury. He clearly preferred the latter.

George Lakoff's world, and George Lakoff's value system, differs greatly from Weaver's, as does his model of partisanship. It is not intellectual argument that distinguishes Democrats from Republicans, says Lakoff (2002, p. 147), but *cultural knowledge* that becomes "physically encoded in the synapses of our brains." Lakoff, a cognitive linguist, argues that Republicans bring a Strict Father model to the national dialogue and Democrats a Nurturant Mother. The former emphasizes strict rules, traditional authority, self-reliance, and moral character, while the latter stresses concern for others, egalitarian modes of communication, empathy, and personal fulfillment. Political discourse in the United States, says Lakoff, bounces between these two poles and, because "new ideas are never entirely new" (p. 147), they are constantly reinscribed within the electorate. While Weaver's model is philosophically based, Lakoff's is psychological, even anthropological, in nature. As such, it better explains voters' feelings about partisan discourse. Not surprisingly, given the tensions between the parties identified by Lakoff, American politics is often a pot ready to boil over.

Weaver and Lakoff are but a few of those who have modeled political partisanship. While indebted to them, we have settled here on an approach that subsumes their views within a four-part schematic. One antinomy features **Restoration vs. Reform,** contrasting preservation of the status quo (or a return to past glories) to politics as an agent of social change. Not surprisingly, given the Republican Party's hierarchical power structure and the Democrats' inherent diversity, different mind sets develop within the parties: "Republicans perceive themselves as insiders even when they are out of power and Democrats perceive themselves as outsiders even when they are in power" (Freeman, 1986, p. 328). Many other party stereotypes are found in the Restoration/Reform pairing: Democrats are fractious while Republicans embrace the eleventh commandment—not to speak ill of one another. Democrats are undisturbed by "the ad-hocness of politics" while Republicans try to impress order "on the anarchy of politics" (Cotter & Hennessy, 1964, p. 183; Lakoff, 2002, p. 33). When Democrats err rhetorically, they do so by "searching for truth rather than brandishing it" (Gitlin, 2007, p. 14) and, when they go too far, "Republicans become authoritarian, intolerant of ambiguity" (Jost et al., 2003). Republicans are comfortable with labels (Morris, Carranza & Fox, 2008), Democrats more trusting of people (McClosky, 1958). Republicans dislike the press because it is presentistic, Democrats dislike the press because it is establishmentarian. People laugh at Republicans because they are stodgy; people laugh at Democrats for becoming overwrought.

A second antinomy sees both Republicans and Democrats as preachy. Republicans often sound as if they had discovered (or perhaps written) some book of Truth. Democrats seem equally self-satisfied when telling people how to live their lives. Republicans are moralists, Democrats fixers, and so both have that "stained-glass window whine." McAdams and his colleagues (2008, p. 978) find that conservatives emphasize moral institutions featuring "purity or sanctity of the self" while liberals are invested in "moral institutions regarding harm and fairness." Democrats attack policy, Republicans attack character. Democrats defer to group will, Republicans to traditional authority. Democrats, being a "big tent" entity, are preoccupied with political constituencies. Republicans are content to be part of a select few, more inclined to use providential truths to justify their actions (Webb, 2008). In other words, the two parties register differently on the axis of **Utility vs. Values**, with Democrats sticking close to the ground and Republicans sailing aloft. When they go too far, Democrats are often charged with expediency and Republicans with tendentiousness.

A third dichotomy is that of **Community vs. Independence**. Studies have long shown that Republicans prize self-sufficiency and self-reliance, while Democrats score highly on prosocial and altruism measures (Sheldon & Nichols, 2009). Democrats embrace redistributive politics, solutions that most Republicans find abhorrent. Conservatives blame poverty on self-indulgence and an absence of moral standards, while liberals see the poor as victims of failed institutions (Feather, 1985; Kluegel, 1990). Interestingly, research shows that conservatives often repudiate social programs for moral, not financial, reasons—"the election imagery of the welfare cheat in his or her Cadillac ... brings them to the boiling point" (Skitka & Tetlock, 1993, p. 1217). In contrast, studies show that Democratic platforms have shifted over time from a rhetoric of "majority rule" to one of "minority rights" (Gerring, 1998). Ultimately, liberals "expand the boundaries of the moral community" while conservatives excoriate free-riding (Skitka & Tetlock, 1993, p. 1221).

A fourth and final polarity is **Populism vs. Nationalism**—the body politic versus the electorate as abstracted. At first this appears to be an academic distinction but it produces quite different outcomes. Democrats stress day-to-day policies—education, health care, Social Security— while Republicans stand further back, emphasizing national defense, foreign policy, and crime and punishment. Both parties understand national identity but they understand it differently, with Democrats celebrating individual differences and Republicans featuring American superiority (Stuckey, 2005). The concept of freedom is also foundational for both parties. It is a quasi-religious notion for Republicans and a license for personal exploration for Democrats. Democrats are permissive about lifestyles, Republicans are permissive about financial derring-do. Democrats see the People as real people; Republicans treat the Nation as transcendent. Given these differences, the parties now "own" certain issues—immigration and voting rights for Democrats, national defense and border security for Republicans (Petrocik, Benoit & Hansen, 2003). These differences also produce rhetorical results: Republicans "speak ex-cathedra, not conversationally" (Gitlin, 2007, p. 42), while Democrats become "playful with ideas" (Kelley, 1977, p. 559).

Figure 3.1 shows how these four contrasts have been operationalized by DICTION. Our approach is admittedly crude; we have standardized the various scores and then summed them (with a constant of 3 being added to the Democratic Tone). The resulting indices are therefore "bulky," with each party's tone containing several pieces and parts. This produces what Smith (2007, p. 139) calls a "menu of arguments" for

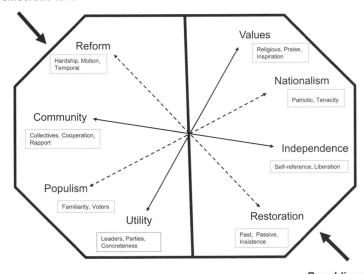

FIGURE 3.1 Operationalizing party tone.

the parties, letting them address different constituencies simultaneously. So, for example, Republicans can stress Independence over Restoration during good times, Values and Nationalism during moments of upheaval. These subcomponents become grafted onto a party's rhetoric over time and do so for a variety of reasons: (1) because a new presidential candidate brings something different to the game (Rapoport & Stone, 2005); (2) because intraparty factions suddenly demand a say (Koger et al., 2010); (3) because the parties "absorb" discourses that have suddenly become popular (Smith, 2007, p. 94); (4) because party discipline waxes and wanes (Bai, 2010a); and (5) because new members introduce novel preferences to party deliberations (Koger et al., 2010).

Our overall contention is that each party uses a "confederation of words" that creates an overall tone for the party. This congeries of elements sets the parameters of what the ancient rhetoricians might call the party's "inventional universe"—that which can be said in a given instance. Individual politicians may appropriate these assemblages differently at times but in the end a discernible tone emerges for the party. Sometimes these mixtures can be philosophically incongruent (e.g., it may become hard for Republicans to reconcile Restoration and Independence on occasion or Democrats may have trouble with Populism vs. Utility) but the *rhetorical matrix* can still function.

Previous scholars have used computerized methods to study party platforms, an undertaking first begun by Zvi Namenwirth and Harold Lasswell in the early 1970s and now pursued with more advanced techniques (e.g., Coffey, 2004; Kidd, 2008; Laver, Benoit & Garry, 2003; Yu, Kaufmann & Diermeier, 2008). Almost all of these studies, however, have been nominal in nature, focusing on the platforms' issue patterns. Issues are important, of course, and nouns signal their presence—*inflation, defense, the environment*. Nouns tell us the *what* of a text. Our hope, in contrast, is to understand the *how* of a text, and that requires more parts of speech. We want to get at things like "partisan flavor" and so we also look at adjectives. We want to know about "ideological force," a construct embedded in verbs. And we are interested in "political responsibility"—who did what to whom—and so the humble pronoun comes into the picture.

Table 3.1 shows what recent party platforms look like when viewed through the schematic outlined above. When laid out in this linear, selective fashion, party differences jump to the surface. But can the DICTION program make these same delineations? Can it track the subtleties required for being "Democratic" but not too Democratic, for being

TABLE 3.1 **Tonal differences in the 2008 party platforms.**

Polarities	Democratic Platform	Republican Platform
Reform vs. Restoration	It is time for a change. We can do better.... If we choose to change, just imagine what we can do. What makes America great has never been its perfection, but the belief that it can be made better. And that people who love this country can change it.	From its founding, America has been an idea as much as a political or geographic entity. It has meant, for untold millions around the world, a set of ideals that speak to the highest aspirations of humanity. From its own beginning, the Republican Party has boldly asserted those ideals, as we now do again.
Utility vs. Values	We will provide immediate relief to working people who have lost their jobs, families who have lost their homes, and people who have lost their way. We will invest in America again—in world-class public education, in our infrastructure, and in green technology—so that our economy can generate the good, high-paying jobs of the future.	Faithful to the first guarantee of the Declaration of Independence, we assert the inherent dignity and sanctity of all human life and affirm that the unborn child has a fundamental individual right to life which cannot be infringed. We support a human life amendment to the Constitution.
Community vs. Independence	For decades, Americans have been told to act for ourselves, by ourselves, on our own. Democrats reject this recipe for division and failure. Today, we commit to renewing our American community by recognizing that solutions to our greatest challenges can only be rooted in common ground and the strength of our civic life.	Decentralized decision-making in the place of official controls empowers individuals and groups to tackle social problems in partnership with government. Bureaucracy is no longer a credible approach to helping those in need. This is especially true in light of alternatives such as faith-based organizations [which better deal] with problems such as substance abuse and domestic violence.
Populism vs. Nationalism	These are not just policy failures. They are failures of a broken politics—a politics. . .that puts our government at the service of the powerful. A politics that creates a state-of-the-art system for doling out favors and shuts out the voice of the American people.	For seven years, the horror of September 11, 2001 has not been repeated on our soil. For that, we are prayerfully grateful and salute all who have played a role in defending our homeland. We pledge to continue their vigilance and to assure they have the authority and resources they need to protect the nation.

"Republican" about just the right issues? To be sure, counting words cannot tell us everything we need to know about partisanship. But it can get us started. And there is so much to learn: Are independents really independent or are they Republicans in disguise? Has partisanship increased over time, as many have claimed, or has it decreased? Do presidents soar above partisanship upon entering the Oval Office? Is political advertising more partisan than stump speaking? Does requiring candidates to engage in formal debates reduce the toxicity of their campaigns? More generally, do Democrats ever sound like Republicans, Republicans like Democrats? About partisanship there is much to learn. We look for some answers here.

Mapping Party Tone

Even though deployment of the Democratic and Republican tones undulates between 1948 and 2008, with some candidates being more experimental than others, the overall result is this: our methods neatly separated Democrats and Republicans. If all one knew was a campaigner's party affiliation, DICTION could predict with some accuracy that person's use of Democratic language (the D-tone), Republican language (the R-tone), and their relative use of both (the Republican-Democratic Differential— the RDD score). The differences were especially sharp for the campaign speeches in our sample, a format in which candidates are given considerable room to maneuver.[2] But it was also true for campaign ads and debates, genres more heavily affected by established conventions (i.e., ads must be short and visual, debates must respond to press agendas).[3]

One of the major differences between the Democratic and Republican tones hinges on what psychologist J. B. Rotter (1990) has famously called the "locus of control"—whether a person sees himself or herself as an active force affecting the world around them or whether they view themselves as being acted upon, a pawn in some larger game. For Democrats, external forces typically inspire the need for change. During the 2008 campaign, for example, Barack Obama framed young people as the products, not the initiators, of social action:

> When I'm President, we'll fight to make sure we're once again first in the world when it comes to high school graduation rates. We'll push our kids to study harder and aim higher. I've worked with Republican Senator Jim DeMint on a

bill that would challenge high school students to take college-level courses—and make sure low-income neighborhoods and rural communities have access to those courses. And I'll make it the law of the land when I'm President. And we'll also set a goal of increasing the number of high school students taking college-level or AP courses by 50 percent in the coming years. Because I believe that when we challenge our kids to succeed, they will. (Obama, 2008, September 9)

Candidate Obama, ever the reformer, reveals an "action bias" here. While not exactly framing young people as flotsam and jetsam, his model of change works from the outside in. That was surely not George W. Bush's model. For him, all that is important lies within the individual, although it sometimes takes some social or metaphysical force to "hail" that potential. In the following excerpt, Bush depicts youth as potential incarnate, clearly rejecting external interventions like those embraced by Obama:

See every child can learn. Every child can learn. And every child in this country deserves to grow in knowledge and character and ideals. Nothing in my view is more important to our prosperity and goodness than cultivated minds and courageous hearts . . . Education is the essential beginning, but we've got to go further. To create communities of promise, we must help people build the confidence and faith to achieve their own dreams. We must put government squarely on the side of opportunity . . . Education helps the young. Empowerment lifts the able. . . . Every day they prove that our worst problems are not hopeless or endless. Every day they perform miracles of renewal. (Bush, 2000, July 10)

These two examples, and thousands more, show how differently the two parties argue. As we see in figure 3.2, the R-tone and the D-tone have waxed and waned over time but the differences between them have persisted. Sometimes the Republicans have been more "progressive" (e.g., their D-tone score ramped up in the 1960s), but all of that changed in 1984 when Ronald Reagan ran for reelection. For their part, the Democrats made greater use of the R-tone in the 1960s, perhaps a reaction to the Cold War politics of the times, and then again in the 1980s, perhaps in response to Reagan's ascendency. Generally, though, each party has a preferred language and each has maintained that preference over time. Indeed, we found that Democrats with lower RDD scores (i.e., those who sounded less "Republican") did better in presidential elections than

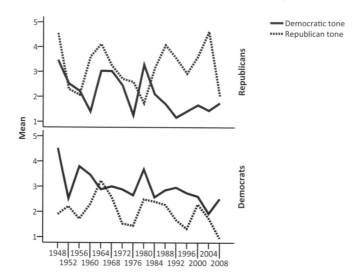

FIGURE 3.2 Use of party tone by politicians over time.

Democrats with higher scores and, similarly, that Republicans with high RDD scores won more often than low scoring Republicans (i.e., those with a more "Democratic" tone). In other words, even when candidates are unsure where to stand policywise, the smartest of them know where to stand rhetorically.[4]

A related set of findings is this: When running for reelection, sitting presidents use their party's tone more profusely than do challengers from that same party. This was true for both Democrats and Republicans.[5] In other words, not only do incumbents have a financial advantage in campaigns, but they also have a rhetorical heritage to depend upon. Perhaps because they already "embody" the party, incumbents are better licensed to draw upon its most revered myths. This effect was especially strong for Republicans, possibly because of that party's structural regularities. Commentators have noted, in contrast, that Democratic campaigns have become more candidate centered over the years, relying increasingly on the unique goals and personae of the candidates du jour (see Galvin, 2010). Those changes may have decreased the Democrats' linguistic discipline as well. Generally speaking, though, sitting presidents are more party allegiant than those running for the presidency for the first time. As a result, each party's "brand" has become fairly identifiable over time.[6]

But these partisan differences do not tell us all we need to know. Other scholars have already told us that Republicans emphasize morality and Democrats empathy (Benoit, 2004, p. 81), that Republicans stress "threat identity" and Democrats "group identity" (Cordingley, 2010, p. 21), that Democrats emphasize "consequentialist reasoning" and Republicans "absolutist reasoning" (Marietta, 2009, p. 391). Having DICTION'S mathematical support for these intuitions is helpful but they can also hide a more complex picture.

We argue here that, for a given politician, the parties' individual tones are not as important as the ratio between them. We argue further that culture, not politics alone, affects candidate tone. Culture, not politics, tells us why Europeans often miss the subtle shifts in intonation when a Republican administration yields to a Democratic administration or vice versa. Instead, Europeans are more likely to notice the similarities between them, that distinctively *American* way of discussing public policy. So, for instance, they would note—and probably be distressed—to find a newly elected Barack Obama singing from the same hymnbook as George W. Bush with regard to Iraq and Afghanistan.

When looking at figure 3.1, then, European observers would miss the line separating the two halves of our octagon. Instead, they would seize on the similarities heard across administrations. They would note that the nation's leaders often call for reform based on traditional principles, urge citizens to accomplish great works but to do so high-mindedly, and tell people to seek their fortunes even while loving their neighbors as themselves. Democrats and Republicans—different but alike; alike but yet not the same. How can all this be true?

We see things this way:

- Both the "Democratic" and "Republican" tones stem from deep-seated, historically reinforced belief systems;
- Regardless of their party of choice, all U.S. politicians must deploy these tones in some measure to be deemed culturally appropriate;
- Republicans must respect popular sentiments and a constant mandate for social improvement; Democrats must confess to the nation's mysteries as well as its destinies;
- The key to understanding a given politician like Michele Bachmann, therefore, is to discover how she deploys these tones *relative to one another*, how she amalgamates the various strains of the American lexicon;
- Sharp deviation from *either* the D-tone or the R-tone is likely to end poorly as, for example, when George McGovern refused to be hyperpatriotic in 1972 or

when Newt Gingrich called Rep. Paul Ryan's Medicare proposal "right-wing social engineering" in 2011.

Throughout this chapter, then, we will pay special attention to the *differentials* between the Democratic and Republican tones because that is where important subtleties come into play. Laypeople sometimes sense these differences. They note, for example, that a barn burner like Harry Truman sounds "antique" to the modern ear—too blunt, too honest, too opinionated—and that a fellow like Bill Clinton is noticeably smoother. They also sense that John Kerry seemed aimless during the 2004 campaign, not nearly as confident as Lyndon Johnson was forty years earlier. What gives people these impressions? Also, why have some observers noted that Ronald Reagan sounded different when running for reelection than he did four years earlier? And what are we to make of independents who run for office? Do they carve out an entirely new way of speaking, one unencumbered by American cultural understandings?

Figure 3.3 presents what we feel is an arresting picture of recent political history. Admittedly, the chart's data are not exhaustive (around 4,000 political speeches) but the resulting picture is stark. Harry Truman, as one might expect, typifies the Classic Democrats and is accompanied by other traditional liberals—Stevenson, Kennedy, McGovern,

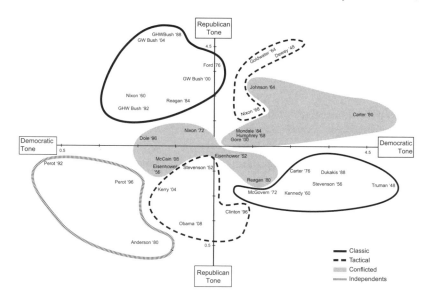

FIGURE 3.3 R-tone/D-tone intercepts for presidential candidates: 1948–2008.

and Dukakis. In contrast, the Classic Republicans include the Bushes, the early Richard Nixon, and the later Ronald Reagan. Nothing too surprising here. But the graph also reveals some interesting blends, including a group of Conflicted Democrats—Humphrey, Mondale, and Gore—and a Goldwater-pressured Lyndon Johnson in 1964 and a Reagan-pressured Jimmy Carter in 1980. We also find some "lost" Republicans—Bob Dole and John McCain—adjacent to the vaguely partisan Dwight Eisenhower.

The chart also reveals an oddly progressive Ronald Reagan in 1980, suggesting that that campaign did exactly what campaigns should do: It made Reagan seek out new constituencies (i.e., the Reagan Democrats) and forced Jimmy Carter to move rightward in response. But Carter was confronted by dwindling energy supplies, hostages in Iran, and supply-side economics, so this strategy failed him. It failed him doubly when he used the D-tone to support the Equal Rights Amendment, environmental legislation, and the windfall profits tax. Figure 3.3 shows Jimmy Carter to be all by himself in semantic space in 1980.

John McCain met a similar fate in 2008. At times, he sounded like a real Republican—"the tax-and-spend policies of Barack Obama will only make matters worse"—but he never captured the Republican language of rugged independence cum family values. He tried to echo Barack Obama's siren call for change from time to time but it sounded vacuous when coming from McCain, devoid as it was of specifics:

> My fellow Americans, Washington is on the wrong track, and even greater financial troubles lay ahead if we don't act quickly . . . But if you give me the chance, I'm going to set it right. You don't have to hope that things will change when you vote for me. You know things will change, because I've been fighting for change in Washington my whole career. I've been fighting for you my whole life. That's what I'm going to do as President of the United States. Fight for you and put the government back on the side of the people. (McCain, 2008, October 11)

Figure 3.3 also reveals an important change in the Democratic Party in recent years. Although it is too soon to declare a "post-partisan" era, the Kerry/Clinton/Obama triumvirate clearly did something different. A New Pragmatism perhaps? Regardless, says Lakoff (2009, p. 389), this has produced a "language advantage" for the Republicans because such a tone is problem centered and not values based. But avoiding traditional political themes can also be useful, says Sidney Milkis (2007), when it lets Democrats bypass hot-button issues. Candidates with the deft political touch of a Bill Clinton or a Barack Obama are especially able to work this particular magic.

But not John Kerry, who spent much of 2004 attacking George W. Bush rather than offering inspiring alternatives. And so one must ask: Are the Wayward Democrats really onto something here or are they politically adrift? Are they the harbingers of a less ideological future or is the party now so riven by special interests that it cannot produce a coherent platform? Another possibility exists: Perhaps Democratic campaigns are being increasingly driven by personality factors, causing the party's historical themes to take a back seat to candidates' idiosyncratic approaches.

Intriguingly, we find independents to be clustered together in quadrant three, neither Republican nor Democratic in tone. There are advantages and disadvantages to such an approach. It has a swashbuckling feel to it, a man-against-the-house quality, but it also lacks coherence (Bastedo & Lodge, 1980) and produces volatility in voters' minds (Courser, 2010). Nancy Rosenblum (2008, p. 348) says that independents often seem like "atoms of the unorganized public bouncing off the structures of a party system," a metaphor connoting high levels of energy and low levels of central tendency. But independent rhetoric can also be appealing. If Republicans produce an "I" discourse and Democrats a "we" discourse, independents have the "you" market all to themselves. Ross Perot provides a fitting example:

> This has not been a typical election year. The two parties would like to have carried on as usual, ignoring real issues, focusing on their special interests. But you spoke out—you, the American people, told the folks in Washington that you own this country. Your job is only half done and if we don't take care of the unfinished business, all of your great work will have been wasted. If you don't show Washington that you are serious about change, we will be stuck with four more years of government in gridlock. (Perot, 1992)

Although it is too early to tell where the Tea Party is going, our (limited) findings show them to be fairly traditional Republicans.[7] When compared to politicians during the last twenty years, independents ranked lowest on the R-tone and second lowest on the D-tone versus conventional Republicans, Democrats, and Tea Party members.[8] In that sense, the two independents who have run for the presidency during the last thirty years really brought something new to the table. That made them attractive to reporters interested in telling colorful campaign stories, but it also made them sound somewhat alien. Traditional Democrats and Republicans, in contrast, share a language—one another's—and most Americans find that comforting. So, although Ross Perot could have lionized Ronald Reagan in the following way, and although George W. Bush or John McCain certainly could have done so, the fact that these are the remarks of Barack Obama shows that American politics is largely a game played between the forty-yard lines:

so "atypical"

> I think Ronald Reagan changed the trajectory of America in a way that Richard Nixon did not ... He put us on a fundamentally different path because the country was ready for it. They felt like with all the excesses of the 60s and the 70s and government had grown and grown but there wasn't much sense of accountability in terms of how it was operating. I think he tapped into what people were already feeling. Which is we want clarity, we want optimism, we want a return to that sense of dynamism and entrepreneurship that had been missing. (Obama as quoted in Stein, 2008, Jan. 16)

A final set of comparisons also sheds light on American political conventions. Figure 3.4 compares a set of cable TV and talk radio "rants" (authored by Keith Olbermann, Rachel Maddow, Bill O'Reilly, Glenn Beck, and Rush Limbaugh) to standard political discourse. The results

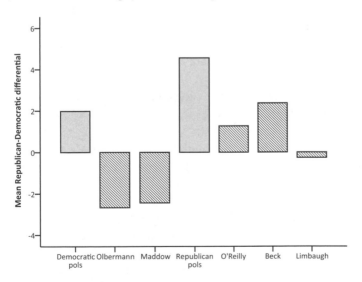

FIGURE 3.4 Party tone for ranters vs. conventional politicians.

are striking. Democrats had far higher RDD scores compared to ranters of similar political persuasion; that was also true when Republicans were contrasted to their counterparts in the media.[9] Overall, the ranters were far more flamboyant than the candidates, which may explain why many mainstream pols avoid cable television whenever they can. Qualities praised on the campaign circuit—earnest knowledgeability, thoughtful delineation of the issues, community involvement—contrast sharply with those preferred on TV: topical zig-zagging, verbal aggression, supercharged emotions, and preening self-regard. Some observers have described ranters as "endlessly confessional," persons who provide a nightly "outlet for anarchy" (Bromwich, 2010, para. 21). Rants are also said to be a "triumph of interactive political performance art" (Chafets, 2008, para. 22), a genre whose practitioners rival the "dunces of burlesque" (Appel, 2003, p. 223).

It is also interesting that the Democrats' RDD scores surpass those of almost all the ranters, again showing the cultural breadth expected of traditional politicians. The liberal ranters (Olbermann and Maddow) stress the Democratic concerns of populism and reform but rarely those of community or utility, not to mention nationalism. Similarly, the conservative ranters pump their chests about independence and restoration (and the Democrats' populism and reform) but largely eschew the Republicans' values-talk and the Democrats' concerns for community.

Politically, then, the ranters are not culturally invested. Being performers they circumvent the demands of nation building. Glenn Beck can be "emotional, dramatic and evocative" (McCollam, 2010, p. 56) and Bill O'Reilly "the plain-talking, straight-shooting classic American hero" (Peters, 2010, p. 863)—a marshal, that is, not a small-town mayor. Rush Limbaugh can weave "political alienation and anger into the illusion of common political ground" (Harris et al., 1996, p. 561) because he does not have to discuss sewer issues with townspeople at the monthly fish fry. The ranters' rhetoric, in short, contrasts sharply with the linguistic discipline found in day-to-day politics, a point recently made by Michael Kazin (2005, p. 114):

> Beginning with the antics of Joe McCarthy, an aggressive populism that rails against a liberal elite in the name of the patriotic, God-fearing masses has all but replaced the earlier conservatism characterized by the defense of social hierarchy, respect for state authority, and an aversion to heated rhetoric and the rapid social changes it seeks to inspire. Edmund Burke and John Adams

might be amused by the likes of Ann Coulter and Rush Limbaugh, but those be-wigged gentlemen would also recognize that such provocateurs have, in effect, rejected the philosophical tradition they cherished.

Overall, then, we have found (1) that Democrats and conventional Republicans have their own rhetorical tones, (2) that they frequently poach in one another's territories, and (3) that they commonly differ from political amateurs (independents, Tea Partyers, and popular commentators). But there is more to our story as well. Politics is a complex business and so too is political language. Not all politicians react in the same way to the same set of circumstances, and these variations can be instructive. While many commentators feel they already know everything that can be known about party politics, we continue to find surprises. We share some of them in the following section.

Balancing Party Tones

Rock impresario Bob Geldof got it wrong when declaring "You can't trust politicians. It doesn't matter who makes a political speech. It's all lies" (Iyer, 2005). What Mr. Geldof should have said is that the real problem, in the U.S. at least, is that there are too many truths to tell, which is why American politicians must be culturally bilingual. No matter what their political affiliation might be, they must adjust the "tolerances" of the R-tone and the D-tone to the task at hand. At first it seems shocking, then bizarre, but ultimately simply American that Barack Obama would author both of the following statements when anticipating his run for the presidency in 2008:

> And now, after three long years of watching the same back and forth in Washington, the American people have sent a clear message that the days of using the war on terror as a political football are over. That policy-by-slogan will no longer pass as an acceptable form of debate in this country. Mission Accomplished, cut and run, stay the course, the American people have determined that all these phrases have become meaningless in the face of a conflict that grows more deadly and chaotic with each passing day. (Obama, 2006, November 20)

> We cannot allow Iran to get a nuclear weapon. It would be a game-changer in the region. Not only would it threaten Israel, our strongest ally in the region

and one of our strongest allies in the world, but it would also create a possibility of nuclear weapons falling into the hands of terrorists. And so it's unacceptable. And I will do everything that's required to prevent it. And we will never take military options off the table. And it is important that we don't provide veto power to the United Nations or anyone else in acting in our interests. (Obama, 2008, October 7)

Like Shakespeare's Iago, presidential candidates like Obama are consistently inconsistent because the country they hope to lead is fashioned out of legion compromises—religious but not too religious, forward-thinking but committed to bedrock values, a democratized nation but a republic too. How can one address these complexities without becoming dizzy? One cannot. To run for the presidency in the United States, for example, is to commit oneself to twenty-four months of pure dizziness.

When viewed through a *rhetorical* lens, then, American political campaigns take on a different look. Table 3.2 is based on a simple measurement of the semantic distance between the two major candidates during each electoral cycle (as reported in figure 3.3). Table 3.2 reports, in essence, the intensity of the dialectic between the two combatants. The Dramatic Confrontations—those involving candidates at the greatest remove—are, not surprisingly, campaigns etched into the national memory: Truman's whistle-stopping, the Kennedy-Nixon debate, the tormenting of John Kerry by the Swift Boaters. All political campaigns, of course, feature sharp arguments, but some campaigns—for example, the Bush-Dukakis confrontation in 1988—become especially pointed: a staunch (if naïve) Democratic vs. a staunch (if distrusted) Republican. Both Bush and Dukakis had strategic problems to solve, so the former tried to out-Reagan Reagan and the latter had himself fatefully photographed in an army tank for the same reason.

The *grounds* of a given campaign can shift rightward or leftward depending on the political times. So, for example, figure 3.3 shows Ronald Reagan moving into enemy territory in 1980 to make himself sound somewhat progressive, while Bill Clinton attacked George H. W. Bush in 1992 for ruining the economy, a "Republican" strategy by most other reckonings. In contrast, the Reciprocal Exchanges find the candidates commonly focused (for example, Johnson and Goldwater in 1964 and Humphrey and Nixon in 1968). In these encounters, the candidates discuss much the same issues and use similar language. Overall, then, table 3.2 reveals a complex political geometry: Party tones are appropriated differently depending on

the issues, on media agendas, and on the candidates' cleverness. So, for example, the most experienced presidential candidate of them all—Richard Nixon—had to deal with a plethora of issues during his three runs for the White House and had to fashion a new rhetorical persona each time he ran.

Bilingual politics is also revealed in figure 3.5, which revisits the cultural "voices" discussed in chapter 2. This is perhaps the sharpest indicator of how similar Republicans and Democrats become when viewed from a distance. While both parties tilt in the expected directions (the R-tone for Republicans, the D-tone for Democrats), we also see an equivalence between them not found among the other spokespersons. Not surprisingly, the preachers embrace the historic values of the R-tone and avoid the utilitarian flavor of the D-tone. The protestors take the opposite approach, embracing reformist and communitarian refrains and circumventing the nationalistic appeals found among even Left-leaning politicians.[10]

None of this is surprising, but the corporate speakers are especially intriguing. Figure 3.5 shows them to be apolitical, really antipolitical, almost completely forsaking both party tones. But what is left to say for a corporate leader when people and their communities, when all transcendent truths, are left off the agenda? It leaves moral issues to be discussed only antiseptically and bureaucratically, as we see in the following:

> Fortunately, real life corporations show a more serious commitment to ethics. One sign of this interest is the number of companies that now issue a corporate code of ethics to employees. My own company does this. And a recent survey found that better than 90 percent of Fortune 500 companies require employees to subscribe to a code of ethics.
>
> These codes map out general principles and philosophy. But they also deal in specifics. For example, when the Pentagon charged General Dynamics with fraudulent billing, the company added this statement to its code: "Shifting of costs to inappropriate contracts is strictly forbidden."
>
> Another sign of corporate commitment is the creation of ethics training programs—and even departments—by many companies, including some that have been rocked by scandals. In the past few years, we've seen companies like Union Carbide, Boeing, McDonnell Douglas, and Chemical Bank set up programs to help employees deal with ethical conflicts. (Wade, 1988, pp. 341–342)

Texts like these help us see politics by contrast; no politician would discuss ethics this legalistically. One senses no passion here, no moral

TABLE 3.2 **Relationship of party tone to election type.**

Election type*	Year	Candidates	Party Tones**	Argument Alignment	Campaign Issues
Dramatic Confrontation	1948	Truman/Dewey	Staunch D/progressive R	Sharp left tilt	Do-nothing Congress; Social Security; civil rights; domestic economy
	1960	Kennedy/Nixon	Staunch D/staunch R	Perfect dialectic	Church and state; economic growth; foreign aid; civil rights; Cuba and Soviets
	1988	Dukakis/GHWBush	Staunch D/staunch R	Perfect dialectic	crime; deficit reduction; Iran-Contra scandal; liberalism; military readiness
	2004	Kerry/GWBush	Wayward D/staunch R	Sharp right tilt	Terrorism; Iraq war; WMDs; free trade; middle-class tax cuts; deficit; joblessness
Classic Conflict	1956	Stevenson/Eisenhower	Staunch D/centrist R	Balanced dialectic	Suez Canal; Brown vs. Board; nuclear disarmamen;; Soviet domination
	1976	Carter/Ford	Staunch D/centrist R	Leftward tilt	Watergate scandal; inflation; abortion; unemployment; energy crisis
	1980	Carter/Reagan	Staunch D/wayward R	Sharp left tilt	Hostage crisis; Cold War; Big Government; energy conservation
	1992	Clinton/GHWBush	Centrist D/staunch R	Sharp right tilt	Tax increases; economy; political scandal; free trade; military readiness

	Year	Candidates			
	1996	Clinton/Dole	Centrist D/centrist R	Sharp right tilt	Political scandal; health care; supply-side economics; campaign donations
	2008	Obama/McCain	Centrist D/centrist R	Rightward tilt	Terrorism; Bush administration; financial crisis; Socialism; Iraq; political change
Reciprocal Exchange	1952	Stevenson/Eisenhower	Centrist D/centrist R	Balanced dialectic	Communist expansion; Korean War; political corruption; civil liberties
	1964	Johnson/Goldwater	Conservative D/progressive R	Balanced dialectic	Racial integration; moral leadership, urban crime; states' rights
	1968	Humphrey/Nixon	Centrist D/centrist R	Leftward tilt	Vietnam war; voting rights; law and order; peace protesters
	1972	McGovern/Nixon	Centrist D/centrist R	Balanced dialectic	Anti-war movement; liberalism; détente with Communists; school busing
	1984	Mondale/Reagan	Centrist D/staunch R	Rightward tilt	Tax increases; national pride; economic recovery; ERA
	2000	Gore/GWBush	Centrist D/staunch R	Rightward tilt	Social Security; health care; nation-building; budget surplus; partisanship

* Based on distance between candidates' positions in figure 3.3
** Based on candidates' locations in figure 3.3.

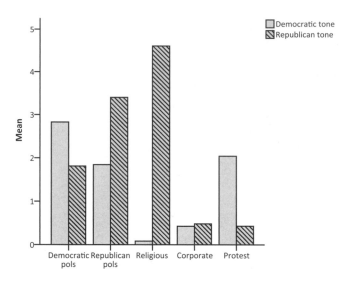

FIGURE 3.5 Party tone for politicians vs. other spokespersons.

certitude. There is nothing glandular in these remarks, no attempt to sort out true good and evil. No politician, in contrast, would treat ethical issues this dispassionately or this abstractly. Instead, they would look to the R-tone for God or to the D-tone for Justice. Sometimes they would look in both directions at once.

In other words, the available party tones give politicians something familiar to say to an often touchy electorate. Accustomed to these rhetorical formulas (hackneyed though they may be), voters come to "listen against" alternative locutions, which may explain why activists like Ralph Nader or Dennis Kucinich had a hard time being taken seriously by Democratic regulars, or why Jerry Falwell and the Christian Coalition unnerved mainstream Republicans. Corporate leaders too—one is reminded of Steve Forbes and Ross Perot—flagged and flailed on the campaign trail. The D-tone/R-tone axis may be boring but it tells the American people who is scary and who is not.

While it is culturally wise for politicians to use both party tones, it also makes strategic sense. Consider the case of George W. Bush who, as we saw in figure 3.3, made ample use of the R-tone during his run for the presidency in 2000 and increased it even more when seeking reelection four years later. The George W. Bush that most Americans remember is the one who sounded clarion calls like the following:

For all Americans these years in our history will always stand apart. There are quiet times in the life of a nation when little is expected of its leaders. This isn't one of those times. This is a time that requires firm resolve, clear vision, and a deep faith in the values that make us a great nation.

None of us will ever forget that week when one era ended and another began. On September the 14th, 2001, I stood in the ruins of the Twin Towers. It is a day I will never forget. I will never forget the voices of those in hard hats yelling at me at the top of their lungs, "Whatever it takes." I will never forget the police or firefighter coming out of the rubble who grabbed me by the arm and he looked me square in the eye, and he said, "Do not let me down." Ever since that day—ever since that day, I wake up every morning thinking about how to better protect our country. I will never relent in defending America, whatever it takes. (Bush, 2004, September 17)

But this is only one version of the nation's forty-third president. As we will see in chapter 7, there is considerably more to Bush than meets the eye. Because we had built a day-by-day compendium of Bush's presidential speeches (roughly 2,300 in total), we were able to get an unusually detailed look at his partisan tendencies. To be sure, Bush made some dramatic statements during his eight years in office, but figure 3.6 shows something else as well: he became more and more "republican" as his

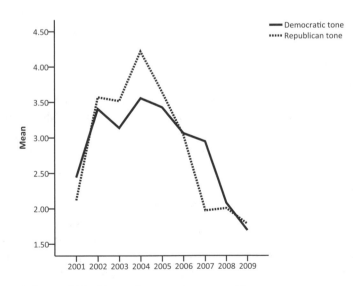

FIGURE 3.6 George W. Bush's use of party tone across presidency.

reelection approached and then quickly returned to a more "presidential" approach. Equally interesting is his simultaneous deployment of the Democratic tone, showing that he pulled out all the stops to win the 2004 election.

In the following passage, for example, we find Mr. Bush bashing corporate malfeasance and even seeming to be an environmental activist, thereby showing voters that he appreciated the full range of American political values:

> In order to make sure there's a hopeful society, we've got to make sure this economy continues to grow. Now, when you're out gathering the vote, remind your friends and neighbors what this economy has been through. We've been through a recession. We've been through corporate scandals—that meant some people forgot what it meant to be a responsible citizen. We passed laws that now make it clear we're not going to tolerate dishonesty in the boardrooms of our country . . . [And] we need an energy plan to make sure jobs stay right here in America. In order to make sure people can find work, this country must have an energy plan. I submitted one to Congress that said we're going to encourage conservation, we'll use renewables like ethanol and biodiesel, we'll use clean coal technologies, we'll use technologies to explore in environmentally friendly ways for natural gas. (Bush, 2004, October 21)

The argument we are making here is not one of political expediency—use whatever you can to get elected—but that elections are certifying moments, moments when politicians from both parties must show they can run a complex and divided nation. Some do this with special creativity, as when John F. Kennedy turned the civil rights issue into a moral argument (Goldzwig & Dionisopoulos, 1989) or when Ronald Reagan equated individualism with community service (Moore, 1991). As Danny Hayes (2005, p. 912) has noted, "The traits that matter the most for candidates are the ones they do not own." As a result, rhetoric on loan from the opposite party becomes a handy adjunct to one's campaign arsenal.

Different electoral settings also demand partisan balance. The formula is to talk like a Republican when debating, and talk like a Democrat in your ads. These effects held true for both parties and were fairly robust statistically.[11] Given what we know about campaign genre, these findings make sense. Campaign debates are highly structured by the press and follow a strict agenda, giving candidates little room for serendipity or obvious pandering. Debates' face-to-face formats, as well as the publicity they afford, make candidates cautious, which leads to protectionist stances—keep us safe, keep us fed, keep us moral—thereby bringing out the Republican even in non-Republicans. Bill Clinton exemplifies:

> Before Senator Dole left the Senate, he and Mr. Gingrich also were recommending that we pass these tax cuts only insofar as we could pay for them. We all assume that the tax cuts will be permanent. But we have to prove we can pay for them. After he left the senate, we abandoned that. That's why most experts say that this tax scheme will blow a huge hole in the deficit, raise interest rates and weaken the economy and that will take away all the benefits of the tax cut with a weaker economy. That's why we have to balance the budget, and I will tell you how I'm going to pay for anything I promise you, line by line. You should expect that from both of us. (Clinton, 1996, October 16)

> We have worked hard to put more and more pressure on the Castro Government to bring about more openness and move toward democracy. In 1992, before I became president, Congress passed the Cuban Democracy Act and I enforced it vigorously. We made the embargo tougher ... Every single country in Latin America, Central America and the Caribbean is a democracy tonight but Cuba. And if we stay firm and strong we will be able to bring Cuba around as well. (Clinton, 1996, October 6)

> One of my proudest moments was signing the Religious Freedom Restoration — !
> Act, which says the government's got to bend over backwards before we interfere with religious practice ... I supported character education programs in our schools, drug-free schools programs. I supported giving parents a V-chip on their television. So, if they don't want their young kids to watch things they shouldn't watch, they wouldn't have to. (Clinton, 1996, October 16)

Bill Clinton, of course, had an uncanny ability to "claim the space beyond partisanship" (Velasco, 2010, p. 7), and this medley of excerpts shows how deft—and how multidirectional—he could be. But these remarks were not his and his alone. They were also fashioned by the debate setting itself, a setting in which he was stared down by his opponent and by testy members of the press. The complexity of the issues, as well as their gravity, prompted Clinton to dip into the conservative arsenal.

Campaign ads, in contrast, permit more rhetorical license. They are shaped by media professionals, not by the candidate, and regularly tap into popular emotions. They are typically short, jaunty, and hard-hitting. They can also be quite personal—the candidate and his wife, the candidate and his horse—and sumptuously visual. They are frequently shot in the nation's villages and towns, featuring the candidate among a gaggle of admirers. Ads are displayed on television, a people's medium, and appeal to needs that voters cannot articulate but nonetheless feel. No matter what candidate is featured, then, advertising has a Democratic cast to it. Even George W. Bush understood that:

- Community: A lot of new Americans arrived today. They were neither Republican nor Democrat, but someone held them close and hoped. (Bush, 2000, July 20)
- Reform: America's having a recession, an education recession, that's hurting our children. Our students rank last in the world in math and physics ... and most fourth graders in our cities can't read. (Bush, 2000, September 26)
- Utility: To keep our commitment to seniors we must strengthen and improve Social Security now, or the retirement of the Baby Boom generation will push it near bankruptcy. (Bush, 2000, June 13)
- Populism: Why vote for George W. Bush? Because he believes in family. Because he supports education. Because he knows we all are the new face of America. Because he wants no child to be left behind. Because it's time for a change. (Bush, 2000, September 9 [advertisement])

So this is our lot: Republicans sounding like Democrats on the even days of the week, Democrats like Republicans on the odd days. For a variety of complex reasons, the U.S. has become a bicameral nation structurally and a bilingual nation rhetorically. Americans want it all: to be old and new at the same time, to be alone, mostly, but neighborly when it suits them. Americans hold fast to certain transcendent values but they also understand what Dwight Eisenhower meant when declaring that "everyone should have a religion, and I don't care which one." Americans do not like to be told what to do except when the pressure is on; then they want answers yesterday, not today. Americans are usually a practical people but they are also prideful, sometimes flying the nation's most sacred symbol from the antennas of their pickup trucks. Somehow, U.S. politicians come to understand all of these pieces and parts. As a result, the best of them learn to talk out of both sides of their mouths.

Conclusion

A quintessential American tragedy occurred on January 8, 2011, when U.S. Congresswoman Gabrielle Giffords, Democrat of Arizona, and several of her fellow citizens were shot by Jared Lee Loughner in Tucson. Like all tragedies, the Giffords attack prompted both grief and introspection. Like all *political* tragedies, it also prompted anger and confusion and a good deal of thrashing about. One perspective held that the Giffords shooting was inspired by the coarsening of political discourse in the United States, by the flame throwers on talk radio and their partisan cousins on Fox News and MSNBC. "We have become intolerant" went the call. "We need more civility" went the response.

Into the breach stepped Sarah Palin and, soon after, Barack Obama. Palin declared that a "blood libel" had been directed at her kind. She argued further that only Jared Loughner was responsible for the crime. "Public discourse and debate isn't a sign of crisis," Palin asserted, "but of our enduring strength. It is part of why America is exceptional." "We are better than the mindless finger-pointing we endured in the wake of the tragedy," she concluded (Palin, 2011). While Palin pummeled the Right's detractors, Obama became quite personal: "Gabby opened her eyes. Gabby opened her eyes, so I can tell you she knows we are here." He soared above the prosaic, urging the nation's people "to look forward, to reflect on the present and the future, on the manner in which we live our lives and nurture our relationships . . . We are reminded that in the fleeting time we have on this Earth, what matters is not wealth, or status, or power or fame but, rather, how well we have loved and what small part we have played in making the lives of other people better" (Obama, 2011, January 13).

The returns poured in immediately and the headlines reported a slam-dunk for Obama:

- The Contrast Couldn't Be Clearer (www.guardian.co.uk)
- Palin, and Media, Created Space for Obama (www.politico.com)
- First Thoughts: Obama Recaptures his 2004 Voice (www.msnbc.com)
- The Non-Accusatory Case for Civility (www.nationalreview.com)
- Obama Takes Opportunity Palin Missed (www.politico.com)
- As Obama Urged Unity, Palin Brought Division (www.washingtonpost.com)
- Mourner-in-Chief's Eulogy Puts Palin to Shame (www.thedailybeast.com)

One could interpret these assessments as more evidence of liberal media bias, but Figure 3.7 undercuts that claim. During her speech, Palin

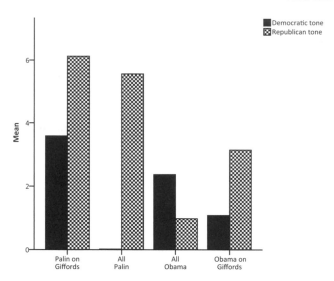

FIGURE 3.7 Palin/Obama reactions to Giffords attack.

was her usual Republican self but she also channeled her inner Democrat with her pugnacious and populist refrains. Obama did just the opposite, ratcheting up the R-tone and modulating the D-tone. The result is that Palin came off as crabbed and sectarian, Obama as statesmanlike, even sermonic. The irony, of course, is that both Palin and Obama could be accused of stealing one another's identities. When doing so, however, Palin botched the job while Obama proved himself the master thief.

The larcenous metaphor, of course, is all wrong. Both Obama and Palin were appropriating their own pluralistic birthright, albeit he better than she. The U.S. has always been attracted to rival discourses, one driving it forward, the other holding it back. During the Giffords affair, Barack Obama was better at working both the clutch and the accelerator. As a result, even the conservative press tipped its hat in his direction. All judged him to be "less partisan" than Palin, although the more accurate claim is that he was fulsomely partisan, brilliantly partisan. Mr. Obama turned a horrific event into a moral lesson while Palin defended the hard to defend. She chose her target poorly and her timing was atrocious. In contrast, Obama knew, as Aristotle knew, that rhetoric is the art of identifying the available means of persuasion in a given case. In the United States, there have always been two ways of getting that done. Political artistry involves knowing how to use which when.

Mailer Wilson on
sp[...] men - 176

Geof Nunberg on "Iraq-list"
shot every [...]
on CNN p106

Drew Gilpin
McCoy - Rep
early America -
"freeze in time" --
spatial
expansion

CHAPTER FOUR

Modernity and the Urgent Tone

Barack Obama soared to the presidency on the wings of time.[1] Everything about his campaign in 2008 was timely: He announced his campaign on February 10, 2007, a full two years before he would take the oath of office as president; he began building a campaign organization much earlier than his Democratic rivals, and he mastered the untested "social media" before most politicians had heard of Facebook or Twitter. Time was also his handmaiden during the general election: He was more vibrant than rival John McCain; he took a perfectly timed trip to Israel in July 2008 to solidify the Jewish vote back home; his campaign's "Fight the Smears" website was informed and agile. In the end, the American people chose "change" over "a steady hand at the tiller." As if to repay his debt to Time, Mr. Obama used 105 temporal words when delivering his inaugural address. Here is what he said in part:

> We remain *a young nation*, but in the words of Scripture, the *time has come* to set aside childish things. The *time has come* to reaffirm our *enduring spirit*; to choose our *better history*; to *carry forward* that precious gift, that noble idea, *passed on* from *generation to generation*: the God-given promise that all are equal, all are free, and all deserve a chance to pursue their full measure of happiness. (Obama, 2009, January 20)

Don't all politicians use the language of time? They do, but not always in the same proportion and that is what intrigues us here. Conservatives, for example, often plan for the future by consulting the past, drawing on the wisdom of the ancients to light the way. Liberals, on the other hand, often point to the present—to pressing needs and recent scandals— and use such tones to open up possibilities. We humans live in time and

(past) fountain of wisdom / something to be spoiled
source of contrast — something to be escaped --

time lives in us. We cannot help but talk about time, pray about it, worry about it.

We also live in space and that too affects how we see the world. Literal space, of course, is just rocks and trees and streams and land. It is agnostic about meaning. Place, on the other hand, is filled with meaning—the secret haunts of childhood, the sacred shrines to which devotees make pilgrimage, the icons surrounding the nation's battlefields (Dickinson, Blair & Ott, 2010). As numerous commentators have observed, to take the place out of politics is to take the politics out of politics. Wherever we roam, politics is there: in the ethnic neighborhoods of Chicago, at the fish fries in the Southland, in the snows of New Hampshire during the primaries.

The presidency of George W. Bush was a spatial presidency far more than a temporal one. Like Barack Obama, he referred to matters of time in his second inaugural but he used far more spatial terms. He spoke of Americans' "journey of progress and justice" and of those living in "the darkest corners of the world." His metaphors were often banal (citizens living in "a chosen nation," others making "their own way") but he occasionally stretched rhetorically, referring to the "truths of Sinai" and to an "edifice of character." Mostly, though, the Bush presidency was about a place savaged (in lower Manhattan) and other places savaged in return (Afghanistan, Iraq). For George W. Bush, space was a very real thing:

> At *this second gathering*, our duties are defined not by the words I use, but by the history we have seen together. For a half century, America defended our own freedom by *standing watch* on *distant borders* . . . We have seen our vulnerability and we have seen its deepest source. For as long as *whole regions of the world* simmer in resentment and tyranny—prone to ideologies that feed hatred and excuse murder—*violence will gather*, and multiply in destructive power, and *cross the most defended borders*, and raise a mortal threat . . . *We are led*, by events and common sense, to one conclusion: The survival of liberty *in our land* increasingly depends on the success of liberty *in other lands*. The best hope for peace *in our world* is the *expansion* of freedom *in all the world*. (Bush, 2005, January 20)

In this chapter, we explore shifts in tone between space and time. Our interest began by our casually noticing that, during the last sixty years, the language of time—Barack Obama's language—seemed to be overtaking the language of space—George W. Bush's language—and that it was doing so in a number of different genres. Not all of these changes were of great statistical magnitude but they kept presenting themselves in political

speeches, candidate advertising, campaign debates, and political news coverage. Between 1948 and 2008, we found that references to place—city,
country, continent—declined while references to time—weeks, months,
years—increased. What does this mean and why should we care?

We sense that these changes are part of a larger cultural story, one that
goes beyond politics but that is also rooted in politics. Politicians are leaders, to be sure, but they are also followers, persons with a special ability
to understand their particular moment in history. Tracking time and space
words helps us see how they struggle with modernity, how much valence
they accord it, and how willing they are to submit to its demands. Modernity, says Elizabeth Goodstein (2005, p. 10), breeds a "democratiza-
tion of skepticism" by calling precedents into question and also the stabilities of the old place-based societies. In modern times, say Giddens &
Pierson (1998, p. 16), "traditions and customs, beliefs and expectations"
become "bendable, plastic resources in a globalized, cosmopolitan world
of intersecting cultures and life styles." Such a condition has direct implications for who can be persuaded to do what. Whereas in earlier times
the "rhythms of the seasons, the cycles of day and night [and] the extremes of weather" set a people's course, their descendants are caught
up in "a twenty-four-hour, three-hundred-and-sixty-five-day-a-year global
economy" (Giddens & Pierson, 1998, pp. 16–17). The result? A perpetually excited, perpetually intrigued, but vaguely worried polity.

Rhetorically, then, modernity presents two strong options to those who
live within its embrace: (1) Go with the flow or (2) resist it fitfully. Submitting to the "tyranny of the moment," says Eriksen (2001, p. 3), makes
the transgeographical technologies of the day popular and fosters a more
international mind set; on the other hand, it can result in some amount
of free-floating anxiety and can even increase a people's diastolic blood
pressure (Patrick et al., 1983). On the other hand, clinging to the old
spatial imaginaries can make one feel trapped—or comforted—by the
place-based determinations of ritual, tribe, religion, kinship, and occupation. What does it mean, then, to think in time? to think in space? What
possibilities do they open up for the nation's leaders and those they lead?

Sampling Modernity

We pursue those questions here. When stumbling upon our findings about
space and time, our initial instinct was to treat them as artifactual, the sort
of random result produced when a great many objects are studied simul-

taneously. Several things prevented us from doing so, however: The risings and fallings were not always linear but they often moved in straight lines and were repeated across different datasets, a suggestion that something broadly cultural was going on. That impression is heightened when one realizes that they result from simple dictionary searches—361 words referring to time, 364 to space. Naturally, this kind of tallying does not tell us how these terms were used, but there is also value in our approach. By keying exclusively on vocabulary, the DICTION program does something that people cannot do: It pays attention to phenomena outside their awareness. This is especially true of temporal and spatial words that are used spontaneously and omnipresently, so central are they to the fundaments of thinking and speaking. Such usages highlight basic ontological forces that, according to Kenneth Burke (1950), "goad" us to achieve more—to win quickly, to displace our opponents, to ascend the social hierarchy.

In focusing on space and time words, we therefore feature large things masked as small things. We also feature two forces central to so much of human creativity—to science fiction's time warping, to religion's concern for the millennial, to road trip movies and to space travel, to journalism's insistence that we stay contemporary. And since politics is both a protective force (e.g., "homeland security") and a vehicle for change (e.g., "a new tomorrow"), space and time are never not at issue.

Hence, we focus in this chapter on two sets of everyday words:

SPATIAL TERMS: Terms referring to geographical entities, physical distances, and modes of measurement. Included are general geographical terms (*abroad, elbow-room, locale*) as well as specific ones (*Ceylon, Kuwait, Poland*). Also included are politically defined locations (*county, fatherland, municipality*), points on the compass (*east, southwest*) and the globe (*latitude, border, snow-belt*), as well as terms of scale (*kilometer, map, spacious*), quality (*vacant, out-of-the-way, disoriented*), and change (*pilgrimage, migrated, frontier.*)

TEMPORAL TERMS: Terms that locate a person, idea, or event within a specific time interval, thereby signaling a concern for processes and measurements. The Temporal dictionary designates literal time (*century, instant, mid-morning*) as well as metaphorical designations (*lingering, seniority, nowadays*). Also included are calendrical terms (*autumn, year-round, weekend*), and elliptical terms (*spontaneously, postpone, transitional*) and judgmental terms (*premature, obsolete, punctual*) having to do with time.

The data being reported here derive from the overall dataset described in chapter 1: (1) campaign speech segments (n = 3,903); (2) political debate segments (n = 907); (3) political ad segments (n = 719); (4) print coverage segments (n = 11,037); (5) broadcast segments (n = 2,370); and (6) letters to the editor (n = 8,125).

The average passage in our study contained 10.2 spatial terms and 15.3 temporal terms.[2] For efficiency's sake, these data were standardized (via z-scores) and then converted into a simple time-space ratio, which distributed itself normally across the 27,231 passages examined. In effect, the time-space ratio became a humble measure of a speaker's preoccupation with the demands of modernity. A high time-space ratio gives an audience the sense that grand happenings are under way, that pressing decisions must be made. A low ratio anchors them in the experienced world, inviting them to survey the scene at a more measured pace. A high ratio signals rhetoric on the move; a low ratio signals rhetoric in reflection.

In the pages that follow, we report how these tones distributed themselves over the years and across genres, and we look for political, cultural, and rhetorical factors to explain them. Our lexical counts do not constitute Grand Science but they were carefully gathered and are far too intriguing to be ignored. While the poet Andrew Marvell's (1994, pp. 22–23) lament—"had we but world enough and time"—may well capture the human condition, it has a special poignancy in the world of politics. That is the story we tell here.

Space, Time, and Politics

In recent years, scholarly questions have been raised about space and time in virtually all disciplines. Historian Andrew Grafton (2003, p. 79), for example, draws on Renaissance thought when calling chronology and geography the "twin eyes of history," while Burnett (2003) reminds us that British technologies of timekeeping in the nineteenth century made round-the-world shipping—and colonial expansion—possible, thereby changing global geopolitics. Almost immediately, time became the handmaiden of industrialization, with timepieces serving as a way of measuring productivity and giving capitalism an empirical scoreboard. Economist S. B. Linder (1970) says that this has produced a "harried leisure class" in the United States, and sociologist Ernst van den Haag (1960, p. 316) reports the inevitable result: "the culture of nearly everybody today" becomes "the culture of nearly nobody yesterday."

Students of cultural studies have examined what happens when modern communication technologies turn place-based societies into "radically open" public spheres (Delanty, 2000) where geographically centered identities, what political scientist Warren Magnusson (2001, p. 201) calls the "old spatial imaginary," yield to global cities. The result, says Weaver (2001, p. 6), is a "rhetoric of nowhere," which leads to "exploitation by destroying any sense of the unique value of any particular place." This rhetoric, he says, is "a language in which particulars"—of places, individuals, and communities—inevitably disappear. As a result, says scientist E. O. Wilson (1998, p. 35), "schools are turning out millions of graduates who do not know, in this sense, where they are."

According to communication scholar John Hartley (2003, p. 258), the mass media are abetting this sense of placelessness: "Journalism as a national discourse . . . the modern . . . equivalent of the agora/forum of the city/polis, is in long, slow decline." "Once virtualized," says Hartley (p. 257), "a sense of civic or national identity is also rendered portable," thereby making ties to a particular nation-state seem quaint at best. Living in a world "that is golly-gosh today" and "chip-wrapper tomorrow," a world in which speed determines everything, privatizes the public. All of this leads to what Carter (1994, p. 39) calls "the law of disappearing nows."

But if Time is a bully, Space makes its demands as well. In *Place Matters*, Peter Dreier and his colleagues (2001) call the roll of spatial politics: exclusionary zoning laws, wasteful land use, Section 8 housing vouchers, regional jurisdiction debates, neighborhood crime rates, urban sprawl, the decline of the inner cities. Problems like these leave little retreat. They are hardy perennials, persistent because they are land based.

Conceptually, then, one can make a case for either space or time as the central term of American political life. Hence this chapter. What sort of politics is heralded by shifts in space and time? Which set of actors—professional politicians, members of the press, the American voter—uses which tone and why? What inspires their locutions and what is their impact? To answer such questions, we need a bit of data.

The politics of time

Figure 4.1 reveals the nation's changing vocabularies of space and time. The mass media, clearly, have become increasingly obsessed with matters of time during the last sixty years. They relentlessly incorporate temporal references in their reportage and the trend is almost linear. Only

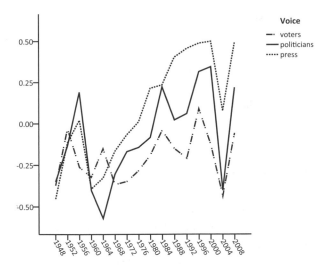

FIGURE 4.1 Time-space ratio by political voice over time.

the 2004 election arrested that trend, giving clear evidence of a "Bush effect," revealing a political candidate who emphasized space more than any presidential candidate since Barry Goldwater in 1964.[3] As they have done historically, the media keep their readers on the edge of time, in part because press norms demand a propulsive narrative. By looking carefully at how the press moves a story along, one realizes that media reportage has become especially "anxious" in recent years. Consider, for example one newspaper report from October 2008:

> John McCain unveiled a feisty **new campaign speech Monday**, but the **talk of change and promise** of a fist-shaking **fight to November** failed to allay Republican concerns that the presidential **race may be slipping** beyond his grasp. With **21 days to the election**, there was widespread agreement that **Wednesday night's third and final presidential debate** would be a crucial opportunity—and **perhaps the last one**—for the Arizona senator to **change the course** of a race that appears to be **moving strongly** in Democrat Barack Obama's direction. (*Los Angeles Times,* October 14, 2008)

Language like this is so thick today that it is almost invisible. Now, it is hard to imagine any other way of telling a story, so accustomed are we to the breathlessness of modern reporting. In the passage above, the *Los Angeles Times* writers keep us enthralled as they careen from campaign stop to campaign stop. A quick tone like this keeps readers asking for more—more details, more speed, more unexpectedness—and that keeps them attentive (or so the theory goes).

To imagine another way of reporting politics, one would have to go back to this same *Los Angeles Times* in September 1968. Even though the following passage is laced with facts, focuses squarely on important matters, and offers nuanced interpretations of the Nixon campaign, its prose is far too labored for the modern eye:

> Former **Pennsylvania Governor** William H. Scranton **said here** Friday that he was **going to Europe** at Richard M. Nixon's request to discuss **the situation there** with **Western leaders**. Scranton told a Statler-Hilton press conference he would leave Sept. 18 for **England, France, West Germany, the Netherlands and Belgium**. He **plans to return** Oct. 19. The leaders he is to meet will be announced when arrangements have been completed, he said.
>
> Nixon believes strongly that the **Soviet Union's invasion** of **Czechoslovakia** makes it important to learn what the **United States allies** are thinking, Scranton said. Scranton said reassessment was important to **world peace,** to **revitalize the free world** and to **strengthen NATO**, not just military but economically and by developing a sense of unity **among the allies**. That unity is important, he said, because only with it can the *free world* have the diplomatic leverage to negotiate a real detente with the **Soviet Union**. (*Los Angeles Times*, September 7, 1968)

The modern eye has a counterpart—the modern ear—and that only adds to the media's preoccupation with time. When we disaggregate our data, we find, not surprisingly, that broadcast news is even more obsessed with temporal issues and less concerned with matters of space, in part because the medium permits it.[4] With television, we can go anywhere, do anything, and return in time for a commercial. "Since Desert Storm," says Roger Stahl (2008, p. 76), "'liveness' has become the prime news value, with all its emphasis on immediacy, presence, and experience." Liveness has become the defining feature of our era of communications.

We also find that time-space ratios are higher for political ads than for speeches or debates, a finding that comports with other research studies.[5] McCarty and Hattwick (1992), for example, show that U.S. advertising, like American politics itself, is more future-oriented than its Mexican counterpart. This also holds true for television programming, where network executives "imbue their lineups with a relentless future orientation,

with the use of common promotional phrases such as 'coming up,' 'just
ahead,' and 'next'" (Weispfenning, 2003, p. 175). Political ads are no different, since they can always describe the next moment as the better moment. "If today's exigencies are weighing you down," the ads tell us, "you
can reinvent yourself tomorrow." If yesterday's policies have run to ruin,
next week's will surely fix things. In so many ways, time offers a rich field
of possibilities to the ambitious politician.

Even though the electronic media make special use of temporal references, that tone has become increasingly attractive to political candidates
on the campaign trail as well, almost as powerfully and almost as broadly.
As we see in figure 4.2, such changes took hold thirty years ago and have
increased steadily since then, with the notable exception of George W.
Bush, a man whose presidency became mired in other people's places.
The contrast between Bush and Obama could not be starker, with Obama
being the "candidate of change" whose central icon was that of a watch
slowing down—of opportunities lost, jobs ended, mortgages cancelled. It
is hard to imagine a speech more rooted in its moment than the one Mr.
Obama gave in Columbus, Ohio, two days before the 2008 election:

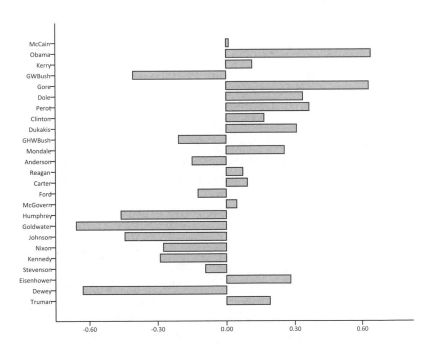

FIGURE 4.2 Time-space ratio for political candidates, 1948–2008.

We *began this journey* in the *depths of winter* nearly *two years ago*, on the steps of the Old State Capitol in Springfield, Illinois. *Back then*, we didn't have much money or many endorsements. We weren't given much of a chance by the polls or the pundits. We knew how steep our climb would be . . . . *Twenty-one months later*, my faith in the American people has been vindicated. That's how *we've come so far* and so close—because of you. That's how *we'll change this country*—with your help. And that's why we *can't afford to slow down*, sit back, or let up for *one day, one minute, or one second* in these *last few days*. *Not now*. Not *when so much is at stake*. (Obama, 2008, November 2)

Mr. Obama shows how tightly intertwined politics and time can be. In part this is because time is more malleable than space. It was more than ironic, then, that just two years later Mr. Obama's words had come back to haunt him. The temporal urgency he emphasized during his run for the highest office in the land still abided in the United States, with the unemployment rate stuck at 9.5% and with Obama being pressured daily to fix a seemingly unfixable economy. But even in the teeth of an apparent Republican resurgence, Mr. Obama clung to time when returning to Ohio two months prior to election day in 2010:

A *lot has changed* since I came here in those *final days* of the *last election*, but what hasn't is the choice facing this country. It's still fear versus hope; the *past versus the future*. It's still a choice between *sliding backward* and *moving forward*. That's what this election is about. That's the choice you'll face *in November*. . .

I know that folks are *worried about the future*. I know there's still a lot of hurt out here. And *when times are tough*, I know it can be tempting to give in to cynicism and fear; to doubt and division—to set our sights lower and settle for something less. But that is not who we are, Ohio. (Obama, 2010, September 9)

As Mr. Obama shows, time is a rhetorically "open text"—its units of measurement are precise (seconds, minutes, etc.) but measuring its *meaning* is something else entirely. That fact was clearly dramatized during the daylight savings debates of the early twentieth century. "It has yet to be proved," declared a newspaper editorial of the time, "that a return to the hours kept by hens and savages confers any ponderable benefits" on the good citizens of the United States (quoted in O'Malley, 1990, p. 270). Discussions of this sort quickly turned political, not just because human resources were at stake (agricultural productivity and urban entertainment zones, for example), but also because the present moment admits to so many different interpretations. The rhetoric of memory is similarly indeterminate. Memorializing events such as the attack on Pearl Harbor, says Richard Fenn (2001, pp. 16–17), "constitutes a rebellion against the passage of time" that turns politics into a "contingency game" where no particular outcome is "foreordained or inevitable."

Strategically, then, time is an omnipresent resource for the politician, especially when more tangible bounties like money, land, or influence are in short supply. "We are running out of time to act" declares the earnest candidate, as if all the nation's clocks would suddenly stop, as if policy time and mechanical time were identical. "Time is the most widely used noun in the English language," reports Barbara Adam (1995, p. 19), so it is not surprising that it has become a kind of universal anxiety machine that lets politicians use all there is to use—the past to memorialize and comfort, the future to challenge and inspire. In other words, politics is always incomplete; it never finishes its work, which can tire out a citizenry longing "for access to primordial time" (Fenn, 2001, p. 16), for once-and-forever solutions.

By discussing time as much as they do, politicians submit themselves to the dictates of modernity and to subtler things as well: time anxiety for an already anxious people, a secular rather than a religious worldview. The language of time addresses people in the most colloquial language of all—at the moment in which they live—but that can be costly from a cultural viewpoint. Fortunately, politics also has another language—the language of space—and it too has its attractions.

The politics of space

Figure 4.1 shows that despite the increasing sense of urgency built into mass media reportage during the last sixty years, the letter writers in our twelve small cities were much more obdurate.[6] Despite a bit more temporal concern in the Bush Sr. and Clinton years, the letters of the citizens who sounded off in their local newspapers were largely place based. These trends were consistent across the sample of newspapers—from Fall River, Massachusetts, to Springfield, Ohio; from St. Charles, Louisiana, to Billings, Montana. But while they emphasized the spatial over the temporal, theirs was not a leisurely discourse. Rather, its forcefulness derived from its geocentric intensity, from its pressing, communal tone:

I semi-agree with letters saying U.S. Rep. Jim Oberstar's having *no property in Minnesota* and paying no taxes *in the state* isn't the main campaign issue, even though *"your heart is where your home is."* The main issue is our *northern Minnesota economy*, and when you have no *vested interest in an area* there is no concern to help it. Oberstar's 5 percent approval rating from the National Federation of Independent Businesses and his zero rating by the *Minnesota Farm Bureau* are the main issues ... Is it any wonder jobs and businesses are **leaving our area**? (D. M., "Losing Jobs," *Duluth News-Tribune and Herald*, October 24, 1992)

I am writing because of the way the *voting places* were set up. I live less than *a mile from the courthouse*, where both Democrats and Republicans can vote together. Yet as I want to vote a Republican ticket, I have to *go across town*, about *4 1/2 miles* in order to vote the way I choose. I wonder why this election is set up this way, as it never has been before. There are *several places near me* where I could vote Democrat, but *no place closer* than said to vote Republican. I had to vote Democrat but my heart wasn't in it, as I didn't have time to *drive that far*. (J. L. S., "Voting Places," *Wichita Falls Record-News*, March 15, 1988)

Roger Evans is the best pick for the state representative of the *73rd District*. He has demonstrated his dedication to the *entire community* through his involvement and service to numerous organizations *in our area*. I want a person *in Columbus* who is *in touch with the citizens* he represents: Evans is the type of leader who will listen to the needs of the people *in our district*. (M.F., "Pick Evans," *Springfield News-Sun*, October 21, 2000)

Citizens like these are rooted in particular towns and that fact makes their arguments less airy than those of a politician. The confidence we see in these passages derives from what they see around them—people queuing up in the local meat market, buildings being erected, old friends being buried. The writers lend credence to Lawrence Cahoone's (2001, p. 32) observation that "the experience of neighborhood is the fundamental civic experience." This lets them decry the distant machinations of Washington, D.C., even while remaining loyal to their own member of Congress. Not being part of the Beltway Crowd, the letter writers can resist abstractions. Their letters sound provincial as a result, a sure sign they were written by people living somewhere.

A number of defenses have been offered for place-based politics. "Social ties and networks," says Alexandra Kogl (2002, pp. 17–18), are important forms of resistance "to the deterritorializations and decodings of

capitalism" because they generate "a sense of stability and security." The
alternative, says Kogl, is a society made up of "technomads" for whom
politics is a theoretical enterprise. But this is not to say that "rooted" individuals are instinctively political by nature. As Robert Lane (1962, p. 305)
observed some fifty years ago, community-based identities can produce
an "immobile" and hence "static" society. Citizens with a more cosmopolitan worldview, Lane determined, possessed a sense of adventure that
let them make "events in distant places more meaningful," thereby letting
them "pluralize the world" in ways that locals could not.

But it would be dangerously wrong to consider cosmopolitanism—
other-placedness, many-placedness—a universal good. Most wars in
human history, for example, have resulted from people trying to occupy
other people's territories ... just because they could. It would also be
wrong to view the politics of place as ignorant or unsophisticated. Especially in a time-obsessed world, which is often a money-obsessed world,
the need to shore up communities undone by environmental degrada-
tion (Buffalo comes to mind) or economic malaise (Detroit is but one example) has never been greater. It will take enormous intelligence and a
sophisticated model of social geography to solve such problems. Place is
central to politics precisely because people live there.

The letter writers in our sample seem especially aware of these matters, while the politicians were more conflicted by the competing demands
of space and time. As we saw in figure 4.2, presidential candidates in the
1970s and 1980s clustered near the midpoint of the continuum, thereby
becoming transitional figures in recent U.S. history. In contrast, politicians
in the 1950s and 1960s—direct heirs to two recent world wars—used spatial arguments to appeal to local truths and situated values. But as we see
in figure 4.3, even the most recent presidents situated themselves somewhere between the press and the people.

Given the equivalent competing demands of space and time, this
should not be surprising. But we also found a number of interesting variations on these trends:

- First-time campaigners had significantly higher time-space ratios than did sit-
  ting presidents running for reelection.[7]
- Most campaigners made significantly more time-based appeals two weeks
  before the election than they did earlier in the campaign.[8]
- Republicans used significantly more spatial appeals than did Democrats.[9]
- The most recent evidence of same: Barack Obama was much more urgent than
  John McCain during the 2008 race.[10]

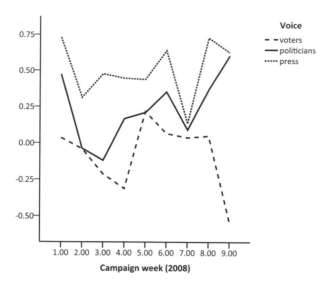

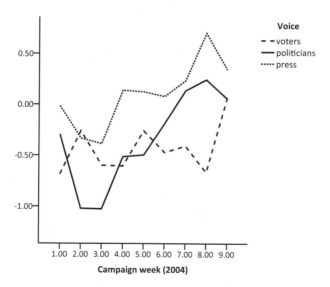

FIGURE 4.3 Time-space ratio by voice during campaign (1996–2008). Dotted lines = the press; solid lines = politicians; dashed lines = letter writers.

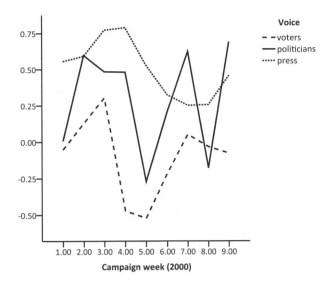

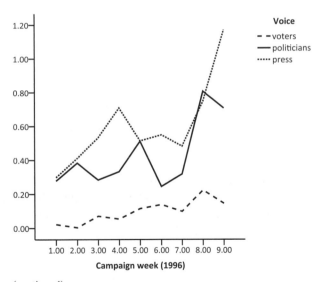

FIGURE 4.3 (continued)

Although American politicians used more temporal than spatial appeals during the last thirty years, George W. Bush became a dramatic exception by staking his reelection on the war in Iraq and by emphasizing his status as commander-in-chief.[11] The Swift Boaters pressed this same theme during that campaign, easily degrading the candidacy of John Kerry despite his service in the Vietnam War. Virtually any speech by Bush during the 2004 campaign explains why his time-space ratio was so low, but a single speech in Iowa displayed that tone as well as any:

- Our first duty in the war on terror is to *protect the homeland.* This morning *at the White House,* I signed a strong law that will make *our nation* more secure.
- Since September the 11th, law enforcement professionals have stopped terrorist activities in *Columbus, Ohio; San Diego, California; Portland, Oregon; Seattle, Washington; Buffalo, New York and other places, including New Jersey,* where we apprehended an arms dealer who was allegedly trying to sell shoulder-fired missiles to terrorists.
- The best way to prevent attacks is to stay on the offense against the *enemy overseas.* We are waging a *global campaign* from the *mountains of Central Asia to the deserts of the Middle East, and from the Horn of Africa to the Philippines.* (Bush, 2004, October 18)

Words such as these work on an audience powerfully when rattled off in quick succession. It is easy to feel primitive in their presence. They make one feel beleaguered, surrounded. The claustrophobia they inspire comes from a jumble of geographical images—some foreign, some domestic—and each possesses its own emotional charge.

Not surprisingly, the Left objects to rhetorics of place. Appeals based on ethnic nationalism, gated communities, and segregated housing lead to a "resurgence of romantic feelings and identifications that construct or reinforce boundaries between insiders and outsiders" says Weaver (2001, p. 2). Karen Piper (2002, p. 14) notes that to map the world is to stake a claim on that which is mapped, making cartography part of "a colonial discourse invested in establishing 'whiteness,' or transparency, as a kind of identity formation." And there is more than one irony here, says Piper (2002, p. 14), since "in reality, indigenous people are the ones who discovered the discoverers, led them to food and water, and shared their territorial knowledge—only to have it betrayed by the final product, the colonial map."

Henri Lefebvre (1991) offers an alternative perspective, arguing that because all places are spaces constructed by people (as, for example, when the American people turned the Gettysburg battlefield into a cemetery and later into a national shrine), their power is a real and legitimate part of the political equation. To dismiss place-based tonalities out of hand, says Cahoone (2001, p. 3), is therefore dangerously elitist. "While neighborhood is not a sufficient condition for wider concern," he continues, "it is a necessary condition" for an enlightened polity. Cahoone goes on to argue that local discussions of this sort are often more reasonable than distanced ones because they force people to deal with the actual conditions under which they live.

Although Mr. Bush pumped up his spatial rhetoric during the 2004 race, he also used the language of time to build a sense of urgency about the rest of his agenda. He, like all leaders, had no alternative. He knew that abandoning space for time would be foolhardy. The new communication technologies, Boyarin (1994) argues, have fundamentally changed people's ideas about proximity and simultaneity, and that harries them. At the same time, says Raka Shome (2003, p. 54), space no longer gives them "a settled source for some settled identity" as it may have in times past. "The hegemony of time is radical, whether to the left or the right," observes Cahoone (2001, p. 11), while place is "conservative in the broadest and homeliest sense of the term." Therein lies the human condition as well as the great struggles of modernity.

The data reported here show that the press emphasizes time, and voters space; the candidates are obeisant to both. *It is this "betweenness" that makes politicians unique.* Any other course of action would be problematic. Too much of a clarion warning that time is running out might seem precipitous. Too heavy an emphasis on space could, as the Bush data show, bring temptations of sovereignty to the surface. Provincialism or presentism? Tradition or modernity? American politicians wrestle constantly with these tonal options. A leader who is unable to say "where she is coming from" or "where she is going" will never make it in the Iowa caucuses. Similarly, candidates who lack a clear sense of "this nation's historic truths" or "the pressing demands of the moment" will fail as well. Space or time? Time or space? Within those Hobson's choices, American politics dwells.

Conclusion

Politicians talk about many things besides space and time. Newspapers write about much else as well. Nevertheless, space and time figure into

American politics in special ways—the Fourth of July is dutifully celebrated each year, presidential terms expire quadrennially on the twentieth
day in January, and CNN's "breaking news" alerts are now permanently
etched onto the nation's television screens. Because of new technological developments (the social media, instant messaging, etc.), time itself
seems to be accelerating. Because of the incessant demands of capitalism,
productivity per unit time is expected to increase exponentially or heads
will roll. Although time is an artificial construct, it rarely feels that way in
social affairs, in business affairs, and especially in political affairs.

Space too presents its challenges. Kurds live in four countries, none
of which is their country of choice. There are two Irelands in Ireland;
there are Palestinians in Israel and Israelis in Palestine; there are Native
Americans who feel like foreigners in their own land. Issues of space have
launched a thousand conflagrations, as have colonialism and ethnic hegemony. And the key political problem with space, of course, is its finitude.
While time unfolds endlessly, land just sits there, locked between oceans.
Nation-states come and go as a result, swapping mountaintops and prai-
ries as time passes. Outer space offers additional possibilities—mytholog-
ically at least—but then there is the travel involved. Politics is about more
things than place but it is always and everywhere about place.

The data reported here lead to important questions. The tendency
of political elites to ratchet up the time machine is ironic since political
change occurs so slowly. At this writing, for example, many Americans
are wondering if meaningful financial regulation beyond Dodd-Frank will
ever occur, given how fraught that discussion became during the Great
Recession. Oddly, the slower Congress's wheels turn, the more we are reminded of time—that we must act today and not tomorrow. Rhetoric of
this sort is what Kenneth Burke (1967) calls "secular prayer," calling upon
the gods to help us resolve the unresolvable. In politics, there is never
enough time to go around.

We need to know more about such matters. What calls forth the
rhetoric of time? Domestic or international problems? Axiological or
policy issues? Who are the agents of political time? Elected politicians?
The people themselves? We must also learn why the past is sometimes
central to our political deliberations and at other times irrelevant (see
Dickinson, Blair & Ott, 2010). We should also ask if the rhetoric of time is
as popular in other democracies or if it is a uniquely American obsession.
The world is modern too, but how modern?

And what of the rhetoric of place? When is it a sign of nativism and when is it emancipatory? Do the new technologies—satellite phones, for example, or the World Wide Web—signal the emergence of a world without fences or do they instead provide an improved delivery system for tribalism and ethnocentrism? In one of his more cryptic moments, Michel Foucault (1986, p. 23) observed that "the anxiety of our era has to do fundamentally with space, no doubt a great deal more than with time." Increasingly, he says, people are looking for a place to be, a task that becomes complicated in a world catering to high-speed consumers and addicted jet-setters. The letter writers in our study seem to be reacting to these modernist conditions and so we should ask what their instinctual tone is telling us. Are they hopelessly nostalgic, longing for a time when chain restaurants and franchised hardware stores were the exception rather than the rule? Or are they calling for a more substantial politics that can touch people more directly?

None of these are zero-sum choices, of course. Rhetorics of time and rhetorics of space have always existed and, more, have been intermingled in complex ways. Nowhere is this better seen than in the discourse of the modern labor union. As Dana Cloud (2011) artfully reports, the old, locale-based union shops are challenged constantly by needs for an international labor force. Also, demands associated with just-in-time production are creating a push-pull, stop-and-go dynamic that makes work routines harder to calibrate, to regularize, and to monetize. What should a union boss ask for under such bewildering conditions? How should a corporate leader respond?

All tones have their cycles. Given the now rather nasty logjam known as the United States Congress, for example, there is ample reason to worry that voting will soon seem passé. How can voters keep the faith when important moments are ballyhooed—a new candidacy, a revolutionary platform—only to be followed by more political torpor? How often can voters be told that they must act *now* without becoming skeptical? And if voters become immune to an urgent rhetoric, what sort of world will be ushered in? To have a virtual media system is one thing. To have a virtual or disengaged electorate is something else entirely. For these reasons, we must continue to ask ourselves what time it is and where we live.

CHAPTER FIVE

Institutions and the Assertive Tone

Lucas and Medhurst (2008) recently surveyed 137 scholars and asked them to rank the top 100 American speeches of the twentieth century. The speeches were rated on two criteria—rhetorical artistry and historical impact—and the results were not unexpected: Martin Luther King's "I Have a Dream" speech was chosen first, followed by the first inaugural addresses of John Kennedy and Franklin Delano Roosevelt, and then a long list of the usual suspects: Barbara Jordan, Huey Long, Douglas MacArthur, Mario Cuomo, Malcolm X, Jesse Jackson, Robert Kennedy, and so forth. Many of the speeches on the list given by sitting presidents were delivered "on location"—Ronald Reagan on the Evil Empire in Orlando, Dwight Eisenhower on atoms for peace in New York City, Lyndon Johnson on the Great Society in Ann Arbor, and Bill Clinton in Oklahoma City to commemorate the bombings. Most of the other presidential speeches were delivered from the Oval Office during prime time—John Kennedy on the Cuban missile crisis, Gerald Ford pardoning Richard Nixon, Jimmy Carter declaring a crisis of confidence, Lyndon Johnson announcing he would not seek reelection, and Richard Nixon on the Cambodian incursion. Not a single Saturday morning radio address made the top-100 list.

Nonetheless, these addresses exist—in plenitude. Ronald Reagan, who got his performance chops via radio early in his career, returned to it when taking office, the same medium he used to keep in touch with his conservative supporters after leaving the California governorship in 1974 (Gould, 2003). George H. W. Bush abandoned the practice of religiously making weekend addresses, but Bill Clinton took it up with gusto in 1993, as did George W. Bush in 2001. Barack Obama made further innovations, presenting his weekend addresses on the radio but also online and usually with video capture. Obama also broke news in this format when announcing some of his cabinet picks, a strategy suggested by his Office of New Media (Cillizza, 2008), which oversees Twitter postings for some 1.7 million of the president's followers (Auletta, 2010).

Substance-wise, the weekend addresses are often forgettable, but their political architecture is interesting. Ronald Reagan, for example, often kept the subject of his speeches top secret to preclude his Democratic respondents from offering substantive retorts. Unlike Bill Clinton, who offered fairly long-winded remarks, Mr. Reagan was usually pithy, often editing his speeches by hand prior to airtime (Rowland & Jones, 2002). Reagan's folksy approach worked well on the radio, says Han (2006), which may be why his rather stiff successor resorted to it only seventeen times during his four years in office. Bill Clinton's tendency to depart from a script drove time-conscious station managers crazy, but he cleverly included fresh material that had not been part of the news cycle, thereby enticing the press to draw near. George W. Bush's strategy was different still. He focused heavily on domestic issues to reach an at-home electorate and used short sentences and upbeat themes to not overstay his welcome (Sigelman & Whissell, 2002).

Given the pedestrian qualities of such rhetoric, why bother with it? Our argument here is that the weekend address sheds light on the broad-based institutionalization that has accelerated in American politics in recent years. Modest though these speeches are, presidents continue to use them. Can ego alone explain their indulgence? If not, why would the president visit the broadcast booth on a Saturday morning when his fellow citizens are overseeing soccer practice or trying out a new sand wedge? Also, why share the spotlight with members of the opposing party, letting them go mano-a-mano with him? Why run the risk of massive overexposure, or worse, of massive underexposure, via such speeches? We argue here that the weekend address has proven to be quite functional, an aggressive response to certain forces of institutionalization that now bedevil all presidents. Psychologically, they also give the president a way of regaining political momentum; they become his rhetorical Camp David.

Institutional Problems

While he may be the leader of the Free World, an American president is not omnipotent; and the signs are everywhere. One goes by the name

of *mass polarization*, the tendency of the American people to sort themselves into rival political camps, which places considerable pressure on
their chief executive (Fiorina & Abrams, 2008). A widening gap in presidential "approval ratings expressed by self-identified Republicans and
Democrats," says Jacobson (2003, p. 1), suggests that certain structural
forces are now at play in the area of public opinion, with mass partisans
engaging in "mental gymnastics" to "buttress their opinions even when
they are demonstrably false" (Hetherington, 2009, p. 414). These lay attitudes are accompanied by *elite polarization*, with congressional battles
now becoming increasingly acrimonious. "No one can have failed to notice," says Cameron (2002, p. 648), "the signs of something unusual, and
rather unpleasant, happening in American politics. The impeachment of
President Clinton, the hyperbolically partisan language and displays on
Capitol Hill, the vituperative tone of dissents in Supreme Court opinions, the mud-flinging displays on media political talk shows, the snide
and nasty language in best-selling political journalism. What is going on?"

What indeed? Studies show that the ideological divides in Congress are
now wider than at any time in the last hundred years and that the White
House has become increasingly strident as well, with the politics of health
care being but one recent example (Kupchan & Trubowitz, 2007). Some
scholars trace this lack of comity to 1983, a year that produced an unusually tight-knit group of Congressional Democrats. "Cross-pressured partisans," members of Congress whose personal viewpoints are sometimes
at odds with their constituents', have also decreased in number (Fleisher
& Bond, 1996) and that has made it difficult for the president to pick
off wavering members of Congress when cutting a deal. Oddly enough,
American voters rather like divided government because it somehow balances power even while producing gridlock (Sinclair, 2000).

Presidents sometimes take advantage of these stalemates by using
their executive powers, but a new Congress often undoes solutions a
president has put in place temporarily (Aberbach & Rockman, 1999).
Presidents have other options, of course. They can recapture momentum
by sponsoring their own policy initiatives, but that often results in institutional—sometimes personal—jealousies between the president and
Congress (Lee, 2008). Indeed, midway through Barack Obama's first four
years in office, the Senate had confirmed only 62 of his judicial nominees
versus 100 at the same point in George W. Bush's administration. In January 2011, over a thousand judgeships (about 10% of the federal judiciary)
were vacant (Zillman, 2011). These data become even starker when one

realizes that judicial nominations had been handled perfunctorily before (no court nominee had appeared before the Senate Judiciary Committee before 1925), but hearings are now a "staple of the process" (Davidson, 2009, p. 130).

The federal bureaucracy, now swollen to gigantic proportions, also puts a check on the president's power, in part because of its sheer size and in part because institutions seek to maintain their established modes of operation. The federal bureaucracy, says Light (1995, p. 1), is "an unwieldy, towering hierarchy in which accountability is diffuse at best and the president is sometimes the last to know." "In 1960 there were 451 senior executives and presidential appointees," says Light (p. 60); "by 1992 there were 2,393." The White House itself has also grown, and that has forced the president to become more of a manager. Thus, even choosing White House staffers is now fraught with politics (enough women? enough minorities?), which cuts into the president's available time (Krause & Cohen, 2000). Hence the advice given to the newly elected Barack Obama by Mike McCurry (2008, p. 702), Bill Clinton's former press secretary: "One person cannot adequately speak on behalf of the institutional presidency. The organization is too complex . . . You must diversify sources of information for the press."

The press. Ah, the press. It has grown larger and more aggressive over the years, an unobtrusive indicator of which is that the president's average sound bite has been reduced from 43 seconds to 9 seconds by one popular estimate (Hallin, 1992). What has replaced the president? Journalists themselves, who were in the limelight for 38.3 seconds per TV story in 2004 (Bucy & Grabe, 2007, p. 664). Reporters constantly try to "shape the issue agenda," says Patterson (1993, p. 146), and so news reports are now highly intertextual, with the president's views artfully mixed into the larger news narrative. And when politicians try to regain control, says Esser (2008), journalists use the tricks of the trade—compressed sound bites, attack segments, and reporter-controlled wrap-ups—to preserve their independence.

But these are fairly benign strategies; the press is capable of much more. In an important series of studies, Steven Clayman of UCLA examined the question-answer sequences in presidential news conferences and found a long-term decline in deference to the president (Clayman et al., 2006; Clayman et al., 2010). Political news has also become deconstructive, so sure is the press that what is going on backstage is more important than what is going on frontstage (Jamieson & Waldman, 2003). Will Web-based technologies change all of this, giving the president a chance to "soar over the heads of the media" so he can "speak directly to the voters"? That is unlikely, says Simendinger (2008, p. 694), because the press has already caught wind of such tricks and increased its White House surveillance. Press and president, it seems, are now perfect codependents.

Another institutional change bears on the weekend address: It has become harder for the president to find a prime-time audience. The list of president turn-downs is a long one: (1) ABC refused to give up airtime for a defense of Reaganomics in October 1982 (DeFrank, 1983); (2) all three networks refused to carry a live speech about the Nicaraguan rebels in February 1988 (Boyer, 1988); (3) the networks also broke with precedent by not carrying a press conference with George H. W. Bush in June 1992, and only CBS carried a Clinton news conference in April 1995 (Harris, 1995); (4) by the time George W. Bush assumed office, the pattern was clear—he could not even be assured of a national audience when talking about terrorism in November 2001 or Iraq in October 2002 (Barnhart, 2001; de Moraes, 2002); (5) and in September 2009, the networks were reluctant to surrender prime-time real estate to Barack Obama for one of his rare presidential news conferences (Andreeva, 2009). Foote (1990) estimates that the presidential share of the TV audience dropped precipitously throughout the 1980s. Since then, televised real estate has only gotten more expensive.

Other institutional actors also conspire against the president. Members of the Supreme Court frequently fail to support the ideological positions of those who appointed them (Gerhardt, 2008), with the Court rejecting not once but three times the Bush administration's attempts to detain terrorism suspects indefinitely (Taylor, 2008). Wall Street too can give the president fits, as when it failed to reform itself after two presidents— George W. Bush and Barack Obama—dressed it down for its risky derivatives and excessive executive compensation. Foreign actors of all sorts, including staunch allies like Great Britain, dependable allies like Germany, and maddening allies like France, have all failed the U.S. chief executive at one time or another, not to mention unwieldy cross-national entities like the United Nations, NATO, and the G8 as well as the U.S.'s bewildering network of allies and enemies in the Middle East and North Africa. Given all of these structural uncertainties, given the self-centered institutions with which an American president must deal, what is he to do?

The White House can no longer speak with one voice, given the leaks that continually bedevil it (Neustadt, 1990), and that has tempted some presidents to secrete themselves with their closest advisors, a natural but ultimately unsatisfactory solution (Lewis, 2003). Another temptation is for the president to take more partisan stances (Wood, 2009), but that only buys him temporary surcease (Mayhew, 2011). To imagine that rhetoric—queen of the arts though it may be—can confront these entrenched institutional forces may seem odd, but recent American presidents disagree. They now treat the weekend address as a kind of presidential *action*, a way of getting things done when other ways of doing things cannot be found. The weekend addresses is an assertive device that helps the president cope. We now consider how and why that is so.

Weekend Solutions

Joshua Scacco (2010) perceptively argues that the weekend address signals a "ubiquitous presidency," a presidency that will use any modality—radio, television, YouTube, iTunes—to occupy our attention. Attention, of course, only gets one so far. Value affirmation is also important, so presidents have also turned to civic ceremonies to link their policy concerns to cultural mores (Hart, 1987; Densmore, 1997). Power maintenance also demands an inventive president. So, for example, George W. Bush used signing statements to circumscribe the powers of Congress despite the legislation it had just passed (Campbell & Jamieson, 2008). "Going local" has also become more common, with the president traveling to the hinterlands, constantly in search of supportive voters and less critical journalists (Cohen, 2010). Presidents sometimes try to gain the upper hand by issuing executive orders, but that can damage a president's credibility if Congress subsequently overrides his actions (Deering & Maltzman, 1999).

"In today's media environment," observes Jennifer Senior (2009), "ubiquity is not the same as overexposure. It's a deliberate strategy . . . A presidency can no longer survive on one message per day or one press conference per year. Instead, you have to turn on a fire hose." Hence the weekend address. While Kernell (2007) notes that presidents have been cautious when adopting new technologies, radio has been the exception. Warren Harding first turned to it in 1921 and even "silent" Cal Coolidge deployed it to some effect. Famously, Franklin Roosevelt initiated a series of Fireside Chats on March 12, 1933, just eight days into his first term as president. David Ryfe (1999, p. 99) notes that Roosevelt used this new medium to such effect that "letter writers referred to Roosevelt variously as a gift from God and a friend next door, a supreme being and a real fellow who did not talk down to the public." Although folklore tells us that Roosevelt's remarks were highly inspirational, Lim (2003, p. 442) notes that they frequently employed "declamation and attacks" as well.

Radio talks have persisted even though there is little direct evidence of their efficacy (Horvit, Schiffer & Wright, 2008). Presidents use them because "94% of the American people 12 years old and older still listen to traditional radio weekly," with another survey finding that even with all the new audio technologies, 82% of the population "planned to listen to traditional radio as much in the future as they did now," a figure that included "70% of 12-to-17 year olds" (Radio Audience Trends, 2006, para. 4, 14). Despite the popularity of visual media, then, radio has endured because it preserves the I-Thou character of human relationships. Some years ago, Walter Ong (1982) argued that oral expression (unlike writing) reaches out to us in special ways: It is situationally based, rooted in the here and now; it builds on others' prior remarks, hence tying people together; and it is bodied forth by a distinct human voice and hence tends to be better remembered.

To better understand the radio address, we sampled the presidential oeuvre broadly, starting with a goal of securing 10 radio addresses each year for each president, a total that was reduced in some cases so we could include a range of direct responses from the opposition party and to avoid oversampling certain speech topics. The result was a database consisting of 63 weekend addresses for Ronald Reagan, 9 for George H. W. Bush, 90 for Bill Clinton, 95 for George W. Bush, and 10 for Barack Obama. (Given the disparity in these totals, we eliminated Obama and the senior Bush from our overall statistical arrays but have included them, when appropriate, for illustrative purposes.) As we see in table 5.1, the remaining 248 speeches—and their responses—produced 527 presidential passages for analysis by DICTION, which we estimate to be a 25% sample of all weekend addresses the three presidents gave while in office. Table 5.1 also shows that the weekend address was used at various times ("tenure in office") and addressed various matters ("topical focus"), but nonetheless was used consistently.[1]

These addresses did not exist in splendid isolation, of course. They generated direct, immediate responses from the opposition. To capture the flavor of these exchanges, we analyzed the remarks of 248 respondents (496 textual passages), the overwhelming majority of whom were members of Congress (86.1%), with state officials (usually governors) being next

TABLE 5.1 **Descriptive data for weekend addresses.**

General variable	Specific variable	Overall	Reagan (n = 63 addresses)	Clinton (n = 90 addresses)	Bush 43 (n = 95 addresses)
No. presidential passages		527 (100%)	139 (25.2%)	210 (39.8%)	178 (33.8%)
President's tenure in office	First 32 months	169 (32.1%)	35 (25.2%)	94 (44.8%)	40 (22.5%)
	Middle 32 months	169 (32.1%)	24 (17.3%)	76 (36.2%)	69 (38.8%)
	Final 32 months	189 (35.9%)	80 (57.6%)	40 (19.0%)	69 (38.8%)
President's topical focus	Foreign Affairs	141 (26.8%)	53 (38.1%)	31 (14.8%)	57 (32.0%)
	Domestic economy	132 (25.0%)	36 (25.9%)	45 (21.4%)	51 (28.7%)
	International trade	15 (2.0%)	12 (8.6%)	3 (1.4%)	0 (0.0%)
	Domestic problems	185 (35.1%)	18 (12.9%)	119 (56.7%)	48 (27.0%)
	Human values	42 (8.0%)	12 (8.6%)	10 (4.8%)	20 (11.2%)
	Partisan politics	12 (2.3%)	8 (5.8%)	2 (1.0%)	2 (1.1%)
Respondents' engagement level	Hi reference/same topic	111 (21.1%)	38 (27.3%)	49 (23.3%)	24 (13.5%)
	Hi reference/different topic	192 (36.4%)	72 (51.8%)	70 (33.3%)	50 (28.1%)
	Lo reference/multiple topics	147 (27.9%)	18 (12.9%)	63 (30.0%)	66 (37.1%)
	No reference/multiple topics	77 (14.6%)	11 (7.9%)	28 (13.3%)	38 (21.3%)

in line at 9.4%. A few lay celebrities like author Jim Wallis and Dr. Jennifer Howse, head of the March of Dimes, delivered responses and even some "ordinary citizens" have been chosen to speak. While only accounting for 3.2% of the total, their remarks were often memorable—for example, twelve-year-old Graeme Frost of Baltimore, who spoke on behalf of children's health insurance, and Afghanistan war vet Elliot Anderson, who talked about Iraq's civil war. Party officials (typically the head of the DNC or RNC) responded to the president less than 1% of the time. Only 12.8% of all respondents were women and, while the great majority of them were sitting members of the House or Senate, women at the state and local levels were twice as likely to respond to the president as were men. These included Arizona governor Jane Hull, who compared herself to Barry Goldwater, State Senator Leticia Van De Putte, who reflected on the Texas governor she once knew who worked across party lines (George W. Bush), and a congressional candidate from Minnesota, Patty Wetterling, who talked about her abducted son and the growing epidemic of school violence.

Our original naïve assumption was that the weekend exchanges would resemble the classic "dialectic" prized by Plato—point/counterpoint and all that. We found, instead, the Sophistic tradition—entrepreneurs hitching a ride to the president's wagon for their own partisan purposes. As we see in table 5.1, only half of them responded to something the president had actually said, with 15% not even mentioning the president by name; 80% of the respondents ignored the president's topic, following the Monty Python dictum "Now for something completely different." On Saturday morning, August 7, 1997, for example, President Bill Clinton gave an impassioned speech on the farm crisis, whereupon Congresswoman Ileana Ros-Lehtinen responded with a talk on sexual predators. George W. Bush addressed tax relief on March 24, 2001, which inspired Senator Russ Feingold to discuss campaign finance regulation. When May 25, 2009, rolled around, Barack Obama talked of fiscal discipline, while Senator Lamar Alexander urged construction of more nuclear power plants.[2]

The weekend address is therefore a liminal entity bridging the gap between policy and promulgation, between education and salesmanship. Han (2006) says the address keeps the White House "on message," but we find, instead, a kaleidoscope of issues. Eshbaugh-Soha and Peake (2008) view it as the president's attempt to narrowcast his message to a more pliable audience, but we find a lot of traditional politicking being done. Scacco (2010) gets it best when describing the address as a "mediated log" recording the president's adjustment to changing conditions. The weekend address is not so much a distinct genre as an amalgamative one, a tool the president uses to stand out against a crowded and confusing backdrop. The weekend address is thus not one thing but many things, and hence it is politics writ large.

Weekend Formulas

Weekend addresses are above all short, a rarity in the world of politics. George W. Bush averaged 518 words each week, with Bill Clinton being a bit more verbose at 880 words (Sigelman & Whissell, 2002). Mr. Clinton gave many of his speeches in front of a small, live audience, while Ronald Reagan geared up for the event by patiently editing prose on paper. Despite the presidents' peculiarities, the weekend addresses are often quite similar. As we see in figure 5.1, for example, they usually focus on something *in particular*, producing a narrow agenda—and high Insistence scores—to help reporters file a specific report on a slow news day (indeed, on a non-news day).[3] High-Insistence speeches are anything but subtle, circling back to the same themes again and again. Even when presented in skeletal form, for example, the speech Ronald Reagan gave on Rosh Hashanah in 1982 is instantly understandable:

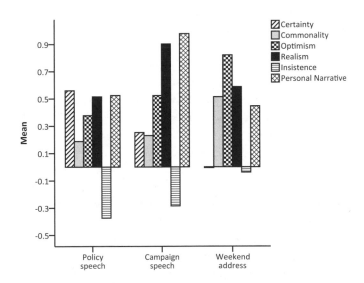

FIGURE 5.1 Tonal characteristics of the weekend address.

- At every crucial turning point in our history Americans have faced and over-come great odds, strengthened by spiritual faith.
- George Washington knelt in prayer at Valley Forge and in the darkest days of our struggle for independence . . .
- Abraham Lincoln vowed "that this nation, under God, shall have a new birth of freedom."
- Yet today we're told that to protect that first amendment, we must suppress prayer and expel God from our children's classrooms . . .
- The time has come for this Congress to [provide] the firm assurance that children can hold voluntary prayers in their schools . . .
- Today, on one of the holiest days of one of our great religious faiths, I urge the Members of the Congress to set aside their differences and . . . help make us "one Nation under God" again. (Reagan, 1982)

Presidential respondents were even more insistent than the chief executive, driving home their points with little grace or nuance.[4] How did Senator Gary Hart respond to Mr. Reagan's prayerful urgings? By accusing the president of subterfuge and, worse, of abandoning the nation in a time of trial. Said Mr. Hart on that same Saturday morning in 1982:

> You might as well have ignored the president's radio message earlier today. There was nothing in it for you. No answers. No solutions. No hope. The president's economic program has failed, and apparently he'd rather not talk about it. Instead, the president spoke about the need for organized school prayer. If you're like me, you have your own faith and your own religious beliefs, but are worried about the condition of our economy. President Reagan, on the other hand, apparently has deep faith in the condition of our economy, but is worried about our private religious beliefs. It's our economy that needs his full attention. For our economy hasn't been in such a precarious position since the Great Depression . . . . (Hart, 1982)

"Take that," Mr. President. "Not to worry," replied Mr. Reagan and his fellow chief executives, "we will use rhetoric as a work-around, drawing on the institution's emotional resources and its cultural resonances." As we see in figure 5.1, the formula they used included both Optimism and group language (Commonality).[5] Even when addressing serious matters, that is, the presidents ladled their speeches with humanity and a studied informality. This made them easy on the ears. None was easier on the ears than Bill Clinton:

- *February 5, 1994*: Good morning. This morning I want to talk with you about jobs, how more Americans can find new jobs and better ones, how we can help business to create those jobs, and how we can prepare our people to hold them. (Clinton, 1994, February 5)
- *April 23, 1994*: Good morning. I'm happy to report to you today that we're closing in on a top priority for the American people: winning a crime bill that will make our homes, our schools, and our streets safer.... (Clinton, 1994, April 23)
- *July 15, 1995:* Good morning. My job here is to make America work well for all of you who work hard. I ran for President to restore the American dream of opportunity for all, the American value of responsibility from all, and to bring the American people together as a community ... (Clinton, 1995, July 15)
- *March 7, 1998*: Good morning. Since I took office I've done everything in my power to protect our children from harm. We've worked to make their streets and their schools safer, to give them something positive to do after school and ... (Clinton, 1998, March 7)
- *May 6, 2000*: Good morning. Warm weather has finally taken hold in most of the country, and millions of families are now taking weekend picnics and hosting backyard barbecues. Today I want to speak with you about the foods we serve at these gatherings and how we can make them even safer than they already are ... (Clinton, 2000, May 6)

These addresses often bore calendrical markings: discussions of picnics on summer's eve, jobs talk for Labor Day, world peace during Yuletide. These cultural touchstones helped the president preside, letting him draw on the institutional history to which he was heir. Figure 5.1 shows two additional routes to transcendence: The presidents were more speculative (lower Realism) on Saturday mornings than on the hustings and they cut back on voter-friendly personal narratives as well.[6] By doing so, they avoided day-to-day minutiae in favor of fundamental principles, giving their remarks an almost homiletic quality.

The weekend addresses were also lower on Certainty than the formal policy speeches. Remarks high in Certainty contain firm directives, including use of the verb *to be* ("It is foreordained—we will be victorious") as well as overstatements ("None can stand in our way"). The presidents were much more indirect on Saturday mornings. Ronald Reagan, the Anecdotalist-in-Chief, had especially deft ways of making his points without being prepossessing. He often let others speak for him, using several different strategies when doing so:

- *Via clever altercasting*: Vice President Bush might be a little embarrassed if he knew I was going to say this, but he's one of those Americans I'm talking about. As a young fighter pilot in the Pacific, his plane was shot down on a military mission. He came perilously close to losing his life. If you know any veterans of the Second World War, you might take the time on August 14th to thank them. There are so many heroes among us, and I'm sure they'd like to know how much we appreciate them. (Reagan, 1985, August 10)
- *Via anonymous quotations*: A woman from California wrote me. "As a home-maker," she said, "I'm the one who shops and budgets for our family. I'm the first one to notice that my dollars are buying more. Little by little, I find I can breathe easier. For the first time in 5 years, I feel I can do some much needed repairs in our home." Well, her letter reflects the growing confidence in our country. (Reagan, 1982, November 6)
- *Via dramatic narratives*: On this point, I like to tell a story about the Geneva summit. Our experts thought the scheduling of any future meetings was a difficult, delicate subject best left to later in the discussions. Yet as we were walking together after our first meeting, I mentioned to Mr. Gorbachev how much I would like him to visit the United States. So, I invited him, and he said, "I accept." And then he told me how much he'd like me to see the Soviet Union. So, he invited me, and I said, "I accept." And there it was, as simple as that. (Reagan, 1986, October 4)
- *Via home-spun asides*: Today I'd like to begin with an expression of gratitude to all who sent get-well cards and letters after my brief hospital stay 9 days ago. Of course, some of my favorites came from young people. Eight-year-old Colin MacDonald, of Holbrook, New York, told me that he liked my speeches— except when they preempted his favorite TV shows. And second-grader Jennifer Carl, of Canton, Ohio, was kind enough to draw a picture of me in bed, Nancy standing at my side, serving me a bowl of—well, of purple soup. Nancy wants the recipe. (Reagan, 1987, January 17)

Ronald Reagan was, admittedly, a rhetorical artist but, artistry aside, there were only minor differences among the presidents.[7] Most followed the same basic script, a script that reveals the speech's basic purpose: To give the president room to gather his thoughts so he could respond sensitively to the issues of the day. The *tone* of these remarks is especially affecting—at times didactic, at times advisory, at times commemorative. The speeches draw on several rhetorical traditions, blending the monarch's pronouncement with the high priest's reminiscences and the soothsayer's warnings. In an environment that often frustrates a president, it lets him take charge for a while.

Weekend Asymmetries

The president is not alone on Saturday mornings. Opposite-party responses have been the norm since Ronald Reagan delivered his first weekend address on April 3, 1982. Most radio stations carried House Majority Leader Jim Wright's rebuttal on that occasion out of concern for the fairness doctrine (Denton, 1982). Since then, the rebuttals have been prepared based on the president's ostensible topic and at other times have been produced in situ. Increasingly, though, both statement and response have been prerecorded earlier in the week.

How do the responses compare to what the president has said? Do they help foster the deliberative democracy championed by Gutmann and Thompson (2004)? Or do they stress wedge issues, as some scholars have warned (Hillygus & Shields, 2008), thereby contributing to greater political polarization (Theriault, 2008)? From what we can tell, they do nothing particularly grand at all. The respondents simply go in their own directions, picking a topic of their liking and largely ignoring what the chief executive has said. As we see in figure 5.2, this tendency has become more prominent recently, with George W. Bush's respondents rarely engaging the president on his own turf. Only 13% of them were maximally

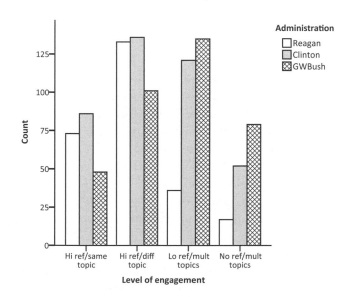

FIGURE 5.2 Discursive engagement over time for weekend addresses.

engaged (high reference, same topic), with 22% never even mentioning the president or his topic-du-jour. These tendencies took hold during the Clinton years and picked up in almost linear fashion throughout George W. Bush's administration. These findings echo John Gastil's wry warning that "voters deliberate leading up to Election Day so that they don't have to deliberate again until the next election" (2008, p. 85). The president's respondents do little to offset such tendencies.

While a few of the responses have been newsworthy, most have been merely dutiful, obligations performed at the urging of party elders. Sometimes the elders themselves have gotten involved (e.g., Orrin Hatch, John McCain, and John Boehner) but little-known personalities have gotten more airtime lately: Senator Johnny Isakson of Georgia, Washington Congresswoman Cathy McMorris Rodgers, and congressional backbencher Kevin Brady of Texas. Taking on this assignment makes some sense (it gets one in the local papers and produces a few TV interviews), but it is mostly a no-win assignment. Here is why: Compared to their respondents, presidents are more Optimistic and use more Personal Narrative.[8] As a result, the presidents hold the upper hand in such encounters: They can use their personal charm and their continuing relationship with voters to maximum advantage, assured that much of what they say will become fodder for the Sunday talk shows. Most important, they do not have to *react* to anything in particular. The respondents draw a much worse card. As former Texas governor Ann Richards would say, like Fred Astaire they must do everything the president does but, like Ginger Rogers, they must do so in high heels and backwards.

As we see in figure 5.3, however, the respondents are learning how to dance, increasing their Optimism both within and across administrations. So, for example, former Senator Bill Bradley (1982) took on Ronald Reagan directly in October 1982: "Yes, interest rates and inflation have come down, but at what price? Businesses are failing at the fastest rate in 50 years. Over 30 percent of our nation's productive capacity lies idle. Most companies have slashed their capital investment budget. So much for rebuilding America." Lamar Alexander, on the other hand, countered Barack Obama in a much more upbeat, if environmentally questionable, way:

> Well, we Republicans like renewable energy, too; we proposed a new Manhattan Project, like the one in World War II, to find ways to make solar power cost competitive and to improve advanced biofuels. But today, renewable electricity from the sun, the wind and the earth provides only about 1-and-a-half percent

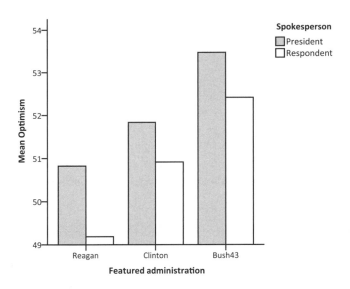

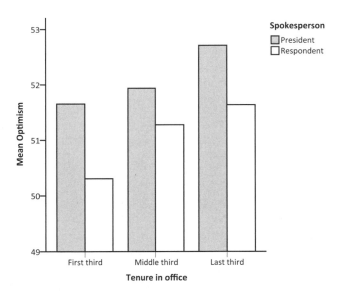

FIGURE 5.3 Optimism scores across and within administrations for presidents and respondents.

of America's electricity. Double it or triple it and we still don't have very much. So there is potentially a dangerous energy gap between the renewable electricity we want and the reliable electricity we must have.

To close that gap, Republicans say start with conservation and efficiency. We have so much electricity at night, for example, we could electrify half our cars and trucks, plug them in while we sleep without building one new power plant. On that, Republicans and Democrats agree. But when it comes to producing more energy, we disagree ... We say find more American energy and use less, energy that's as clean as possible, as reliable as possible and at as low a cost as possible. And one place to start is with 100 more nuclear power plants. (Alexander, 2009)

Increasingly, then, the weekend addresses have become a sporting match and the old rules have changed. All contestants are now wilier, more willing to experiment with different political styles. With Barack Obama doing sports commentary during a Georgetown-Duke basketball game, says Scacco (2010), the Ubiquitous Presidency has finally become a reality. But so too has the Unending Response, and, as we have seen here, it is becoming harder to distinguish between them. As a result, the direct political dialectic envisioned by the nation's founders is becoming harder to find. The weekend exchanges have turned into something odd: the sound of four hands clapping in separate, soundproof rooms.

Conclusion

When he gave the very first weekend address on international trade on November 20, 1982, Ronald Reagan began dolefully: "Well, as you've probably heard on news reports, America's problems are not unique. Other nations face very severe economic difficulties. In fact, both developed and developing countries alike have been in the grip of the longest worldwide recession in postwar history. And that's bad news for all of us." Mr. Reagan then went on to discuss the consequences of the recession: "When other countries don't grow, they buy less from us, and we see fewer jobs created at home. When we don't grow, we buy less from them, which weakens their economies and, of course, their ability to buy from us. It's a vicious cycle." He continued in this vein for some time and then reached the most optimistic portion of his address, such as it was: "Let no one misunderstand us. We're generous and farsighted in our goals, and we intend to use our full power to achieve these goals. We seek to plug the holes in the boat of free markets and free trade and get it moving again in the direction of prosperity. And no one should mistake our determination to use our full power and influence to prevent others from destroying the boat and sinking us all."

Mr. Reagan's speech scored in the 19th percentile on Optimism and in the 20th percentile on Commonality. Speaking on a similar topic some thirty years later, and in a more dire economic climate, Barack Obama began with a Personal Narrative, showing that he grasped the financial difficulties besetting the nation, but he then got plucky, scoring in the 50th percentile on Optimism and in the 82nd percentile on Commonality. Said Mr. Obama:

> Over the last month, I've been traveling the country, talking to Americans about how we can out-educate, out-innovate, and out-build the rest of the world. Doing that will require a government that lives within its means, and cuts whatever spending we can afford to do without. But it will also require investing in our nation's future . . . In cities and towns throughout America, I've seen the benefits of these investments. The schools and colleges of Oregon are providing Intel—the state's largest private employer—with a steady stream of highly-educated workers and engineers. At Parkville Middle School outside of Baltimore, engineering is the most popular subject, thanks to outstanding teachers who are inspiring students to focus on their math and science skills.
>
> In Wisconsin, a company called Orion is putting hundreds of people to work manufacturing energy-efficient lights in a once-shuttered plant. And in the small community of Marquette, in Michigan's Upper Peninsula, widely accessible high-speed internet has allowed students and entrepreneurs to connect to the global economy. One small business, a third-generation, family-owned clothing shop called Getz's is now selling their products online, which has helped them double their workforce and make them one of America's 5,000 fastest-growing companies in a recent listing. (Obama, 2011, February 26)

In these passages, Presidents Reagan and Obama describe the arc of the weekend address. Obama commences his upbeat itinerary in the fourth sentence of his remarks, while Mr. Reagan sings the blues throughout, only to offer what at best can be described as a melancholy conclusion when he imagines the international boat "sinking us all."

Why these changes over the years? Are we now a more fitful nation, unable to listen to a trenchant economic report, all too ready to turn our attention elsewhere? Are we now addicted to a saccharine presidency, one that comforts rather than challenges, that preaches rather than analyzes, that diverts rather than leads? To be sure, the weekend address helps the president sell his wares; it has turned into a kind of political infomercial as a result. The president's respondents have taken his cue and together they produce independent public relations ventures linked not by topic or purpose but only by their simultaneity.

Will the weekend address continue? Some observers doubt it since so few stations now carry the president's speech. Also, although these speeches may help set the press's agenda (for Sunday morning, anyway), they seem incapable of reliably shifting attitudes in the president's direction. Given all this, perhaps they will be abandoned altogether, although we suspect not. The weekend address is a presidential embodiment, a way for the chief executive to stake his claim to the issues of the day in a manner of his choosing. Like the presidency itself, the weekend address has morphed over the years, both substantively and methodologically, and that is likely to continue as well. When all else fails in Washington, these little speeches are a way for the president to get something done each week, his way of striking back and striking forward at the same time. In political life, that often counts as progress.

The weekend address opens a window on the institutionalized forces that have now captured Washington, D.C. These forces, and their resulting calcifications, are now a major irritant for many Americans. But even a moment's reflection can find solace in institutions. Currently, for example, many in the world are hoping that Egyptians will institutionalize the popular will first heard in the Arab Spring, while others are hoping that the Palestinians will find some kind—any kind—of structural permanency. In Libya, the challenge is one of tearing down autocratic institutions without tearing down all institutions and, in Pakistan, of keeping the military involved without it becoming totalizing. In many parts of the world, people are praying for institutions.

In light of these conditions, democratic gridlock seems a less tragic matter. In light of these conditions, the weekend address seems an acceptable way of getting something done when doing seems otherwise impossible. Ultimately, the weekend address is an agenda-setting device, a way of calling voters' attention to new policy options or to possibilities long since forgotten. It is also a way of keeping spirits up and of rallying the troops without shutting off avenues of compromise with one's rivals. Institutional politics is a complex thing, so rhetoric is often its adjunct.

PART III
Personal Forces

CHAPTER SIX

Scandal and the Resilient Tone

The story most often told in the future about the William Jefferson Clinton administration will probably be about impeachment.[1] But which impeachment story? There are several available narratives: overweening arrogance; sexual predation; the mystique of power; innocence gone awry; a slathering right wing; a meddlesome Congress; a salacious press; a constitutional crisis; a man who knew no bounds. Here, we add another chapter to the impeachment story by arguing that insufficient attention has been given to Bill Clinton's rhetorical skills during the crisis, skills that let him govern the nation successfully for eight full years. Applauding such talents does not vindicate his indiscretions, but it does make his story more complicated. It is within these complications that Clinton's richest story lies.

This chapter looks at a short but crucial moment during the Clinton administration. By examining the president's responses to the impeachment charges, we discover certain language features that sustained his legitimacy for many Americans (60–70% of them, by most measures). In contrast to the oft-painted picture of an embattled president holed up at 1600 Pennsylvania Avenue, we describe a man who aggressively made his case and who never lost the ability to connect to the American people. The result was a presidency saved—for good, for ill, or for both.

The Clinton Miracle

Although there is still much to debate about the 2000 campaign between Al Gore and George W. Bush, one thing was clear at the end of that race: Bill Clinton was still the most popular politician in the United States, and he became even more popular as each day of the Bush administration dawned. Few Americans respected Mr. Clinton's morals and most wanted a person of sterner stuff to replace him in office. But if the forty-second president had been allowed by the Constitution to succeed himself in office once more, he would have done so. Why? How could a serial adulterer and admitted perjurer retain such popularity and political muscle? Was it because the electorate had lost its moral compass, or because no electorate can afford a moral compass when the Dow hovers near 12,000? Was it because the president's domestic and international initiatives worked out especially well, or was it because the seductions he used on Monica Lewinsky and Jennifer Flowers worked on the American people too? Was it because the congressional Republicans were inept at the time, because the threat of war was low, or because the American people had stopped caring about politics?

Even a seasoned politician like Trent Lott could not explain how Clinton emerged from the Lewinsky scandal unscathed. As Lott told Ken Gormley (2010, p. 646), the legal scholar who has penned the most detailed account of the whole affair, "There are only a couple of political things in my career that I still have not been able to understand. . . . One is the fact that the American people apparently continued to support Clinton throughout the whole thing, knowing what he did, knowing what he said, knowing how he had demeaned the office." Lott's confusion was so profound that he felt compelled to add, "I still think history needs to try to explain why the American people thought that all that was okay. Was it just the pure charm of [Clinton's] personality? Was it just that they thought Republicans were being mean? I don't know."

Nobody yet knows the answers to such questions, but there is little doubt that the Lewinsky debacle left nary a scratch on Bill Clinton. Indeed, as political scientist Arthur Miller (1999, p. 722) notes, "two-thirds of the people felt that Clinton has, at some point, lied about the affair," and yet "throughout 1998, in contradistinction to the repeated predictions of virtually every media commentator, political pundit, and Republican party leader, Clinton's job approval rating rose after every new revelation." Even after one of Clinton's early speeches during the Lewinsky affair (when it finally became clear to many that he had had numerous dalliances), the polls showed that Clinton's post-speech job approval rating was 73% (Zaller, 1998, p. 184).

Indeed, Clinton's ability to withstand the scrutinies of Monicagate may have actually strengthened the presidency because it let the president have "the authority to assert executive privilege over a broader set of communications, including communications with the First Lady and among top advisors ... Most importantly, the Clinton acquittal will restore presidential immunity from impeachment save in egregious circumstances" (R. Miller, 1999, p. 729).

How could this have happened? Six explanations have become popular:

1. *Voter psychology*. Some say that modern voters, living in an age of specialization and differentiation, now make sharp distinctions between a mere "sex scandal" and an event with "important political consequences" (Owen, 2000, p. 162). These modes of compartmentalization, says Gronbeck (1997), are fostered by media narratives that frame sexual relations as matters for titillation rather than for substantive discussion. As psychologist John Gartner (2008, p. 336) has suggested, Clinton himself may have helped the voters feel this way: "While it would have been understandable if Clinton had become distracted by the crisis, Clinton's focus on the presidency, paradoxically, seemed to increase."

2. *Voter morality*. In an age of postmodern ethics that no longer adheres to essentialist notions of morality, the Clinton saga just didn't add up to something important. In such an age, say Stuckey and Wabshall (2000, p. 529), the need for presidential heroism dissipates, "for in the absence of pure 'evil' ... we do not need a president to embody pure good." As a result, "definitions based on the president as an unambiguously moral leader have clearly lost much of their persuasive traction." Indeed, as Parry-Giles and Parry-Giles (2002, p. 127) note, Clinton's ambiguous morality may have served him well since he "personified many of the challenges to political authenticity that characterized most of the late twentieth century in the United States."

3. *Political deliverables*. Analyses of Monicagate became too subtle too quickly, says political scientist John Zaller, by stressing the psychology of the affair. "It was not admiration for Bill Clinton's character that first buttressed and then boosted his approval ratings," says Zaller (1998, p. 185), but "the public's reactions to the delivery of outcomes and policies that the public want[ed]." Raw, empirical success, says Zaller, provides ideal political insulation for even a morally challenged leader like Bill Clinton. Even a recent reassessment of Zaller's hypothesis by Carol Silva and her coauthors (2007, p. 481) finds that "economic factors contributed to the president's survival indirectly by promoting higher approval ratings."

4. *Political exigencies.* According to this notion, the Clinton impeachment was nothing more than partisan theater designed to increase Republicans' electoral chances. After the off-year elections of 1998, that is, the animus needed to deliver the coup de grace simply subsided. "Electoral considerations," argue Lanoue and Emmert (1999, p. 253), "apparently had a greater impact on the October, 1998 vote on holding impeachment hearings than on the actual impeachment votes two months later." Clinton had a special knack for appropriating the Republican agenda as his own, Klein (2002, p. 183) notes: "Clinton's political hermaphroditism had something to do with the excessive hatefulness that crippled his opponents." With so few other targets of opportunity available to them, the Republicans went after the president's personal character. Had there been no off-year elections, this theory goes, Clinton would have been saved considerable personal embarrassment.

5. *Media reactivity.* Many Americans now revile the mass media more than they dislike their elected leaders. Appalled by the steady barrage leveled at Clinton by commentators like Fox's Bill O'Reilly and CNBC's Chris Matthews, voters may have instinctively sided with Clinton. "Given that the public came to question the credibility and impartiality of the media," says Miller (A. Miller, 1999, p. 728), "the potential impact of the media's coverage was reduced." Robert Busby (2001, p. 186) concludes that Mr. Clinton was helped by a press establishment that "appeared to have put itself above the commonplace interplay of politics—much as the Republicans in the House sought to do—and indeed appeared to pay little heed to public opinion."

6. *Comparative superiority.* There is little doubt that Mr. Clinton's opponents came at him with guns blazing. But they may well have overplayed their hands, pushing for full-bodied impeachment when Fox News and a 24–7 campaign of embarrassment might have done just as much damage. Strategically, says Klein (2002), Clinton's opponents were blinded by blood lust and hypocrisy, making the president often seem worthy of pity in contrast. Indeed, says Gerhardt (2001), congressional Republicans may have actually *strengthened* the institution of the presidency by pushing too fast, too hard, with too little. Gerhardt believes, as a result, that even intense partisans in the future will think twice before trying to impeach a chief executive based on largely personal and/or moral shortcomings.

Each of these explanations has an element of truth, but each shares a fatal flaw: They posit an inert president who was mere flotsam on the tides during impeachment. Agentless theories like these are too deterministic for explaining someone like Bill Clinton, we argue. We also argue that one must pay attention to what Clinton himself did during Monicagate. Because rhetorical action is so central in an age of media, we focus here on an important series of statements made by Mr. Clinton between August 17, 1998, and February 12, 1999, that explain how he kept his presidency afloat.

Studying the Clinton Crisis

Textual analysis can be conducted at both the manifest level (i.e., the arguments offered by the speaker, the policies endorsed, the evidence provided) as well as at the latent level—what a message says about its circumstances. Rhetorical studies operating at the latent level are often subtle, focusing on such matters as the patterns of imagery a rhetor uses, the tacit assumptions undergirding a particular line of logic, the value claims being made, or the psycholinguistic habits signaling a speaker's demographic or psychographic identity. We operate here at the latent level to discover what President Clinton may have said covertly during the Lewinsky scandal when public surveillance was at its peak. Our assumption is that the social impressions Mr. Clinton created by his language choices were especially influential during the impeachment ordeal.

We make this assumption because Mr. Clinton himself said very little about the Lewinsky situation, although his lawyers and defenders supplemented his reticence. As for Mr. Clinton himself, between August 17, 1998, when he addressed the nation from the Map Room in the White House at 10:00 p.m., and February 19, 1999, a week after the Senate failed to remove him from office, he discussed (or failed to discuss) impeachment matters on twenty-eight occasions. The longest of these remarks (1,142 words) was his speech at a prayer breakfast in the White House on September 11, and his shortest consisted of 11 words spoken on October 9 during joint remarks with Germany's Gerhard Schroeder: "I don't have anything to add to what I said yesterday." Fourteen of these speech acts were of the latter sort—either outright refusals by Clinton to discuss the matter or public resolve to keep his eye on the big picture:

REPORTER'S QUESTION: "Mr. President, do you see any way out of an impeachment inquiry?"

THE PRESIDENT: "Well, let me answer you this way: the right thing to do is for us all to focus on what's best for the American people. And the right thing for me to do is what I'm doing. I'm working on leading our country, and I'm working on healing my family." (Clinton, 1998, September 24)

Five additional sets of remarks were metapolitical comments on the fallout of the Lewinsky affair. These comments came in snatches—at the Kremlin, in the office of the Taoiseach in Dublin, during a single-question exchange with reporters at the White House, just before entering the Cabinet Room for a meeting on Social Security, and during a joint press conference with Prime Minister Netanyahu during a trip to Jerusalem. Most such remarks were brief and, while casual, not unsophisticated. For example, when asked how the impeachment issue might affect voter turnout, Clinton shifted to a partisan frame: "The answer to your question is, I don't know. I know that this is no ordinary election, no ordinary time. What is at issue are big things that will affect every American and every American family's children. What is at issue is the future of Social Security . . . " (Clinton, 1998, October 30).

But most interesting of all were the nine statements dealing directly with the Lewinsky affair itself. Averaging only six hundred words in length, these remarks included his oft-maligned address to the nation on August 17, 1998, and his "victory" speech in the Rose Garden on February 12, 1999. Sandwiched between them was a brief reflection at Union Chapel on Cape Cod during the president's summer vacation (on August 28), remarks to the Florida Democratic Party in Orlando on September 9, the prayer breakfast of September 11, a joint press conference with Vaclav Havel on September 16, a wide-ranging interview on Black Entertainment Network on November 2, the "better apology" to the nation broadcast from the Rose Garden on December 11, and the "rally-the-troops" remarks with Democratic leaders on December 19, just after a bill of impeachment had been reported out by the House of Representatives. The tone of these addresses differed in interesting ways but, collectively, they represented Mr. Clinton's attempt to take the initiative during the Lewinsky situation.

To get at the subtexture of these remarks, we analyzed Clinton's lexical choices. The operating assumption was that a speaker's political vocabulary contains within it important clues about his or her philosophical worldview, psychic disposition, and social expectations. Few speakers—especially those in emotionally charged situations—give conscious attention to their minute lexical choices, which makes computerized language analysis especially handy in those situations. Here, in addition to looking at DICTION's standard variables, we examined Mr. Clinton's use of Patriotic Terms since he faced such a constitutionally charged set of issues. Did he avoid the nation's sacred values or take refuge in them? Did he tilt toward his adversaries or away from them?

We also examined the president's crisis remarks with respect to his personal rhetorical history by comparing his impeachment statements to a broad assemblage of policy speeches and campaign remarks from both 1992 and 1996. Our hope was that examining the impeachment statements in light of the Clinton oeuvre would show how he dealt with the pressures of the moment and hence something about his implicit theory of discourse. Such an approach seems particularly suited to Bill Clinton, who demonstrated throughout his life that he could manage almost any situation with words.

But do the facts bear out Mr. Clinton's confidence? Did his language skills give him the edge during impeachment? We believe that the answer to both questions is yes. We also believe that Zaller's (1998) claim that policy alignment alone insulated Clinton from his detractors is too restrictive a view of modern politics. Bill Clinton delivered the goods economically but he also crafted an appealing set of images during impeachment and attached them to a suitable public vocabulary. The result was a presidency saved.

The August 17 Disaster

On August 18, 1998, this latter claim would have seemed comically wrong. The speech Mr. Clinton had given the day before met nobody's expectations, containing as it did an odd mixture of the self-serving and the petulant. While the speech did have its tender moments—"Now this matter is between me, the two people I love most, my wife and our daughter and our God. I must put it right."—they were overshadowed by his odd circumlocutions ("Indeed, I did have a relationship with Ms. Lewinsky that was not appropriate") and, most memorably, by his attacks on his tormentors:

> I had real and serious concerns about an independent counsel investigation that began with private business dealings 20 years ago—dealings, I might add, about which an independent federal agency found no evidence of any wrongdoing by me or my wife over two years ago. The independent counsel investi-

gation moved on to my staff and friends, then into my private life, and now the
investigation itself is under investigation. This has gone on too long, cost too
much, and hurt too many innocent people. (Clinton, 1998, August 17)

Clinton's combination of attack, defense, and self-absorption was
too much for most observers. As Simons (2000, p. 448) reports, his failure "to express genuine remorse, his retreat to legal hairsplitting, his
tarnishing of the office of the Presidency, and his assault on the very
meaning of moral responsibility" served him poorly indeed. These ethical failings were attended by a complete tactical meltdown, says Simons: "Reaction to the four and a half minute speech by the media,
and by politicians on both sides of the aisle, was nearly uniform. Clinton had failed to achieve his objectives. Worse yet, he had reinforced
doubts about his ... ability to govern." Simons goes on to explain why
the speech turned out so poorly, with Clinton trying to manage unman-
ageable dilemmas: ethical challenges, conflicting role requirements, generic conflicts between legal and political speech, and multiple audience involvement. Given this complexity, the popular press was hard
on the speech:

- He [Clinton] essentially did not say he was sorry for what he had done; he was
  just sorry he got caught.... The language also had that Clinton smell. Seven
  months of lies and the famous finger wag somehow amounted only to an admission that he "gave a false impression." As for defending answers as "legally
  accurate," most people think something is accurate or it is not. (Gibbs & Duffy,
  1998, p. 34)
- The speech did not elicit sympathy because he was not tough on himself ... His
  demeanor was not that of a strong man in a moment of contrition but that of
  a defensive man in a moment of aggression. There was no trust in his speech,
  no sense that he knew he could trust the compassion of the people he leads.
  (Noonan, 1998, p. 36)
- Perhaps the Founders should have listed "high crimes and corruptions of language" as grounds for impeachment. Other presidents have lied—and about
  things more important than sex. But Clinton has turned weasel words and tor-
  tured legalisms into a way of life. (Alter, 1998, p. 45)
- So what if he was angry after four years of investigations and four hours of intimate questioning? He could have had the grace to at least sound a little more
  apologetic for his behavior. He might have even thrown in a pinch of humility
  for good measure. (Hayden, 1998)

In trying to account for Clinton's petulance, political psychologist Stanley Renshon (2000) suggests that the "openness" of the public platform (vs. the constrictions of the legal depositions he had given immediately prior to the speech) tempted Clinton to let off steam. Clinton's "character psychology," says Renshon, was one that almost never let him accept responsibility for his own actions. "A president with a strong capacity to be in touch with the concerns of others" but also a president who "has a tendency to exploit others for his own purposes," says Renshon (p. 58), ensured that he would try to meet all of his incommensurate goals on August 17.

DICTION analysis of the August 17 speech confirms what many suspected: the address was completely uncharacteristic of Bill Clinton. As we see in figure 6.1, for example, one of Clinton's greatest strengths was his ability to combine two features that are hard to combine: hard-headed practicality with a sense of group harmony.[2] Compared to others, these were his signal strengths. As something of a "policy wonk," Realism came naturally to Mr. Clinton. This was the Georgetown-Yale-Oxford Clinton, the Clinton who intimidated aides with his need to know. At the same time, there was the Bill Clinton from Hope, Arkansas, who could enter any black church in the United States (or any McDonald's restaurant, for that matter) and feel immediate kinship with the people and they with him. Somehow, this back-slapping son of the South had become intertwined with a technocrat of the Nineties and, together, they sustained a presidency for eight memorable years.

But the speech of August 17 contained no such refrains. Clinton's Realism score for the speech (40.9) was almost four standard deviations below his normal mean of 52.5. Similarly, his Commonality score was 47.1, almost two standard deviations below his typical score (based on a comparison sample of 645 speech passages). In addition, the speech's practiced evasions dramatically drew down his Certainty score; his Optimism and Activity levels dropped as well (although not as precipitously). As if to compensate, Clinton's self-references doubled in the speech, which is not surprising given the personal circumstances confronting him.[3]

These tonal features do not exist in isolation, of course, but instead combine to form a master lexicon. The sensibility implied on August 17 was that of a self-absorbed man who had gotten caught for doing something he should not have been doing and who refused to admit it. Instead, Mr. Clinton offered a mélange of observations that never really comported to an overall argument. Some of his remarks were too careful by

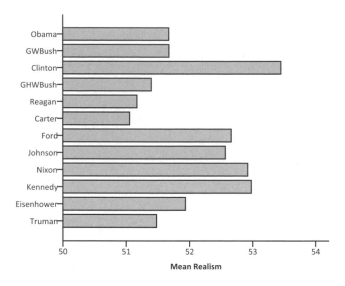

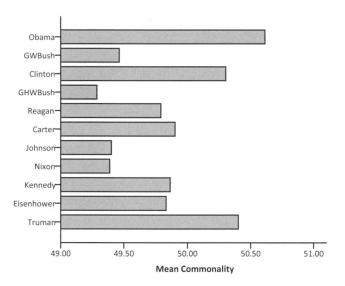

FIGURE 6.1 Clinton vs. other presidents on *realism* and *commonality*.

half ("while my answers were legally accurate, I did not volunteer information"), while others were starkly self-pitying ("I answered their questions truthfully, including questions about my private life—questions no American citizen would ever want to answer"). Instead of looking outward to the nation, to the community, he looked inward to his own sorry circumstance ("the independent counsel investigation moved on to my staff and friends, then into my private life"). His conclusion ended the discussion ("we have important work to do—real opportunities to seize, real problems to solve"), but it was a flat and unspecific conclusion. His call to arms had a Nixonian cast to it: "I ask you to turn away from the spectacle of the past seven months, to repair the fabric of our national discourse."

The fact that Clinton's speech was atypical of him is not surprising. Few individuals have faced the circumstances he faced, and no rule book has been written for those who did. Clinton's "rhetorical signature" (Hillbruner, 1974)—his normal clarity, buoyancy, and sense of the commonweal—abandoned him at just the wrong time. If he had waited and cooled off a bit, says David Gergen (1998, p. 36), Clinton might have righted the ship:

> Steaming from his afternoon confrontation with Starr, under pressure from his wife and lawyer, he rejected his better instincts and a better speech that had been drafted for him. Instead of addressing the needs of the nation, he used his talk to try to save his marriage and his own fanny. Had he waited 24 hours to calm down, he might have given apologies to everyone who deserved them . . . He could have healed, not polarized.

Writing *My Life* several years after leaving office, even Bill Clinton himself found fault with the speech he had made on that fateful evening: "I believed every word I said, but my anger hadn't worn off enough for me to be as contrite as I should have been" (2004, p. 803).

Rhetoric and Resurrection

While the speech of August 17 still sticks in the craws of many Americans, it was not the end of the Clinton story. According to most election experts, the impeachment imbroglio had no discernible effect on the congressional races held two months later. But why? Our argument is that Clinton quickly recovered from his unwise indulgence of August 17 by reinscribing his rhetorical signature. Slowly, steadily, he deployed his favored political vocabularies and did so in campaign style, choosing his speaking situations carefully and making precise adaptations to those situations. In doing so, he followed a path he had trod before: "President Clinton is both determined and resilient. His persistence has been a great political asset. As governor and president, he has had a number of serious setbacks from which he has recovered and from which he has gone on to new achievements. Clinton's capacity to recover is obvious; the question is why he has to do it so often" (Renshon, 2000, p. 48).

Apparently, Mr. Clinton had within him a rhetorical compass that told him when he had gone astray. When that happened, he returned to true north, to his base instincts. Voters, it appears, also employ such orienting devices once they have learned a leader's favored tone and then use it to gauge his or her subsequent behavior. When voters listen to a speech, that is, they may be half-listening as well to all previous remarks the speaker has made. As a result, an apologist not only faces an immediate situation but also that which came before and that which can be anticipated (see Achter, 2000).

Thus, despite the problems with the August 17 speech, all of that changed in short order. As we see in figure 6.2, during the next several months Mr. Clinton transcended his August address, consistently ratcheting up his preferred vocabularies until they once again approached his normal tone (see the dotted lines in figure 6.2). The important thing to remember here is that all of these speeches dealt with the Monica Lewinsky situation. In other words, Clinton consistently found new ways of talking about his travails, which is to say, he found old ways of talking about his travails. He abandoned the self-centeredness of August 17 (low Commonality); he abandoned the evasiveness (low Certainty); he abandoned the pontifications (low Realism); and he abandoned the legalisms (low Familiarity). In their stead, he substituted a generosity of spirit and vision not seen on August 17. Especially remarkable is how quickly Mr. Clinton made these changes, as can be seen in a speech given just eleven days later in Union Chapel on Cape Cod:

> All of you know, I'm having to become quite an expert in this business of asking for forgiveness. (Applause.) It gets a little easier the more you do it. And if you have a family, an administration, a Congress and a whole country to ask, you—you're going to get a lot of practice. (Laughter.)
>
> But I have to tell you that in these last days, it has come home to me, again, something I first learned as President, but it wasn't burned in my bones, and that is that in order to get it, you have to be willing to give it. (Applause.)

And all of us—the anger, the resentment, the bitterness, the desire for recrimination against people you believe have wronged you, they harden the heart and deaden the spirit and lead to self-inflicted wounds. And so it is important that we are able to forgive those we believe have wronged us, even as we ask for forgiveness from people we have wronged. And I heard that first— first—in the civil rights movement: "Love thy neighbor as thyself." (Clinton, 1998, August 28)

Pronouns tell the story of this speech. Plurals substitute for singulars; second person for first person. The tonal shift is remarkable: Suddenly, Bill Clinton merges with the collective, he feels their feelings and they his. Even though he focuses on his misdeeds in the speech, he finds time to generalize beyond his situation ("you're going to get a lot of practice") and to seek reincorporation into the American community ("we ask for forgiveness from people we have wronged"). The Union Chapel speech's Commonality score is sharply higher than the August 17 address, letting voters once again hear the president they had come to know, the president who was one with his people.

It was this rhetorical feature, say Benoit and McHale (1999, p. 266), that made Clinton a popular president and that, ironically, caused special prosecutor Kenneth Starr to suffer "worse image problems than Clinton, who admitted to misleading the public and cheating on his wife." Clinton's language of commonality established his legitimacy as "representative of the community" (Brovero, 2000, p. 223), a key factor in any political (vs. purely legal) proceeding. Clinton's "compulsive need to meet people, to know them, to like them, to have them like him," says Greenstein (1998, p. 180) was both his ambition and his salvation. Clinton's detractors could wonder "What does it say about us as a country if we let him get away with this?" (quoted in Stuckey & Wabshall, 2000, p. 527), but in doing so they missed Clinton's magic: He appeared to see no distinction between himself and the nation he served. He spoke that way too.

If the Union Chapel speech reestablished Clinton's social ties to the nation, his short speech to the Florida Democratic Party signaled he was now back in the political business. His Familiarity score (use of common, everyday words) doubled on that occasion and his Realism score jumped dramatically as well. In contrast to the peregrinations found in his August 17 speech, the Orlando remarks never strayed from the bottom line: "I have no one to blame but myself for my self-inflicted wounds ... [but that] doesn't take away from whether we're right or wrong on the issues

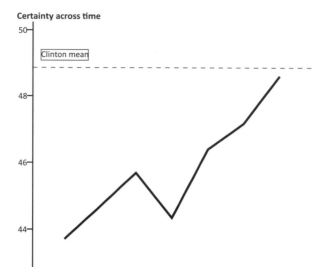

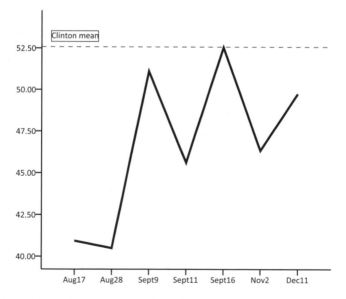

FIGURE 6.2 Clinton on August 17 vs. other impeachment remarks.

Commonality across time

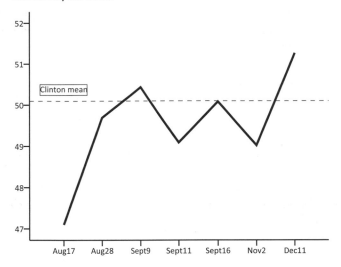

Familiarity across time

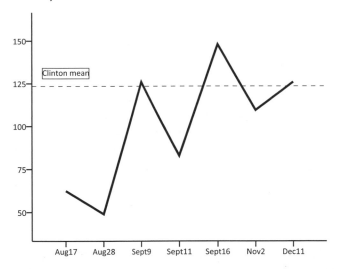

FIGURE 6.2 (continued)

or what we've done for the last six years or what this election is about."
When combined adroitly, Familiarity and Realism conduce to narrative, a
Clinton stock-in-trade. His introduction to the Orlando speech was par-
ticularly affecting:

> When I was over at the Hillcrest School—Buddy and I were over there a few
> minutes ago—and I was shaking hands with all these little kids out there. And
> this kid that reminded me a lot of myself when I was that young—he was big-
> ger than the other students and kind of husky—he said, "Mr. President, I want
> to grow up to be President. I want to be a President like you." And I said—I
> thought, I want to be able to conduct my life and my presidency so that all the
> parents of the country could feel good if their children were able to say that
> again. I'll never forget that little boy, and it's a big guide for me. (Clinton, 1998,
> September 9)

Once he had gotten through the doldrums of August, even seasoned
reporters could not throw Clinton off the track. Note in the following exchange, for example, how quickly he shifts from the philosophical to the
practical:

> REPORTER'S QUESTION: Mr. President, from your understanding of events, is Mon-
>   ica Lewinsky's account of your relationship accurate and truthful? And do you
>   still maintain that you did not lie under oath in your testimony?
> PRESIDENT CLINTON: Mr. Hunt, I have said for a month now that I did something
>   that was wrong .... but ... with only two weeks left to go in this budget year,
>   a very, very large range of items before the American people here at home—
>   doing our part to deal with this financial crisis, with funding the International
>   Monetary Fund, saving the Social Security system before we spend the surplus,
>   doing the important work that we can do to help educate our children, dealing
>   with the patients' bill of rights for these people, 160 million of them, in HMOs.
>   These are the things, to me, that I should be talking about as President. (Clin-
>   ton, 1998, September 16)

One should not be misled by the speed of Mr. Clinton's transition here.
The ellipsis in the above passage consists of a frank admission of wrong-
doing ("On last Friday at the prayer breakfast, I laid out as carefully and
as brutally honestly as I could what I believe the essential truth to be"),
along with a candid assessment of his ongoing struggles: "[I need] to focus
on what I did, to acknowledge it, to atone for it, and then to work on my

family—where I still have a lot of work to do, difficult work"). But even here the moral turned into the utilitarian ("a lot of work to do") and an ethical crisis became an agenda item. The assumptions undergirding American pragmatism can be used to supply all of the missing warrants in his address.

It is also worth noting that Clinton's resurrection proceeded campaign-like, which may explain why news coverage, as well as public opinion, moved in his direction over time (Kiousis, 2003). As we see in figure 6.2, there was a doggedness to Clinton's approach, a slow, steady, ever-onward quality. He was also clever to distribute his remarks across different settings: a speech in church, a political rally, a press conference, a TV interview. This let him mask his relentlessness, thereby allowing Clinton to "become himself" once again . . . but slowly. It takes a computer to notice such a glacial approach.

Rhetoric and Specialization

The story so far is one of Mr. Clinton refinding his natural voice but it is also worth noting what he did not do. He did not, for example, make heavy use of Denial words (*can't, won't, shouldn't,* etc.). Clinton's normal score on this variable was 5.69, but his "Lewinsky" speeches averaged only 5.13 denials per passage (a statistically significant difference). That is, he did not offer his detractors a line-by-line rebuttal nor did he make empty-sounding resolutions about the future. Instead, Clinton was as Optimistic in his crisis speeches as he was on the stump and when addressing policy matters from the Oval Office. "Going negative" was simply not his favored tone as it was, say, for an apologist like Richard Nixon. The key to the Clinton approach was consistency, a tendency to stay within his established parameters.

On special occasions, though, Clinton made some telling adaptations and they are part of the resurrection story too. His crisis speeches averaged 21 self-references per passage, compared to only 7 for his policy addresses and 12 for his campaign remarks. This is in keeping with the scholarly literature on apologia (Ware & Linkugel, 1973; Benoit, 1995) as well as with common sense: When accused, one should go to the source of the problem—the self.

But Clinton's approach was distinctive: He did not project himself against a social or political backdrop (as, for example, Gary Hart did when attacking the press for his undoing, or as Ronald Reagan did when linking his perfidy to the Iranian government). Instead, Clinton went inside. As a child of the Sixties and as an adherent to a confessional religion, Clinton knew that all salvation—political as well as moral—is ultimately a matter of conscience. This approach was easy for Clinton because he never saw a distinction between the interior and the exterior. He talked about his undershorts on television, about his brother's addictions, about his abusive father and, incessantly it seemed, about his moral failings.

Clinton's forays into the Self made for late-night parody ("I feel your pain") but it also made him approachable to others. His was therefore a pedestrian presidency but also a Rogerian presidency, one that used self-disclosure as political coinage. Television's intimacies—its chatty talk shows and soap operas—encouraged him on this score. During the Lewinsky affair he turned empirical challenges into interior challenges and then dismissed them, as he did when asked about his marital difficulties on the Black Entertainment Network: "All I can tell you is I'm working at it very hard and I think it's terribly important. It's more important than anything else in the world to me ... but I think the less I say about it, the better" (Clinton, 1998, November 2).

What about the Whitewater affair? Again, he interiorized the exterior: "Neither my wife nor I did anything wrong. And eventually that will become clear to the American people ... and so I'm at peace about that." And what of his detractors? Clinton's strategy is consistent—hear a crime, report an emotion: "So there are some, again, whose life is solely—they evaluate themselves solely on whether they're in or out, who are very angry about that. And I'm sorry for them. I'm not even angry at them anymore, I'm just sorry" (Clinton, 1998, November 2).

There was another, more subtle, aspect to Clinton's recovery. He used certain speech acts to punctuate his resurrection. For example, in the friendly confines of the BET interview he scored high on Embellishment, using adjectives and adverbs to embroider his claims about those who had wronged him. When asked what he thought of Washington's "right-wing conspirators," for example, Clinton unburdened himself:

> [For] most of these people, it doesn't matter to them whether there's a patients' bill of rights or not, to make sure doctors, instead of accountants, make health care decisions. It certainly doesn't matter to them whether there's a minimum wage increase. It doesn't matter to them whether we have 100,000 more teachers and modernized schools. It doesn't matter to them whether we save Social Security for the 21st century. (Clinton, 1998, November 2)

In a similar way, Clinton used his address at the annual prayer breakfast to emphasize his faithfulness to eternal truths. This speech was extremely high on Optimism, which is surprising since he did a good amount of atoning in the address (as, for example, when he apologized to the Lewinsky family). But most of the speech was upbeat, giving it an almost salvific quality. Said the Reverend Clinton:

> I am very grateful for the many, many people—clergy and ordinary citizens alike—who have written me with wise counsel. I am profoundly grateful for the support of so many Americans who somehow through it all seem to still know that I care about them a great deal, that I care about their problems and their dreams. I am grateful for those who have stood by me and who say that in this case and many others, the bounds of privacy have been excessively and unwisely invaded. That may be. Nevertheless, in this case, it may be a blessing, because I still sinned. And if my repentance is genuine and sustained, and if I can maintain both a broken spirit and a strong heart, then good can come of this for our country as well as for me and my family. (Clinton, 1998, September 11)

Ironically, even though Clinton's remarks had a New Testament flavor, the Lewinsky family's rabbi, David Wolby of Sinai Temple in Los Angeles, said of the speech: "Sometimes it's precisely such moments of despair that enable somebody, at least in the Jewish tradition, to elevate themselves beyond anything they imagine they could be" (Cannon, 1998, p. 7).

But it would be another two months before Mr. Clinton would strike the right tone of repentance. It was not until he spoke in the Rose Garden on December 11, 1998 (a week before his impeachment), that Clinton said what many wished he had said on August 17. His December speech was crisp and clear (very high on Certainty) and also high on Commonality, giving it a kind of congregational fervor. Most important, the speech was low on Optimism, the lowest of any of his crisis addresses.

The mixture was attractive: Contrition combined with group destiny. Mr. Clinton admitted what he did wrong ("I never should have misled the country") and explained why ("I gave into my shame"). He apologized for what "members of both parties in Congress are now forced to deal with" and even admitted he had learned from his critics ("they do show us our faults"). "Like anyone who honestly faces the shame of wrongful conduct," said Clinton, "I would give anything to go back and undo what I did." Dramatically, the president declared that should the Congress "determine that my errors of word and deed require their rebuke and censure," he was ready to accept it (Clinton, 1998, December 11). In the popular mind, Mr. Clinton finally got his apology right. For the House of Representatives, of course, it was too little too late.

Bill Clinton was a president for all seasons, and so the address he gave to congressional Democrats one week later was different still. It contained a heavy dollop of Patriotic language, with Clinton using six times the nationalistic terms he used in his other crisis addresses. In doing so, he tied himself to the political traditions of the nation (versus its religious and cultural roots). Even though the House of Representatives had just impeached him, this was also the most optimistic speech he made during the Lewinsky drama. In it, he thanked the members of the Democratic Caucus, he thanked those who had supported his family, and he lionized such traits as the "presumption of good faith," the "need to pull together," "constructive debate," and "defense of the Constitution." Above all, he urged his listeners to "rise above the rancor" and to be "repairer[s] of the breach" so that all could move into "the new century about to dawn" (Clinton, 1998, December 19). Even during Clinton's midnight, the dawn was near.

Conclusion

In his discussion of political crisis, Randall Miller (1999, p. 714) notes that the "purpose of impeachment is to halt further injury to the polity." For Miller, punishment is a subordinate function of impeachment, with protection of the nation being primary. This distinction explains how rhetoric becomes important in such instances. During a remarkable three-month period, William Jefferson Clinton found ways of reusing the same political vocabularies that had twice elected him to office, thereby giving voters the sense that the nation was still in good stead. Additionally, but secondarily, he used rhetoric to punish himself, and that too was good enough for most Americans.

The media pundits and Washington politicians never understood any of this. Although they were professional wordsmiths, they never really appreciated Clinton's power of language nor how it alone could stand up to legal and constitutional challenges. But Clinton knew that words can serve both protective and penitential functions. Impeachment happened to Bill Clinton, but Bill Clinton also happened back, causing the American people to engage in a serious kind of political, and emotional, deliberation (Lawrence & Bennett, 2001).

We feel that too many observers have unwisely dismissed the symbolic aspects of the Clinton impeachment, although they are no doubt correct that the president's accomplishments insulated him from his antagonists in many ways and made Ken Starr seem an interfering prig. But an old principle of social psychology holds that people's attitudes do not stay in place unless they have satisfactory ways of explaining those attitudes to others. To keep Bill Clinton as their president, that is, the American people needed a language that did not make themselves seem venal or self-serving. As a person who had "always worked the middle ground" (Murphy, 2005, p. 664), Mr. Clinton easily supplied the needed language. He used Realism to distinguish himself from the ideologues and Commonality to separate group concerns from individual misdeeds. He also used Certainty and Familiarity to give voters an abiding sense of confidence. In doing so, he gave people a language they could use to embrace the status quo. In a sense, then, Bill Clinton became the nation's ventriloquist.

Another claim being made here (and throughout this book) is that lexical force is a more important facet of politics than has heretofore been acknowledged. This study traced words, not ideas or arguments or philosophies or worldviews. Such tracings will be inadequate for some, for there is a natural human arrogance that assumes that mere word choice is either random (and hence not theorizable) or obscure (and hence politically ineffectual). While that is true in some cases, words become especially powerful when entire lexical families are deployed across time. In such cases, their slow and steady deployment works its way into public discussion and then changes the nature of that discussion.

As we have seen here, Bill Clinton never let the Lewinsky scandal throw him off stride, but his language behavior says as much about the American people as it does about him. The August 17 address upset most of his fellow citizens because of its emotional indulgence. Clinton quickly recovered, however, launching a low-key campaign to win them back. His critics were outraged by all of this, wondering why adultery, perjury, and (possibly) blackmail were insufficient to remove a president from office. The only possible response to such charges is that, in a democracy, an electorate usually gets what it wants. In Clinton's case, it wanted a clear-headed, forceful chief executive with a sense for the people. Perhaps it should have wanted more. But what? Bill Clinton was no better than those he governed and, in a democracy, that is often enough.

CHAPTER SEVEN

Complexity and the Measured Tone

When George W. Bush's administration drew to a close, it seemed like nothing remained unknown about the president. Bush was a commander-in-chief who fought a two-front war in Iraq and Afghanistan, who rallied the nation in the aftermath of September 11, who helped his fellow Republicans capture both houses of Congress in 2002, who signed the No Child Left Behind Act in 2003, and who was handily reelected in 2004. He then lost control of Congress two years later, oversaw a jaw-dropping deficit, and eventually suffered one of the more precipitous declines in public approval of any U.S. president (he ended his term in office with the backing of only 30% of the electorate). The Bush presidency was tumultuous beyond belief, and by now it is hard to imagine anything new about it.

Our data suggest otherwise. This chapter examines a great many of Bush's public pronouncements with a particular eye to his ideological tendencies. But why bother? How else could Mr. Bush be described other than as the "most divisive occupant of the White House in 50 years" (Jacobson, 2008, p. 13)? Mr. Bush's "style, agenda, and tactics," says Gary Jacobson (2008, p. 240), "ultimately provoked the most divergent partisan assessments of any president since the advent of regular polling on the president's job performance." Jacobson argues that Bush's tendency to control the national agenda, make policies in secret, and then sell his solutions vigorously while ignoring the press produced a level of divisiveness not seen since the Vietnam War. And all of this from a president who promised to "change the tone in Washington" when elected.

Despite his best intentions, Bush was often called "cocky," "uncritical," "messianic," "pontifical," and almost every other adjective associated with undue self-assurance. The anecdotes that travel furthest about Bush are anecdotes like this: "Three months ago . . . in a private meeting with Amish farmers in Lancaster County, Pa., Bush was reported to have said, 'I trust God speaks through me'" (Suskind, 2004, p. 51). Even if apocryphal, such tales were widely believed—both by Bush's supporters and his detractors—suggesting that they capture something essential about the man.

Other scholars have noted that only some of the divisiveness seen during the Bush years could be attributed to the president himself. Midway through his administration, for example, "party identifiers" in the U.S. had reached the 90% level (Campbell, 2005, pp. 224–25), leaving little room for open-ended dialogue. In addition, because reporters with their "big-story mentality" were naturally attracted to a "binary discourse," the Bush presidency was particularly ripe with narrative possibilities (Coe et al., 2004, pp. 247, 248). Other scholars argue that the crisis of 9/11 fundamentally "transformed the relationship between the President and the U.S. citizenry toward something that is, by degree, more heavily grounded in charismatic leadership" (Bligh, Kohles & Meindl, 2004, p. 227).

What else might explain Bush the ideologue? Hugh Heclo (2003, p. 46) attributes such traits to the president's worldview, where "the idée fixe locked in the confines of its own idiom" requires manifestation. Other scholars reverse this polarity, declaring that the Radical Right made Bush their captive, adding an "imprint of righteousness" to his words and actions (Danner, 2005). While "the Democrats lately have become the party of nuance and complexity," says Packer (2004, p. 30), "the Republicans have become the party of monolithic will," thereby leaving Bush no choice but to adopt their refrains. Kellner (2007, p. 640) adds more fuel to the fire when arguing that "the Bush administration, aided and abetted by the U.S. corporate media, manipulated a politics of fear to push through a right-wing agenda that included the Patriot Act, massive changes in the legal system, a dramatic expansion of the U.S. military, and the U.S.-led military intervention in Afghanistan and Iraq." The result, says Rogers Smith (2008, p. 273), was a rhetoric containing "anti-democratic features discouraging deliberation and dissent." For Robert Ivie and Oscar Giner (2007, p. 594), Bush's discourse implicitly acknowledged that an "Orwellian state was necessary in order to protect democracy from its enemies."

So the popular view of Bush is that he prosecuted an unpopular war with gusto, was irresolute with respect to Guantanamo detainees, curried favor with religious conservatives regarding stem cell research, and turned a deaf ear on environmental concerns. All of this is true. But it is also true that he was moderate on immigration, treaded carefully on Social Security reform, and was a staunch ally of Israel while trying to accommodate Arab sensibilities.

Indeed, despite Bush's alleged ideologies, the political right never really trusted him: he opposed gutting the Department of Energy, whose abolition had been in every GOP platform since 1980 (Shirley & Devine, 2010); many conservatives vilified Bush for his lack of fiscal discipline (York, 2009); some detested his "federalist" inclinations (Milkis & Rhodes, 2007); and pro-lifers were dismayed when he ruled out a litmus test for Supreme Court nominees (Savage, 2005). Perhaps because he increased spending on domestic programs, refused to criticize his opponents' patriotism, and tried to extend the ban on assault weapons (Starr & Dunham, 2003), George W. Bush never really became a darling of the right.

Policy matters aside, what else might Mr. Bush have done to reinforce such conflicting views of his presidency? Can he be rightly seen as an ideologue when his remarks are compared to those of his predecessors and contemporaries? Did he become more ideological as his administration wore on or did he throttle back after learning the ways of Washington? Did special events, topics, or circumstances bring forth the strident Bush? Is it possible that he governed in one way but spoke in another? Or should popular images of Bush the ideologue be rethought?

Our answers to these questions are not uncontroversial. They call into question much existing press commentary and a considerable amount of scholarly research about the nation's forty-third president. We find Mr. Bush to be more a pragmatist than an ideologue, a person often bedeviled by the intricacies of his job but whose remarks contained considerable nuance nonetheless. Above all, we argue, the Bush presidency cannot be understood unless one examines the political complexities confronting him and how he responded to them—via the tone of his remarks. In many ways, we also argue, the rhetorical facts are on Mr. Bush's side.

Studying Bush's Tone

In investigating President Bush, we gathered almost all of his public remarks (our corpus contains just under 2,300 full texts). In addition to examining the standard DICTION variables, we also created a special measure dubbed the **Hortatory Tone**, defined as *the tendency to focus on core beliefs of politics, religion, and community in assured and dramatic ways*. To create this variable, two of DICTION's built-in scores and three customized dictionaries were combined: Hortatory Tone = Patriotic Language + Religious Language + Voter References + Certainty (all-encompassing language) + Embellishment (heavy use of adjectival constructions).

More specifically, we monitored the use of standard American tokens ($n = 31$), including constitutional language, celebratory terms, and words related to fundamental rights and historic truths (e.g., "freedom," "justice," "republic"), as well as sacred language ($n = 200$)—broad-based Judeo-Christian terminology, including value-laden terms, religious personalities, and theological constructs (e.g., "worship," "disciple," "prophecy"). To this we added references ($n = 48$) to the American citizenry writ large ("people," "constituents," "nation," etc.). The numerical totals of these word lists were standardized (because of their different mathematical ranges) and then combined to build the Hortatory measure used throughout this study.

We looked at roughly 275 speeches per year during the Bush presidency. For each speech, the date, topic, length, location, occasion, audience, and purpose were recorded, permitting a fairly thorough look at Bush's rhetorical architecture. We found that Mr. Bush's speeches were delivered to government or military audiences 10.4% of the time, to national or press audiences 40.2% of the time, and to local or invited listeners 49.4% of the time. Location-wise, 59.2% of his addresses were delivered in the environs of Washington, D.C., and 33.2% elsewhere in the U.S. Roughly 38% of his speeches were formal briefings, 49% were partisan rallies, and 13% were delivered in ceremonial settings. Interestingly enough, these proportions remained constant over time—including the political rallies—again validating the notion of the modern presidency's "perpetual campaign." There was some topical variation over the years but, generally speaking, our sample is quite robust.[1] We estimate that it contains 80% of all speeches Bush gave during his eight-plus years in office.

Noticing the Unnoticed Bush

The common description of George W. Bush as an ideologue could mean many things. It could mean that he refused to compromise with his opponents in Congress, and there is considerable evidence supporting that charge. It could also mean that he aligned himself with the right wing of his party, restricting himself to a narrow set of political optics, and there is some truth to that claim as well. Further, it could mean that he refused to break bread with his detractors and, indeed, 72% of his domestic speeches were given in "red" states and only 28% in "blue" states. And it could also mean that the legislation he sponsored, the cabinet officers he chose, and the advisers who influenced him were drawn from an exceedingly narrow band of the political continuum. All these things may be true, but this is also true: George W. Bush did not speak like an ideologue (at least not very often).

Overall, the Bush data on the Hortatory Tone generated an almost perfectly normal curve (even a left-skewed curve), suggesting that while he was not averse to using strong language, he did not deploy it excessively. In these ways and more he contrasted sharply with Barry Goldwater, who was variously called an extremist, a crusader, a zealot, and a New Deal detractor during his run for the presidency in 1964. He also differed from Ronald Reagan, who described Russia as an evil empire, who fought (and paid for) the Contra rebels, who bombed Libya and invaded Grenada, and who staunchly embraced supply-side economics. Compared to "hard cases" like these, Mr. Bush was sparing of speech.

Figure 7.1 provides a clearer indication of Bush's approach.[2] No matter how provocative his policies might have been, George W. Bush was the least ideological presidential candidate the nation saw during the last half century. How can this be true? How can the Bush stereotypes be so misguided? Is George W. Bush truly milder than his father, wilier than Bill Clinton, more diplomatic than Dwight Eisenhower? Can DICTION get something right that others have gotten wrong?

These are fair questions but a bit more texture is needed to answer them. Consider figure 7.2, for example, which shows that, when first running for office in 2004, Bush came on stronger than usual before returning to a more placid approach in his second term. During the '04 campaign, Mr. Bush found a good story to tell. The story he told—that the times were dangerous and that the nation's destiny was linked to his continued leadership—had strong, martial overtones, precisely what the Republican strategists had prescribed for victory. There was a politics to this choice but there was also an aesthetic. Note in the passage below, for example, how Bush begins with a well-wrought narrative but then seamlessly moves to an uncompromising conclusion:

Two-and-a-half years ago, our nation saw war and grief arrive on a quiet September morning. From that day to this, we have pursued a clear strategy: We

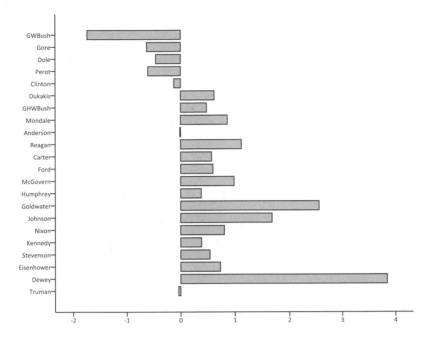

FIGURE 7.1 Use of Hortatory Tone in presidential contests, 1948–2000 ($n = 3,986$).

are taking the offensive against the terrorists abroad. We're taking unprecedented measures to protect the American people here at home. The goal of the
terrorists is to kill our citizens—that's their goal—and to make Americans live
in fear. This nation refuses to live in fear. We will stand together until this threat
to our nation and to the civilized world is ended. (Bush, 2004, March 2)

Bush's rhetoric during the 2004 campaign was considerably more strident than it was during the 2000 election, in part because the times were
more challenging and in part because Bush ran a single-minded campaign
in '04, focusing largely on national defense. In 2000, in contrast, he and Al
Gore confronted one another on a panoply of issues—international diplomacy, the nation's economy, education and infrastructure, the Clinton
scandals, etc.—all of which required suppleness.[3] In short, although stridency was not his preferred tone, Mr. Bush found it suitable when running for reelection:

Before September the 11th, of 2001, Afghanistan served as the home base of al
Qaeda, which trained and deployed thousands of killers to set up terror cells

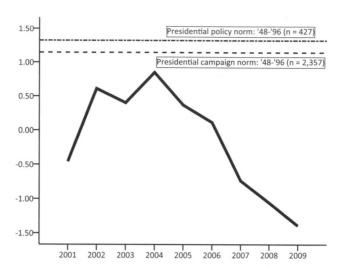

FIGURE 7.2 George W. Bush's use of the Hortatory Tone over time.

around the world, including our own country. Because we acted, Afghanistan is a rising democracy. Because we acted, over ten million people have registered to vote in a country that a short time ago was brutalized by a barbaric regime called the Taliban. Because we acted, Afghanistan is an ally in the war on terror. Because we acted, many young girls go to school for the first time. Because we acted, America and the world are safer. (Bush, 2004, August 26)

Although Bush's hortatory climb reached its zenith during the 2004 election, it was rapidly abandoned thereafter. But even in 2004 his oratory stayed well below the presidential norm (as we see in figure 7.2). One reason for Bush's reluctance to "go nuclear" is that a hortatory rhetoric forces one to trade in abstractions—truth, justice, and the like—and philosophical matters were never his strong suit. Indeed, there was something in Bush that seemed to hate rhetoric—artful tropes and all that. In its place, he constantly looked for a good story, one with a clear plot line and a satisfactory denouement. Thanks to Ashley Pearson, he found one, just as the 2004 campaign was getting underway:

Last month a girl in Lincoln, Rhode Island, sent me a letter. It began, "Dear George W. Bush. If there's anything you know, I, Ashley Pearson, age 10, can do to help anyone, please send me a letter and tell me what I can do to save our country." She added this P.S.: "If you can send a letter to the troops, please put,

'Ashley Pearson believes in you.'" Tonight, Ashley, your message to our troops has just been conveyed. (Bush, 2004, January 20)

Our data show that while Bush often let loose on the stump, he behaved more prudently in most ceremonial settings and, especially, in formal briefings where he temporized, perhaps because he knew the press would pore over his every word.[4] On the electoral circuit, however, Bush came on strong. Never really a creature of Washington, D.C., he felt uncomfortable there but felt at ease when stumping across the country on his issues. Indeed, the 2004 campaign was a campaign based on a single day—September 11, 2001—and that day dominated virtually everything George W. Bush said during the election. The approach was well-suited to a linear person like Bush and showed that, in times of great stress, the American electorate would rather hear a strong story than no story at all.

Looking back, it is clear that Bush's policy platform in '04 was not radically different from John Kerry's: neither knew how to win the war in Iraq, neither had a plan for rescuing Social Security, neither knew how to stop global warming nor how to eliminate corporate malfeasance. Given the absence of fresh ideas, George Bush's platform and his rhetoric became coterminous, a way of telling the same tale of perfidy he told at the beginning of his presidency when the great towers came down. Said Bush: "Sometimes I'm a little too blunt . . . I get that from my mother." "You always know where I stand," he declared on another occasion. "You can't say that for my opponent." "If America shows uncertainty or weakness in these troubling times," he warned, "the world will drift toward tragedy— and this will not happen on my watch" (quoted in Danner, 2005).

Given how thin Bush's résumé was when running for the presidency in 2000—some draft dodging as a young man, an undistinguished business career, service as a foot soldier in his father's administration, and a moderately successful stint as governor—if the Bush43 presidency should have been anything it should have been a domestic presidency. History intervened, however, and his presidency became international to the core. The attacks of 9/11 sucked up all the political oxygen and terrorism came to dominate the Bush agenda. Even though the remarks below were atypical of Bush, *this* is the George Bush that most Americans remember:

As freedom advances across a troubled part of the world, it is once again opposed by fanatical adherence of a murderous ideology. And once again, the stakes are high. Now, as then, our enemies have made their fight a test of American credibility and resolve. Now, as then, they are trying to intimidate free people and break our will. And now, as then, they will fail. (Bush, 2005, August 30)

The Other Side of the Coin

Three things can be concluded from the foregoing: (1) Mr. Bush sometimes engaged in hyperbole, especially with regard to the wars in Iraq and Afghanistan, but (2) these were the exception rather than the rule, and (3) our findings differ from those of most critics, who have roundly denounced Bush for his excesses. The scholarly unanimity has been so impressive that we quote from the best of them at length:[5]

- *Bush the Heedless*: His rhetoric served to truncate the deliberative process, leading to an impoverished debate over the merits of his proposal, and ultimately to incoherent policies. (Crockett, 2003, p. 480)
- *Bush the Isolationist*: While the values expressed in the West Point speech seem unexceptionable to some, others noted that Bush's monolithic world view seemingly obviated the need for seeking an understanding of others—and appeared to disregard the sovereignty of nations. (Jarratt, 2006, p. 94)
- *Bush the Calvinist*: Bush's World War II analogies in his covenant renewal messages encouraged Americans to perceive the war on terror in the same black and white fashion in which they thought about World War II. In this way, the president's discourse illustrated what Jasinski describes as the potential of epideictic rhetoric to be used for "subversive" ends. (Bostdorff , 2003, p. 305)
- *Bush the Exorcist*: The president positioned himself as St. George slaying the mythical dragon. Behind the armor of St. George were more familiar masks: the Jesuits exorcising devils in London or the ministers pursuing compacts with the devil in Salem. (Ivie & Giner, 2007, p. 585)
- *Bush the Manichean*: For President Bush, the world is, as it ever was, divided between good and evil. People of character oppose evil. Policy is justified not by expediency arguments, but by metaphysical ends—by character and by faith. (Murphy, 2003, p. 626)
- *Bush the Fascist*: Bush's rhetoric, like that of fascism, deploys a mistrust of language, reducing it to manipulative speechifying, speaking in codes, repeating the same phrases over and over. This is grounded in anti-intellectualism and contempt for democracy and rational argument. (Kellner, 2007, p. 636)

Speaking into the teeth of such an impressive assemblage is daunting. After all, these scholars were hard on Bush because of their deep commitment to multiordinal debate and their rejection of blind ideology. But did the scholars treat Bush fairly? Did they consider the full swath of his discourse? Did they examine its several pieces and parts?

To address those questions, we used DICTION's ability to examine a text regardless of its derivation. We identified eleven of the most thoughtful essays on Bush's rhetoric, especially those focusing on his war-time remarks. From them, we extracted all direct quotations from Bush's speeches dealing with the war in the Middle East. This produced a sample of 8,507 words, which we then subjected to DICTION analysis. After doing so, we analyzed the 288 Bush speeches on national defense in our databank and compared the two datasets

As we see in figure 7.3, the results are startling. While the Hortatory mean for Original Bush was −1.10, the mean for Excerpted Bush was 8.44—more than three standard deviations higher.[6] Moreover, the scholars' quotations consistently omitted the upbeat, communal flavor of Bush's rhetoric, features which he used to keep his countrymen buoyed up during a long and frustrating war.[7] In other words, our data show that *this* was the George W. Bush who most often appeared before the American people. Indeed, even Bush's best remembered speech—that given on the evening of September 11, 2001—registered a 1.69 on our Hortatory scale but a 9.23 when the scholarly excerpts from that speech were analyzed by the program.

To be sure, George Bush was often his own worst press agent. Also, his image frequently outpaced his reality, an outcome that often befalls the nation's chief executive. Still, the contrast between the Original and Excerpted Bush is so stark that it leaves one wondering how people can process the same discourse and arrive at such different interpretations. According to DICTION, the following passage perfectly captures Mr. Bush's wartime refrains even though it diverges sharply from the Bush described in the scholarly studies:

> I know of America's greatness because I get to see it up close, and it is a privilege to see it up close. I see it in the foot soldiers in the armies of compassion, who perform acts of kindness and hope every single day. I see it in the courage of ordinary citizens, like those who rushed toward danger when the Twin Towers fell and our Pentagon burned. I see it with military families who've lost loved ones. And every time I come away moved and inspired by their valor, grit, pride, and love of country. (Bush, 2008, February 7)

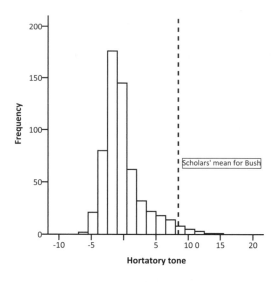

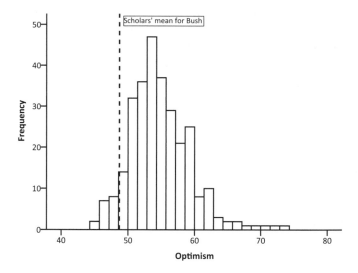

FIGURE 7.3 Variable distributions for Bush speeches on national defense ($n = 288$).

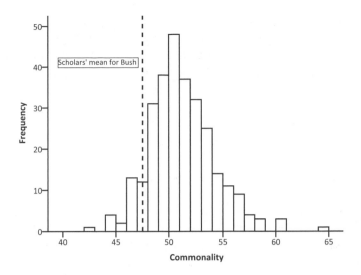

FIGURE 7.3 (continued)

Explaining the Unexplained Bush

What explains the gap between our data and the George W. Bush described by most researchers? This is a question of genuine importance, a
question having both political and theoretical implications. It is a question that exposes alternative epistemologies and that asks how, and by
whom, political histories are best written. It is a question that touches on
the value (and shortcomings) of statistical data and one that highlights the
prismatic nature of language. It is also an existential question: When can
we trust our gut impressions and when must we be more reflective? Why
is it hard to see the political within ourselves and easy to see it in others?
When do words point unerringly to human truths and when do they lead
us astray? Why does it take so little effort to deconstruct an American
president and so much effort to examine our own biases dispassionately?

Our findings point up a number of tensions—some academic, some
political, some merely human—but all of which offer important insights
for how politics should be studied. To wit:

1. *Art vs. science.* This is the most obvious antimony exposed in the
Bush case study. Art's attack on our project is a direct one: to reduce
something as complex as "ideology" and "partisanship" to a series of lexical counts is reductionistic to the core. To assume that words—the most

fundamental embodiments of thought and feeling—are quantities and not qualities, such detractors might argue, is inherently fallacious. They would observe, further, that automated language analysis examines words out of context, something that people themselves never do. By permitting such practices, computers are rendered insensitive to meaning and hence to what it is to be human.

DICTION's defense, as was mentioned in chapter 1, is this: (a) the dictionaries included in the program have considerable face validity and are completely transparent to the user; (b) the program examines hundreds of thousands of words in just a few minutes and cannot be distracted by a researcher's political biases or theoretical expectations; (c) examining a large number of words deployed across time, context, speaker, and location triangulates insights that could never be garnered by human observers; and (d) as a decoding mechanism, DICTION tracks minute verbal patterns that even the canniest encoder can neither monitor nor control but that may have considerable rhetorical impact. DICTION, in short, is a limited modality but so too are human observers.

2. *Intimacy vs. distance.* One of DICTION's greatest strengths is also its greatest weakness: it pushes a user away from a passage by exposing so much data that it is hard to see its nuances. The close textual critic, in contrast, looks into the very sinews of a passage and can thus track even minor verbal phenomena with sensitivity. But there is danger here as well. By becoming enmeshed in the details of a text, a critic does something that ordinary receivers never do and, hence, can misappreciate the here-then-gone phenomenological experiences of everyday audiences. Getting the big picture of a text therefore prevents at least as much bias as it encourages. DICTION helps a researcher "step back," and stepping back is important in a world where ordinary citizens are confronted hourly, daily, and weekly with a blizzard of stimuli, any one of which—or several of which—can shape their political realities. Because listeners engage in much more forgetting than remembering, DICTION keeps things in proper, human perspective.

3. *Discourse vs. policy.* One simple way of rejecting the arguments made in this chapter is to reason that words are one thing but that money, armaments, and power are something else entirely. No matter what Mr. Bush *said*, that is, what he *did* by sponsoring legislation, signing executive orders, or appointing federal judges remains the best measure of his ideological bent. From this perspective, words take a backseat to laws written, monies distributed, and troops deployed. George W. Bush raised par-

tisanship to a new high, reports Skinner (2008), and whether he did so with words or not is beside the point (or so DICTION'S detractors might claim).

On the other hand, finding reliable metrics for gauging ideology has not been easy for scholars. Moreover, since all legislation must be first debated in public, language inevitably helps shape policy determination. In short, DICTION knows what it knows and measures what it measures. And it does so identically each time it is used, thereby providing a useful baseline for other collateral assessments. While it is tempting to dismiss words as mere effluvia, words do matter, a fact that George "Mission Accomplished" Bush himself once acknowledged: "I regret saying some things I shouldn't have said, like 'Dead or Alive' and 'Bring 'em on.' My wife reminded me that, hey, as president of the United States be careful what you say" (quoted in Mooney, 2008).

4. *Description vs. judgment.* Computers count but critics criticize. They inspect a text looking for unsavoriness and then issue warnings. "A critic is a gong at a railroad crossing clanging loudly," says Christopher Morley, although that bell is sometimes rung in vain since ordinary voters are often so busy living their lives. "A good critic is the sorcerer that makes some hidden spring gush forth unexpectedly under our feet," says Francois Mauriac, although people do not always respond well to such gushings. "An important job of the critic is to savage what is mediocre or meretricious," says Susan Sontag, although such judgments are often greeted with a yawn.[8] Still, in their best moments, critics are important safeguards for an enlightened polity.

Computers know nothing of such stuff. They just stupidly do what they have been asked to do. They cannot separate right from wrong nor the excellent from the banal. They can count some things but are mystified by most things. Ultimately, they are no smarter than their users. But that, ironically, can be an adjunct to traditional textual analysis. It is one thing, for example, to know ideology when one sees it and quite another to specify its parameters and modes of measurement ahead of time. In their rush to judgment, that is, critics often fail to connect their assumptions to their methods and their data to their claims. DICTION, in contrast, operationalizes everything it touches and can only report that which is there. DICTION knows nothing of aporia or simulacra, but it has an exquisite understanding that 10 is four more than 6.

5. *President vs. administration.* It is entirely possible that ideology reached new heights during George W. Bush's administration even though

he, himself, may have resisted it. An administration containing such bellig-
erent characters as Dick Cheney, Karl Rove, and Donald Rumsfeld may
well have spiked the national quotient of moral rigidity even while encouraging Bush to stay above the fray. This good cop/bad cop scenario
has played itself out in previous administrations. Ronald Reagan, for example, was particularly deft at such maneuvers, rallying the nation while
his henchmen carried out the Reagan revolution. This is exactly the point
made by White & Zogby (2004, p. 81): "Rove was determined that, unlike
George H. W. Bush, the younger Bush should do nothing to alienate the
core Republican base on domestic issues—especially taxes. At the same
time, Rove made sure that while Bush would be a tough partisan behind
closed doors, he would not strike a harsh tone in public, as Speaker Gingrich had." Our data suggest that Rove's strategy may have been exe-
cuted throughout the Bush administration, with the president speaking
prudence and his henchmen certainty.

    6. *Cause vs. effect*. There is considerable collateral evidence that the
U.S. has witnessed extreme partisanship in recent years. George W. Bush
may have been part of that trend but other forces may have intervened
as well. For example, Mark Brewer sees signs in the electorate itself: "All
evidence points to the increased importance of partisanship in the general
electorate, and it certainly appears that individuals have become increasingly likely to recognize partisan differences on issues related to economic equality, race, and cultural concerns" (2005, p. 223). Barbara Sinclair (2005, p. 121) observes similar trends, but sees political elites at the
center of things: "In the latter part of the twentieth century, Congress polarized along partisan and ideological lines. Observers and members alike
complained about the bitter partisan warfare that pervaded Washington.
Presidents could expect less and less support from members of the opposition party and, given the frequency of divided partisan control of Congress and the White House, encountered increasing difficulty in enacting
their programs."

    In other words, it is possible that people "pre-heard" ideology in
Bush even though he himself spoke carefully. Presidents are influential,
to be sure, but sometimes they just ride the waves of popular sentiment.
Whether or not George W. Bush was an ideological donor or an ideological recipient, that is, deserves further study.

    7. *Sample vs. population*. Given how small the news hole has become,
it is possible that media selectivity explains why Bush has been judged an
ideologue. For example, although Mr. Bush discussed economic issues five

times more often than terrorism, that fact is not well known. Because the press pays special attention to "red meat" speeches containing clear ideological cues, some of Bush's remarks—such as those on terrorism—may have been overrepresented in media reportage and formal scholarship. Consider, for example, table 7.1, which contrasts Bush's passages quoted and not-quoted in the mass media. A quick inspection shows that "quotability" results from the speeches' ideological cues, cues that dramatize regnant polarities. Editorial choices like these are understandable because they help voters get to the heart of an issue. At the same time, however, this selectivity can misrepresent a presidency to a nation. We believe that is what happened to the Bush administration.

8. *Quantity vs. impact.* By assembling a great many of Bush's speeches, we have accounted for more of his rhetoric than have most scholars. Some will find that irrelevant since not all speeches are created equal. A State of the Union address witnessed by millions surely has more impact than one observed by two hundred brave souls standing in the rain outside a VFW hall in Des Moines. By aggregating these speeches, DICTION implies that all texts are somehow equivalent, thereby ignoring their differential political valence. In contrast, newspapers cover what they cover, and scholars study what they study, because they can sort out the relevant from the irrelevant. So, for example, a great many scholars have dissected Mr. Bush's 9/11 speech and judged it a representative anecdote for his entire administration.

We, on the other hand, know of no valid way of assessing an anecdote's representativeness. All we do know is that when Bush's 288 national defense speeches are examined together, he emerges as far less ideological than his predecessors in office. We also know that those speeches were one-sixth as ideological as those he gave on human values and were fairly equivalent to his remarks on law and order. We also know that his low-Hortatory speeches were ten times as typical of Bush as the excerpts found in press reports or the scholarly journals. Naturally, DICTION's skeptics can argue that some speeches are more influential than others— not witnessed more often, not more readily remembered, but actually more influential. But influential to whom, influential about what, and how is that influence measured? Speeches described on the front page of *The New York Times* are no doubt important, but what is the half-life of their importance and, again, how can it be measured?

DICTION is agnostic about such matters. It assumes that Quantity and Impact are separate issues and, until such matters are sorted out, there is

TABLE 7.1 **Partisan differences in quoted vs. nonquoted passages in statements of George W. Bush.**

Speech Location	Topic	Quoted passage	Nonquoted passage
Veterans Day, Tobyhanna, PA 11/11/05	War in Iraq	While it is perfectly legitimate to criticize my decision or the conduct of the war, it is deeply irresponsible to rewrite the history of how that war began. Some Democrats and antiwar critics are now claiming we manipulated the intelligence and misled the American people about why we went to war.	And our debate at home must also be fair-minded. One of the hallmarks of a free society and what makes our country strong is that our political leaders can discuss their differences openly, even in times of war.
National Association of Realtors, Washington, D.C., 5/13/05	Social Security	The American people now understand that Social Security is headed for serious financial trouble. And they expect the folks here in Washington, D.C. to do something about it. They expect us to put aside partisan differences and focus on the good of the country.	Franklin Roosevelt did a smart thing when he created Social Security. The system has meant a lot to a lot of people. Social Security has brought peace of mind to millions of Americans in their retirement.
President's Address to the Nation, Washington D.C., 12/18/05	Iraq	I will make decisions on troop levels based on the progress we see on the ground and the advice of our military leaders—not based on artificial timetables set by politicians in Washington.	All who had a part in this achievement—Iraqis, and Americans and our coalition partners—can be proud. Yet our work is not done. There is more testing and sacrifice before us.
Six Point Plan for the Economy, Kansas City, MO; 9/4/03	Economy	Instead, because we did act, the recession was one of the shallowest in modern economic history. Some critics, who opposed tax relief to start with, are still opposing it. They argue we should return to the way things were in 2001. What they're really saying is they want to raise taxes.	There's a lot we can do now that the Congress is back in town. And I look forward to working with both Republicans and Democrats to set the framework for continued economic prosperity and growth.
President Promotes Compassionate Conservatism, San Jose, CA: 4/30/02	Economy	It is compassionate to actively help our fellow citizens in need. It is conservative to insist on responsibility and on results.	It's important to be a confident country. And I'm confident in the ability of American entrepreneurs and producers to compete in the world. I'm confident that our farmers and ranchers can compete in the world.

2002 Unity Luncheon, Atlanta, GA; 12/17/02	Appointments	If the Senate had its way, I would have the authority to suspend the work rules in the Department of Agriculture, but not in the office of homeland security. The Senate Democrat leaders want to tie the hands of this department as we determine who to hire, who to fire, and whether or not people can be moved.	I believe America will lead the world to peace. And at the same time, here at home—same time here at home, we can make sure, by following our hearts, by being the compassionate country we are, to make sure this American experience shines brightly for every single citizen who lives in our country.
Plan for Economic Growth, Canton, OH; 4/24/03	Economy	Some in Congress say the plan is too big. Well, it seems like to me they might have some explaining to do. If they agree that tax relief creates jobs, then why are they for a little bitty tax relief package?	But the greatest strength of the American economy is found right here, right in this room, found in the pride and skill of the American work force. Last year, productivity growth in America was 4.8 percent—that is the best annual increase since 1980.
Women's Entrepreneurship Forum, Cleveland, Ohio; 3/10/04	Trade	Some politicians in Washington see this new challenge, and yet they want to respond in old ways. Their agenda is to increase federal taxes, to build a wall around this country and to isolate America from the rest of the world.	This is a land of great wealth, and it's a land of great opportunity, and you're seizing the opportunity. Through the hard work of our people, the innovation of our businesses, and the good policies now in place, we have put a recession behind us.
Bob Riley for Governor Luncheon, 9/28/06	Homeland Security	Five years after 9/11, the worst attack on American homeland in our history, the Democrats offer nothing but criticism and obstruction, and endless second-guessing. The party of FDR and the party of Harry Truman has become the party of cut-and-run.	Now is the time for the United States of America to lay the foundation of peace, to confront the challenges we have square on, to protect our country, to do our duty so that generations will look back and say, thank God this generation of Americans was willing to serve and serve strong.
President Discusses Health Care, Dublin, OH; 2/15/06	Health Care	That's kind of a Washington attitude, isn't it—we'll decide for you, you can't figure it out yourself. I think a lot of folks here at Wendy's would argue that point of view is just simply backwards and not true.	Let me start by giving you kind of a state of the economy—it's strong. I recognize there's parts of Ohio that aren't necessarily as strong as other parts of the country, but from an overall perspective, when you look at the nation's economy, it's strong, and it's getting stronger.

more than enough descriptive work to keep people busy. Were it able to make suggestions (which it cannot), DICTION would therefore urge critics to pay more attention to establishing fact patterns about George W. Bush. As we see in table 7.2, for example, Bush speeches declared "most important" by scholars have varied widely in Hortatoriness, thereby calling into question the easy generalization that Mr. Bush blustered and fumed his way through the forty-third presidency.[9]

TABLE 7.2 **Hortatory scores for George W. Bush's most important speeches.[1]**

Date	Topic and location	Hortatory score
1/20/2005	Second Inaugural Address, U.S. Capitol	10.94
2/2/2005	State of the Union, U.S. Capitol	10.41
9/2/2004	Nomination Acceptance, New York, NY	9.53
1/28/2008	State of the Union, U.S. Capitol	9.44
1/31/2006	State of the Union, U.S. Capitol	8.31
1/20/2004	State of the Union, U.S. Capitol	7.14
1/29/2002	State of the Union, U.S. Capitol	6.98
6/28/2005	War on Terror, Fort Bragg, NC	6.78
1/23/2007	State of the Union, U.S. Capitol	5.64
11/8/2001	Homeland Security, Atlanta, GA	4.36
1/20/2001	Inaugural Address, U.S. Capitol	3.72
9/7/2003	War on Terror, White House	3.43
9/11/2002	9/11 Anniversary, Ellis Island, NY	3.36
1/15/2009	Farewell Address, White House	3.15
9/14/2001	9/11 Remembrance, Washington, DC	2.91
9/11/2006	War on Terror, White House	2.86
1/28/2003	State of the Union, U.S. Capitol	2.76
1/10/2007	War on Terror in Iraq, White House	2.74
8/9/2001	Stem Cell Research, Crawford, TX	2.03
5/1/2003	Mission Accomplished, San Diego, CA	1.94
9/15/2005	Hurricane Katrina, New Orleans, LA	1.90
9/20/2001	War on Terror Announcement, U.S. Capitol	1.69
5/15/2006	Immigration Reform, White House	1.32
9/13/2007	War on Terror in Iraq, White House	1.15
12/18/2005	War on Terror in Iraq, White House	0.86
10/7/2001	Strikes Against Al Qaida and Taliban, White House	0.77
7/19/2005	Supreme Court Nomination, White House	0.39
3/19/2003	Invasion of Iraq, White House	0.14
9/24/2008	National Economy, White House	−0.52
10/7/2002	Iraq War, Cincinnati, OH	−0.57
9/11/2001	9/11 Terrorism, White House	−0.76
1/30/2005	Iraqi Elections, White House	−0.77
3/17/2003	Ultimatum for Iraq, White House	−1.35
2/27/2001	Administration Goals, U.S. Capitol	−1.52
6/6/2002	Department of Homeland Security, White House	−2.24
2/1/2003	Loss of Space Shuttle Columbia, White House	−2.37
12/14/2003	Capture of Saddam Hussein, White House	−2.96

[1] As identified by Coe, K., & Neumann, R. (2011). The major addresses of modern presidents: Parameters of a data set. *Presidential Studies Quarterly 41*, 727–751.

9. *Independence vs. contagion.* The study reported in this chapter was prompted by our reading a single sentence in a single scholarly study. It went like this: "Bush's discourse displayed Orwellian features of Double-speak, where war against Iraq is for peace, the occupation of Iraq is its liberation, destroying its food and water supplies enables 'humanitarian' action, and the killing of countless Iraqis and destruction of the country will produce 'freedom' and 'democracy'" (Kellner, 2007, p. 636). We were instinctively suspicious of this claim because it seemed so overwrought. But as we read more of the literature, it was clear that Kellner spoke for many scholars, although most were less polemical when making their claims.

But what inspired this intellectual chorus? The raw facts in the case? Common intellectual predispositions? A similar take on the political cosmos? The presence of an "invisible college" guiding critics' understandings of rhetorical acceptability? These are all possibilities and so are these: Researchers' inability to detach themselves from the currents of popular opinion; the overweening influence of the nation's press on the scholarly agenda; a set of unwritten rules about what can and cannot be said about a conservative Republican in the scholarly journals.

10. *Argument vs. tone.* It is possible, although unlikely, that our analysis of Bush and those from the critical community are equally correct. The case for this cheery option goes like this: argument and tone, thought and word choice, are simply different phenomena. "Argument," is an intellectual exchange between two or more participants acting on contrasting philosophical assumptions when deliberating about some policy matter. "Tone," in contrast, references behavioral phenomena—words spoken or written—that bear no isomorphic relationship to the thought-world producing them. By accepting these distinctions, one could imagine George W. Bush as an ideologue, philosophically speaking, who could somehow hide that fact in public.

Theoretically, it may be possible to force such a distinction but how would that turn out pragmatically? In the everyday world, it would seem, ideas exist only when given empirical instantiation—as art, music, architecture, poetry, oratory. Until made manifest, ideas can only waft about in Plato's noumenal sphere, an unlikely place for getting the work of the world done. For these reasons, we find it hard to imagine George Bush as an ideologue unless that quality is somehow signaled by his language choices, choices that can be measured empirically. An ideologue-once-removed, we suspect, is an ideologue that cannot exist.

Nevertheless, all of these are matters worth exploring and we encourage those explorations. Our main call here is for greater scholarly pluralism, for letting a thousand flowers bloom. We especially urge critics to become more inquisitive about social scientific studies of rhetorical behavior, not because they offer more truth, but because they question existing answers and prompt new ones as well.

Conclusion

We have made no brief for George W. Bush here. He was, at best, a middling president dealt a harsh blow by the forces of fate nine months into his administration. He was not brilliant and surely not eloquent. At this remove, Mr. Bush's lasting contribution seems a dangerous one—an exacerbation of tensions between the industrial West and the Muslim nations. He would have hoped for a better legacy. From our perspective, however, Bush's legacy is this: He responded to the complexities of his times by pulling his punches, using ideological rhetoric sparingly and for largely practical reasons. His was a measured tone.

Rhetorically, Mr. Bush was neither baldly partisan nor unthinkingly ideological, and he was considerably more prudent than the other pols who ran for the presidency between 1948 and 2004. In that sense, Bush may have been a "hidden-hand president" who operated genially in public and differently behind the scenes. As we have seen, incongruities like these suggest (1) that rhetoric and policy often run counter to one another, (2) that the press sometimes pursues its own agenda while ignoring the facts on the ground, and (3) that once a president's popular image is established, it resists contradiction. At the very least, these propositions lend themselves to further inquiry.

Sometimes the most parsimonious explanation of conflicting data is the simplest. That is our conclusion: George W. Bush was an adaptive animal—partisan at times, ideological at times, but mostly careful. He ran to the right to get reelected in 2004 but became more prudent thereafter (unless speaking about national defense). In short, our data show Bush to be a smart politician who understood human sentiments. His political skills have generally been ignored but a few commentators have pointed them up:

- President Bush does not evoke a stuffy aristocratic air when he speaks and interacts with the public; rather, his frequent self-deprecation creates an impression of instant familiarity and accessibility, that he's simply an ordinary fellow who happens to occupy an extraordinary job. (Datta, 2007)

- One of the reasons Bush has survived his troubles is that he doesn't do things that increase those woes. He takes the blows, stays the course, tries to move on. To be a good president, you have to be a good politician—and Bush is that. (Podhoretz, 2004, p. 25)

- The President has an array of interpersonal gifts that fit well with this fearlessness—a headlong, unalloyed quality, best suited to ranging among different types of people, searching for the outlines of what will take shape as principles. (Suskind, 2004, p. 44)

It is possible that these observers are wrong about Bush. It is also possible that word-counting programs cannot capture something as powerful as political ideology. It is further possible that the Bush stereotypes are true and the findings reported here misguided. In our defense, we ask this question: Can one speak ideologically without using tenacious language or embellished prose and without fervently praising sacred traditions and the nation's electorate? We suggest not. While DICTION is only a counting machine, it counts what it counts accurately, and what it counts is important. Our data show George W. Bush to be a skilled politician who dealt with complex events in textured ways. Others' opinions to the contrary, we stand with that conclusion.

CHAPTER EIGHT

Inexperience and the Neighborly Tone

E verything about Barack Obama was new. He was the first president not born in the continental United States, the first multi-racial president, the first African-American, the third to be married to a career professional, one of the youngest presidents, the first to pass major health care and financial reforms simultaneously, the first commander-in-chief with no military service to fight two wars, the first sitting president to receive the Nobel Prize. In a political institution prizing football and baseball, Mr. Obama was the first chief executive with a decent jump shot.

Mr. Obama's presidential campaign in 2008 was also new: the first to upend a viable female candidate in the primaries, the second to confront a team comprising a woman in the general election. His was the first campaign to raise over a half-billion dollars and the first to use Facebook, YouTube, blogs, podcasting, and Twitter comprehensively. Interest in Obama's newness never slacked, with 38.4 million Americans watching his convention address, twice as many as those who watched John Kerry's speech in 2004. News coverage soared during the '08 campaign, with Fox News increasing its viewership 29% over the previous year and CNN up 44% over 2007 (Greppi, 2009).

The issues of the 2008 election were also novel—climate change, immigration reform, gay marriage, Wall Street regulations. But it was really Barack Obama who commanded the scene. *The Washington Post*'s David Broder knew that something special was happening when he watched people file into the Des Moines convention hall in December 2007 for an Obama political rally. Says Broder (2008, para. 3): "It was startling that almost a year before Election Day, 18,000 people had given up their Saturday shopping time to stand (there were no chairs) and listen to an hour of political rhetoric. In all the eight Iowa caucus campaigns I'd covered over four decades, I'd never seen anything like this. In fact, I'd not seen voters so turned on since my first campaign as a political reporter, the classic Kennedy-Nixon race of 1960."

Obama was new, which is also to say he was inexperienced. During the primaries, John Edwards reasoned that Obama's thin resume would undo him in Iowa (Brooks, 2007) and Hillary Clinton observed that he was dangerously naïve about foreign policy (Zeleny, 2007). During the general election, Mr. Obama's own running mate, Joe Biden, warned that he would be "tested" by foreign leaders because of his inexperience, a comment that led to "a chilly conversation on the phone" between Biden and Obama (Alter, 2010, p. 30). For many voters on Election Day, the question was this: Could Obama overcome his political immaturity like John Kennedy, or would he be a ditherer like Jimmy Carter? (Gergen & Zelleke, 2008).

We focus in this chapter on how Barack Obama met these challenges of inexperience: he channeled who he had already been, not who he might someday become. In making this argument, we depart from conventional explanations for Obama's success. Many observers claim, for example, that Obama's appeal lay in the future he offered the electorate, but we find him to be rather presentistic. Still others say that Obama painted florid pictures for his listeners, but we find him to be quite linear. Our basic argument is that Obama drew on his background as a community organizer when campaigning but did so in an especially exacting manner.

Two years later, though, Mr. Obama's magic seemed to be fading. He had "lost the narrative" in the words of one political consultant (Balz, 2010), perhaps because he abandoned the qualities that resonated so strongly with the American people during the campaign. Another possibility is that his inexperience, once charming, finally wore thin. After all, the Oval Office is not the campaign trail. It has its own perquisites and requisites and Mr. Obama had to learn to deal with both. The result: When the 2012 election rolled around, the Obama tone was still a work in progress. We trace that progress here.

A Discourse Born of the Times

Political campaigns have changed dramatically over the years: they have become more expensive, and partisanship has increased; candidates must now cope with media framing and media priming; voter turnout has become less predictable; and special interest groups—PACs, 527s, etc.—have become deft at promulgating countermessages. Presidential campaigns have also lengthened—Obama's campaign began in the summer of 2006, thirty or so months before he would take the oath of office as president. Does such a jam-packed schedule hasten a candidate's maturation or turn him into a mere message machine? Does the rhetoric of the primary season collapse upon that of the general election, or is it distinctive? Do media pressures, the policy agenda, popular opinion, or idiosyncratic forces presage how issues will be discussed on the stump? We touch on all of these matters when assessing the 2008 campaign.

Mostly, that campaign was deadly serious, producing less bloviating than any campaign since 1948. The times were tough and the candidates addressed that fact directly, especially with regard to the nation's finances. Note, for example, that the following passages from Obama and McCain are virtually interchangeable. It is as if both were running against a third candidate—The Economy—and only mildly certain they could vanquish it:

> Now, I know times are hard. I know they're hard. They're hard here in Nevada. They're hard here all across the country. They're hard in Michigan; they're hard in Ohio; they're hard in Pennsylvania; they're hard in my home state of Illinois. I know they're hard and I'm not going to pretend that the change we need will come without a cost—although, I will tell you that I make sure that we can pay for every program I've proposed in a fiscally responsible way so that we're not loading up debt for our children and our grandchildren! (Obama, 2008, September 17)

> My friends, a little straight talk—a little straight talk. These are tough times. Today, the jobs report is another reminder, these are tough times. There're tough times in Wisconsin, there're tough times in Ohio, there're tough times all over America. You're worried about keeping your jobs and finding a new one, struggling to put food on the table and stay in your home. All you ever asked of government is to stand on your side, not in your way. And that's just what I intend to do: stand on your side and fight for your future. (McCain, 2008, September 5)

Four years earlier, things were different. The rhetoric was different as well—far more upbeat, far more expansive. In the following passage, George W. Bush paints a picture largely with primary colors:

And you're helping people realizing that success. It must be a fantastic feeling to be a part of the American Dream. It must be great to see—it must be magnificent to see somebody walk in to their home and feel the pride of ownership, the fantastic feeling of saying to a son or daughter: Here's your room; here's our piece of property. [So] I want to thank you, very much, for what you're doing. I want to thank you for helping pull our economy through some tough times and helping this nation get on that hopeful path for a bright future. I appreciate your hard work, I appreciate your optimism, I appreciate your love for America. (Bush, 2004, October 2)

Previous research (Lichter & Smith, 1996; Hart, 2000) has shown that media reportage is much more pessimistic than political discourse, and reliably so. Reporters take their roles as guardians of the Fourth Estate seriously and, according to Luke (1978), they sometimes deploy an "artificial negativity" to make bad news out of nothingness so that their role of guard dog is preserved. Our data show that the press has reliably performed that function, but they also show that the "optimism gap" between candidates and reporters narrowed considerably in 2008. While there are robust statistical differences in Optimism between candidate and press from 1948 to 2004, that differential dropped sharply in 2008, as we see in figure 8.1.[1]

During that campaign, both Obama and McCain took a cold, analytical look at the issues confronting the nation. "The economic crisis we face is

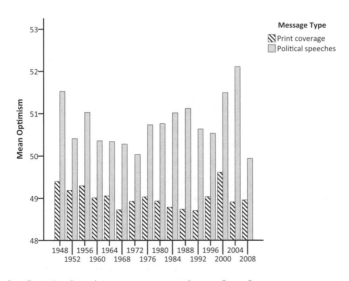

FIGURE 8.1 *Optimism* for print coverage vs. speeches, 1948–2008.

the worst since the Great Depression," said Mr. Obama in Tampa, Florida, on October 20. "Businesses large and small are finding it impossible to get loans," he continued, "which means they can't buy new equipment, or hire new workers, or even make payroll for the workers they have" (Obama, 2008, October 20). The American people are unaccustomed to such stark recountings, especially from a political candidate and especially just two weeks before the votes are cast. John McCain behaved similarly. While he began the campaign a bit more optimistically than Obama, the candidates synchronized their tones by mid-September and remained joined at the hip until Election Day.

Our data also show that the 2008 campaign witnessed the lowest use of the Hortatory Tone (see chapter 7) ever recorded in the Campaign Mapping Project.[2] Combined with our findings on Optimism, a number of questions present themselves: How could an *American* political campaign be so short on homiletics? How could candidates refrain from being fulsome when so many of their fellow citizens needed a boost? How could there be no invocation of the Founding Fathers? No reference to the "huddled masses" or the "essential dignity of the American worker"? Remarks about "change" were heard, but often that word hung in midair, unaccompanied by policy specifics.

We have found a steady decline in the Hortatory Tone over the last half century, a decline in what Richard Weaver (1953) has called the "spaciousness" of American oratory. The possible reasons for this are many. The rise of the television era, for example, may have put the kibosh on overweening rhetoric, with candidates now submitting to what Jamieson (1988) has called the "conversational" demands of an intimate medium. Also, the increasing sociological diversity of the United States may have made references to a single Deity or to ageless truths passé. Modernity may also have rendered overblown language—"a good and great nation," "a dastardly enemy"—increasingly antique. Whatever the reason, the voters in 2008 were treated to a spare discourse.

Avoidance of the Hortatory Tone could also be a function of the candidates themselves: Obama the restrained attorney, McCain the functional bottom-liner; Obama the product of the Academy, McCain the career military officer. But the times, too, demanded prudence. The nation that invented the automobile was no longer buying cars; the nation that designed the first silicon chip was finding few new devices into which they could be inserted; familiar businesses—Linens 'n Things, Foot Locker, Steak and Ale—were being shuttered completely and, what was especially shocking for a technological nation, CompUSA and Circuit City were closing their doors as well. Ann Taylor, Home Depot, Sharper Image, and even Starbucks also cut back significantly on their single-store locations. News of this sort began leaking out in 2007 and became a torrent a year later. The candidates adjusted accordingly, significantly increasing their Realism scores as the general election took hold, eschewing abstractions and focusing on the real-world vicissitudes facing the American people.[3]

Our data also reveal over-time increases in Insistence, a handy measure of code restriction and agenda maintenance.[4] The assumption here is that repetition of key terms (all of which are nouns or noun-derived adjectives) reflects a preference for a limited discussion of issues. In other words, while the primary campaign encouraged the candidates to cover the waterfront of topics, the general election concentrated their minds wonderfully. In addition, the candidates' time-space ratios (see chapter 4) significantly increased once they entered the general election, with the shift toward temporal language being especially pronounced for Obama.[5] The cumulative result: The campaign became focused and rapidly paced, with Obama and McCain racking up the highest time-space ratio between 1948 and 2008 and the third highest set of Insistence scores. Consequently, the candidates were neither poetic nor leisurely. They produced a nagging discourse that stayed on message. Barack Obama nagged most often:

I've got a different economic philosophy than John McCain—I believe that building a strong middle class is the key to making our economy strong. And that's what we'll do when I'm President of the United States. So, yes, we'll create millions of new jobs, and yes, we'll put more money back into the pockets of hardworking families. (Obama, 2008, October 20)

And under my plan, if you make less than $250,000 a year—which includes 98 percent of small business owners—you won't see your taxes increase one single dime. Not your payroll taxes, not your income taxes, not your capital gains taxes—nothing. It's time to give the middle class a break, and that's what I'll do as President of the United States. (Obama, 2008, October 18)

But if you want real change, if you want an economy that rewards work, and that works for Main Street and Wall Street, if you want tax relief for the middle class and millions of new jobs; if you want health care you can afford and education that helps your kids compete, then I ask you to knock on some doors, make some calls, talk to our neighbors, and give me your vote. (Obama, 2008, October 25)

Broadly speaking, then, the 2008 campaign was distinctive: the candidates were abstinent, a full standard deviation lower on Optimism than the 2000 and 2004 candidates. They also eschewed the Hortatory Tone, replacing it with a far more pragmatic discourse. Compared to the primary season, both Obama and McCain were exceedingly task-driven during the general election. Not surprisingly, voters celebrated when the campaign ended, either because their candidate had won or because the two-year ordeal of electing a president was finally over. But their celebrations were low-keyed, with many voters sounding just as sober as the candidates. For many Americans, 2008 was a difficult year, and the next two years gave them little respite. It was out of these trying times that Obama's rhetoric was fashioned but there were other factors at work as well.

A Discourse Born of the Man

During 2008, many Americans were smitten by Barack Obama. His speech on race in March 2008 was declared an instant classic. His acceptance of his party's nomination in August matched the elaborate stagecraft of the convention itself. And his celebratory address on election night to some 250,000 persons in Grant Park was said to be the most powerful speech in recent memory. But there was also something odd about Obama's oratory: It was a Rorschach for many—people saw what they wanted to see or, to be fairer, they worked overtime to capture its essence:

- **A tutorial tone**: We all stopped to listen to him as he explained this extremely complicated, sensitive topic ... It was a teaching moment. He's been unusually good at that. Not all presidents are good teachers, but he has shown great potential for that. (Ted Widmer, quoted in Seelye, 2009, para. 30)
- **A careful tone**: [Obama] grows large and impressive, filling Americans with cockeyed hope even as he warns them not to expect too much too soon. Even Obama's caution—a commodity notably absent from the White House for eight years—fills people with optimism. (Dowd, 2009, para. 8–9)
- **A reportorial tone**: Obama's speeches have been additionally unusual in having a life beyond the moment in which they are given ... Obama has mastered

the performance part and more, because his major speeches are written to be read, rather than just watched and heard. (Fallows, 2008, section IV, para. 6)

• **An oral tone:** I believe Barack Obama embodies, more than any other politician, the ideal of American eloquence . . . I've been going through his speeches textually. The text alone cannot tell us why they are so powerful, it is about delivery. (Ekaterina Haskins, quoted in Holmes, 2008, para. 2, 30)

One commentator gave up completely when trying to explain Obama's appeal. "Barack Obama inhabits this region of the unknown-known, this space of incipience" (Conley, 2008, p. 310).

The DICTION program cannot measure the space of incipience but it can tell us that Barack Obama generated the highest Commonality scores of any presidential candidate during the last sixty years. When this datum is combined (as we see in figure 8.2) with his lower-than-normal Optimism scores and his high Realism scores, his campaign message becomes clear: "The times are not good. War and the economy press upon us. We must sustain one another."[6] Despite all of the commentators' disquisitions on "hope" during the 2008 campaign, that is, it was Commonality, not Optimism, that propelled his campaign. Of the twenty-three major-party candidates to run for office since 1948, Obama's Optimism scores were third from the bottom; only George McGovern and Barry Goldwater were lower. For Commonality, however, Obama was a full standard deviation

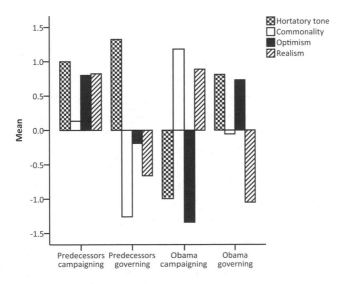

FIGURE 8.2 Complex variables over time: Obama vs. predecessors.

higher than seventeen of his predecessors and half a standard deviation higher than the remaining five (except for Al Gore). In short, the Obama campaign was quite direct about the nation's problems and looked to the people themselves—in their small towns, in their churches and union halls—to bail themselves out.

This reading of the Obama method reveals his background as a community organizer in Chicago, a job that treated *people themselves* as the solution to their problems. In linguist George Lakoff's (2009, para. 10) terms, Obama had empathy, the ability to put "himself in other people's shoes, seeing the world through their eyes, and therefore caring about them." In psychologist David Winter's (2009) terms, Obama's power sprung from his "high affiliation" needs, while political scientist Thomas Dumm (2008, p. 319) says that "Obama emphasized how he himself embodies all races, how he is, in essence, post-racial." An even more practical interpretation of Obama's strategy is this: He cashed in his experience as a community organizer to overcome his inexperience as a national leader.

But if there is a special magic in Obama's tone, it lies in his *combination* of Commonality and Realism, his ability to "make local" the solutions of the day. His approach grew out of the streets he walked during his prior occupation, from the doors he knocked on, and on the succor provided by those he met. He drew on those encounters day in and day out during the 2008 race, ultimately fashioning a kind of pedestrian eloquence that had three subproperties:

- *Historical resiliency:* This time—this election—is our chance to stand up and say: Enough—enough. We—Denver, we can do this. We can do this because Americans have done this before. Time and again, we've battled back from adversity by recognizing that common stake we have in each other's success. That's why our economy hasn't just been the world's greatest wealth generator, it's bound us together as Americans. It's created jobs, and it's made the dream of opportunity a reality for generation after generation after generation of Americans. (Obama, 2008, September 16)
- *Transcendent capacity:* When the American people decide that now is the time to bring about real change in America, nothing can stop them. Nothing can stop the American people when they are unified: black, white, Hispanic, Asian, Native American, young, old, rich, poor, Democrats and independents and Republicans deciding that we are going to transform this country so that we give a better life to our children and our grandchildren. (Obama, 2008, September 12)

- *Sociological sensitivity:* There are no real or fake parts of this country. We are not separated by the pro-America and anti-America parts of this nation—we all love this country, no matter where we live or where we come from. There are patriots who supported this war in Iraq and patriots who opposed it; patriots who believe in Democratic policies and those who believe in Republican policies. The men and women from Nevada and all across America who serve on our battlefields may be Democrats and Republicans and Independents, but they have fought together and bled together and some died together under the same proud flag. They have not served a Red America or a Blue America—they have served the United States of America. (Obama, 2008, October 25)

Obama's ability to combine linguistic families was, according to Zadie Smith, his signal strength. Smith is especially impressed by the powerful associations Obama's experiences and sensibilities bring to mind:

Throughout his campaign Obama was careful always to say we. He was noticeably wary of "I." By speaking so, he wasn't simply avoiding a singularity he didn't feel, he was also drawing us in with him. He had the audacity to suggest that, even if you can't see it stamped on their faces, most people come from Dream City, too. Most of us have complicated back stories, messy histories, multiple narratives.

It was a high-wire strategy, for Obama, this invocation of our collective human messiness. His enemies latched on to its imprecision, emphasizing the exotic, un-American nature of Dream City, this ill-defined place where you could be from Hawaii and Kenya, Kansas and Indonesia all at the same time, where you could jive talk like a street hustler and orate like a senator. What kind of a crazy place is that? But they underestimated how many people come from Dream City, how many Americans, in their daily lives, conjure contrasting voices and seek a synthesis between disparate things. Turns out, Dream City wasn't so strange to them. (Smith, 2009, February 26, para. 22–23)

As we see in figure 8.3 (and as we previously saw in chapter 4), Mr. Obama's campaign was also distinguished by his sense of urgency, the natural language of a thoroughgoing modernist. As columnist E. J. Dionne (2009, para. 1, 4) observed, "For the past two years, Barack Obama has made it hard for anyone to pin him down philosophically. . . . his references to ideology are disdainful and dismissive. In discussing his economic stimulus package, he speaks of judging his proposals by how many jobs they produce and how quickly they will move the economy. Other criteria

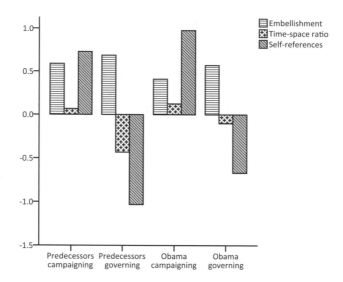

FIGURE 8.3 Simple variables over time: Obama vs. predecessors.

are inadmissible." What is perhaps most interesting about Obama's pragmatism was that it moved people powerfully or even, as some would have it, spiritually.

DICTION cannot explain such complex reactions. It only notices the words people choose. It takes a sensitive observer like Thomas Palaima (2009, para. 50) to shed light on Obama's linguistic superstructure. It was Obama's use of *rhythms*, says Palaima, his iambic cadences, that let him turn quotidian claims into moving oratory. His "rhythmic patterns . . . are entrancing," says Palaima. "They are the inheritance of a long tradition in blues, in gospel, in church preaching, in field calls and responses, in rap and hip hop. They result from long attention paid to how words fall upon our ears, not how they are picked up off printed pages. They result from paying attention to how words get embedded in our minds."

Figure 8.3 offers an interesting contrast to John McCain by tracking Obama's use of Embellishment, a simple ratio of adjectives to verbs based on David Boder's (1940) conception that heavy modifiers "slows down" a verbal passage by deemphasizing human and material action. As can be seen, Obama used the sparest of lexicons, sticking to nouns devoid of coloration and verbs bereft of modification.[7] (This may in part be why he was often referred to as "No Drama Obama" by his campaign staff.) Obama's is a staccato tone, a propulsive tone, one that turns simple phrases into boxcars on a train picking up speed. The oral power of such an approach becomes clear when its components are detached from paragraphs and presented serially:

> People might have been taking out credit cards to try to make ends meet.
> If they got sick, that was the way they tried to deal with it.
> But now they realize those teaser rates of zero percent have skyrocketed to 28 or 29 percent.
> And they've fallen behind.
> And we have higher bankruptcies than we've seen in a generation.
> And so it's harder to save.
> It's harder to retire.
> It's harder to figure out how to send your child to college.
> People are struggling.
> And it's not just the immediate struggle.
> You know, contrary to what John McCain's adviser said.
> The American people aren't whiners.
> People are willing to put up with a lot.
> Because we are a self-reliant and independent people.
> So we don't expect government to solve all our problems. (Obama, 2008, September 8)

John McCain could not have been more different. He was, in so many senses, a "pol" from the old school who ran on the basis of his personality and biography rather than staunch ideology. He was also an emotional man who had a temper but who somehow refrained from rashness (Renshon, 2008). These traits produced a garrulousness in McCain, but it also gave him an attractive sense of immediacy. Whereas Obama spoke in five-word bursts, McCain dilated, forcing his audiences through a thicket of modifiers.[8] The result was usually worth it because John McCain was consistently and delightfully colorful.

McCain's campaign was also his biography. In that sense, he was the exact opposite of his opponent: while Obama had to compensate for his political inexperience, McCain emphasized his status as a Senate leader, a war hero, and an informed student of politics. The result: he used many more Self-references than Obama.[9] Freie (2009) argues that McCain chose this strategy for two reasons: (1) Hillary Clinton had won eight of twelve late primary contests by focusing on Obama's inexperience and (2) McCain's own issue positions were admittedly out of touch with the popular sentiments of the day. This calculus ultimately determined that McCain should emphasize his personality, which is probably why he preferred the town hall format. There he could stress his background as a former POW, a man gifted at building cross-party alliances, and a person who preferred pragmatism over ideology. So his campaign let McCain be McCain, preventing him from becoming a Hollywood tintype.

Obama was less forthcoming. He spoke in the first-person plural, not singular, and despite his Ivy League education and diffident (some say professorial) manner, he somehow managed to reach out to people who felt excluded. Obama's approach was therefore curious by traditional standards—hard-headed but friendly, cerebral yet realistic. Perhaps this odd approach should not have worked, but the times, the Obama persona, and the sorry state of the Republican Party permitted it. Inevitably, though, his inexperience caught up with him and Mr. Obama was forced to reinvent himself.

A Discourse Born of the Office

The American presidency is larger than the person holding the job. The office bespeaks its inhabitants, at least in part, and that is true for Barack Obama as well. Our research shows that he made a number of rhetorical changes dictated by his new political duties in the postcampaign period. Modifications like these are neither universal nor determinative, but scholars have noticed them in the past (see Hart, 2000). President Obama's new job changed him in ways not entirely of his choosing.

Figure 8.2 shows how: Obama's Hortatory Tone went up dramatically and his Realism dropped.[10] This made him sound more philosophical than pragmatic as he began targeting bedrock American values. Mr. Obama's Optimism also increased as he imagined new horizons for a troubled nation.[11] Not surprisingly, as figure 8.3 shows, his Self-references decreased as well, making him less convivial than he was on the stump, perhaps because of the formality expected of a sitting president. And Mr. Obama's Embellishment scores also increased slightly, a change for a man given to unadorned sentences.[12] In short, the office made Obama more oracular—not really a pontificator, not yet a demagogue, but a man becoming accustomed to speaking axiology. As Fineman (2009, para. 3) notes, "Like Reagan, Obama shares a celebrity's sense of comfort on the (public) stage, a belief in sticking to the script, and a faith in the power of the written word spoken from an imposing rostrum. He also shares Reagan's reverence for the power of a narrative in politics—Reagan, because he was an actor; Obama, because he is a writer."

In making these changes, Mr. Obama often resembled his predecessors. They too became more hortatory upon taking office, although only marginally so compared to Obama. They also referred to their own beliefs and experiences less often and embroidered their remarks a tad more. And, like Obama, they explored more abstract concepts when speaking as chief executives, causing their Realism scores to drop considerably.[13] Collectively, these changes reflect the role change expected of American presidents, who are expected to "perform" their office without rising above their audience.

Some of Obama's changes were pronounced, especially his sudden preference for the Hortatory Tone. The explanation seems obvious: on inauguration day, Obama was confronted with unprecedented domestic challenges even as he tried to figure out how to wind down one war (in Iraq) and gin up another (in Afghanistan). As Kenski, Hardy, and Jamieson (2010) report, heavy news consumers were obsessed with the economy during the 2008 election (tipping things heavily in Obama's favor), but the news got no better during the next eighteen months and so the political tides turned. Obama soon faced a political juggernaut, a fact well evidenced in a speech he gave in Cleveland two weeks before the midterm elections. That speech shows the New Obama—forceful argument supplemented by a dollop of judgmentalism:

> This country is emerging from an incredibly difficult period in its history—an era of irresponsibility that stretched from Wall Street to Washington, and had a devastating effect on a lot of people. We have started turning the corner on that era. But part of moving forward is returning to the time-honored values that built this country: hard work and self-reliance; responsibility for ourselves, but also responsibility for one another. It's about moving from an attitude that said "What's in it for me?" to one that asks, "What's best for America? What's best for all our workers? What's best for all of our businesses? What's best for all of our children?" (Obama, 2010, September 10)

The Cleveland speech reveals two other changes in Obama's tone. As figure 8.2 shows, he ratcheted up his Optimism after becoming president but decreased his Commonality a bit, an odd juxtaposition.[14] These two instincts—envisioning new initiatives while licking old wounds—play against one another in the speech and diminish its inspirational capacity. The result is that Obama seems almost haunted by his opponents:

> But with the nation losing nearly 800,000 jobs the month that I was sworn into office, my most urgent task was to stop a financial meltdown and prevent this recession from becoming a second depression. And, Ohio, we have done that. The economy is growing again. The financial markets have stabilized. The private sector has created jobs for the last eight months in a row. And there are roughly 3 million Americans who are working today because of the economic plan we put into place ... [And yet] a few weeks ago, the Republican leader of the House came here to Cleveland and offered his party's answer to our economic challenges. Now, it would be one thing if he had admitted his party's mistakes during the eight years that they were in power, if they had gone off for a while and meditated, and come back and offered a credible new approach to solving our country's problems. But that's not what happened. There were no new policies from Mr. Boehner. There were no new ideas. (Obama, 2010, September 10)

This approach stands in contrast to the Obama the American people had gotten to know in the fall of 2008. According to Ivie and Giner (2009, p. 363), that Obama "exuded pluralism, eschewed the arrogance of rigid ideology, and abandoned the conceit of enforcing a narrow code of international conduct." According to Murphy (2009, p 311), for Obama the campaigner there was "always a transcendent place of agreement above [any] two opposing theses." For Gunn (2010), Obama's use of Commonality distinguished him from the stereotypical Angry Black Man; for Terrill (2009), it let the nation see itself as a union without being literally unified; for Bowden (2010), it made Obama a Weberian leader whose charisma depended on his affiliative instincts.

But this Obama became harder to find as president, as if his experiences in office were overriding his earlier charming inexperience. To be sure, his Commonality scores were still higher than those of his predecessors and he still tried "to broaden the parameters of American national identity" (Stuckey, Curry & Barnes, 2010, p. 426). We find those refrains in his Cleveland speech, but, again, they are offset by discordances:

> We are here today because in the worst of times, the people who came before us brought out the best in America. Because our parents and our grandparents and our great-grandparents were willing to work and sacrifice for us. They were

willing to take great risks, and face great hardship, and reach for a future that would give us the chance at a better life. They knew that this country is greater than the sum of its parts—that America is not about the ambitions of any one individual, but the aspirations of an entire people, an entire nation. That's who we are. That is our legacy. And I'm convinced that if we're willing to summon those values today, and if we're willing to choose hope over fear, and choose the future over the past, and come together once more around the great project of national renewal, then we will restore our economy and rebuild our middle class and reclaim the American Dream for the next generation. (Obama, 2010, September 10)

Politics is nothing if not dialectical. Even as he was intoning these words, Nancy Pelosi was telling him to do a better job of taking on the Republicans. Even as Obama tried to build new bridges, still other Democrats demanded that he relaunch his campaign's rhetoric of urgency (see figure 8.3) and embrace a more progressive politics.[15] Even as he spoke of overarching goals, he was said to be failing as the nation's First Democrat. According to journalist Matt Bai (2010b, p. 38), "Obama's brand management" of inclusivity and transcendence ran up "against the culture of his party." He typically avoided the Jefferson-Jackson dinners of the state parties, says Bai, preferring "venues, preferably outdoors or in large theaters when he can reach voters who aren't party regulars."

Were the changes in Obama's tone inevitable? The result of a natural maturation process, or even of Beltway determinism? Perhaps so. Figure 8.4 shows what happened when he engaged the Republicans in an unprecedented face-to-face encounter. Meeting with the House Issues Conference in Baltimore on January 30, 2010, the President spent some ninety nationally televised minutes engaged in what the *Washington Post* described as "a muscular defense of his first year in office," remarks containing "both tense drama and bipartisan comity" (Kane & Bacon, 2010, para. 1). The give-and-take was sharp, with Mr. Obama making his case stoutly and then being sharply questioned by eight House members on issues both domestic and foreign.

At one point during the exchange, the president declared "I am not an ideologue" only to be met with a chorus of guffaws. As we see in figure 8.4, though, that statement became increasingly correct as the encounter progressed, with his Hortatory Tone dropping steadily only to be accompanied by parallel declines in Optimism and Commonality. In a sense, figure 8.4 represents Washington on its best days, where bipartisan ex-

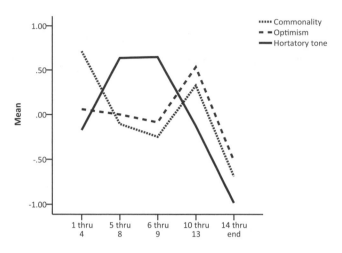

FIGURE 8.4 Obama to GOP House Issues Conference, January 30, 2010: variables across speech segments.

changes can stir up unpleasant emotions but occasionally produce interpersonal openness and greater flexibility of thought. While this is a fitful kind of progress, it may be the best a democracy can produce in a time of political stress.

We conclude that Obama the campaigner and Obama the president are not the same person but that they bear a family resemblance. Rhetorically, his group concern, born out of his background as a community organizer, remained a strength, even though his scores on Commonality dipped a bit during his first two years in office. His increases in Optimism buttressed those declines, but mere buoyancy is a language many politicians speak and not what made Obama distinctive. Obama was special, says Robert Terrill (2009, p. 381), because of his ability to show that "we might share a common stake without sharing common experiences," that if "we are to achieve a more perfect union, we must become able to divide ourselves." Mr. Obama's biography—a man both black and white, both Ivy League and middle-class, both an intellectual and a neighborhood leader—let him embody what his rhetoric also embodied, an ability to turn complexity into community. It takes much work to effect such transformations, and Barack Obama brilliantly achieved them when campaigning for president.

Things looked different when he became president. Ron Suskind (2011) imagines that Obama didn't "feel like himself" when taking office, "someone who could bring people together, who could map common ground and, upon it, build a future" (p. 11). "A president who doesn't feel quite like himself," Suskind continues, "often portends a crisis of leadership," so the president's aides worked feverishly to help him overcome the steep learning curves (p. 12). Obama's inexperience—that appealing untainted quality that endeared him to so many on the hustings—suddenly portrayed him as a ship's captain "practicing his knots belowdecks" (p. 461). Mr. Obama's new job demanded a new Obama, at least in part.

Conclusion

Barack Obama's presidency is still feeling its way. His rhetoric is emerging as well. As we have seen in this chapter, the rhetorical moves that served him well in his run for the presidency slipped a bit two years later. The increased Optimism was nice, but the declines in Realism and Commonality were worrisome. Combined, they made it harder for Obama to connect to the ordinary voters who had welcomed his candidacy with such enthusiasm in 2008. "The sad truth is that he has left the little guys—the unemployed, the people whose mortgage loan rates increased to the point where they couldn't afford them anymore," said Rabbi Michael Lerner (2009, para. 8), an avowed supporter. Another supporter, Colin Powell (2010, para. 6) argued similarly: "He has lost some of the ability to connect that he had during the campaign. And it is not just me picking on the president. It's reflected in the polling." Even Mr. Obama agreed that abandoning his distinctive rhetorical moves had cost him political capital: "If there's one thing that I regret this year is that we were so busy just getting stuff done and dealing with the immediate crises that were in front of us that I think we lost some of that sense of speaking directly to the American people about what their core values are" (quoted in Travers, 2010).

But if Obama's drops in Commonality and Realism cost him support, his increasingly hortatory speechmaking only compounded the problem. When commenting on Obama's rhetoric, for example, columnist Michael Gerson (2010, para. 4) gave him no quarter: "Self-pitying: *'They talk about me like a dog.'* Self-absorbed: *'I spent some time, as I often do, with our soldiers and our veterans.'* Snappish: *'If I said fish live in the sea, they'd say no.'* Pedestrian: *'Their slogan is 'No we can't.' Nope, no, no, no.'* Humorless. Negative. [And yet] his challenge reaches beyond rhetoric and beyond the midterm elections: finding not only a new agenda but a new persona."

Despite such brickbats, considerable money has been lost underestimating Barack Obama. One must not forget his astonishing accomplishments two years earlier, accomplishments that were largely the result of having done things in unorthodox ways. Although Mr. Obama himself had precious little political experience, he was extremely bright and learned from the experiences of others. So, for example, one commentator says that in 2008 Obama reran the Depression-era campaign of Franklin Roosevelt (Brunschwig, 2009). In addition, he somehow overcame the divisiveness of the Democratic primary and built a huge war chest for the general election (Gurian, 2009). Not only that, says Ditonto (2009), Obama effected significant changes in the basic sociological makeup of the American electorate.

His rhetoric alone did not produce these dividends, but it was part of the story. Some scholars argue, for example, that Mr. Obama reappropriated the "American dream" from Ronald Reagan (Rowland & Jones, 2007) in 2008 even as he borrowed the familial refrains of George W. Bush (Elder & Greene, 2009). Also, John McCain's secularism may have created an opening for Obama—a Democrat—among religious voters (Eitmann, 2009). And while some have argued that Obama's mainstream appeals papered over the nation's racial and ethnic balkanization (Lacy, 2008), there is little doubt that he brought something entirely new to the scene when running for the highest office in the land.

Returning to those refrains would be wise for Obama so that he does not fall victim to the high-blown oratory that presidents use when feeling cornered, the very approach that right-wing populists have used to combat his presidency. Returning to the more sober refrains of earlier times would set a better course. Obama's rhetoric in 2008 had an "astringency" to it (Kinsley, 2008, para. 6) that told people what they did not want to hear but that gave them a vital sense of common cause. Obama's ability to comfort and inspire people is prodigious, and he can surely reproduce that voice when he hears it inside himself once again.

Programs like DICTION only tell part of a political story. It merely roughs out the rhetorical facts. Taken together, our data show that Barack Obama ran one of the most understated campaigns in recent history. His coolness and professionalism led him to victory even though he was new to the national stage. But past is not always prologue, and as the 2012 election approached, Obama was charged with reigniting an electorate grown disenchanted with Washington's rhetoric. Above all, Obama needed a simpler, galvanizing discourse, the discourse that had brought him to office. Could he find it again? A nation waited, its people listening.

CHAPTER NINE

Ambition and the Wandering Tone

Sometimes Sarah Palin seems more phenomenon than person. She has several children, as do many Americans, and she has governed a state, as have some. She goes ice fishing and moose hunting and played competitive basketball as a young woman—all things that people do. She ran for vice president of the United States, as have others, and dressed handsomely during her travels. Also things that people do. But then there are the oddities: Although her "presidential viability" for the 2012 presidential race trailed that of Mitt Romney, Newt Gingrich, and Mike Huckabee in mid-2011, none of them could fill up a conference center like Sarah Palin. Also, while decrying the "lamestream media," Palin made a small fortune as a Fox News commentator and as author of several best-selling books. As governor, she endorsed birth control but was also pro-life; she supported natural gas drilling in the Arctic National Wildlife Refuge but raised taxes on oil company profits. She was once declared Miss Congeniality in a beauty pageant but later became known for eviscerating her political opponents. She championed religiosity but was the object of a $100,000 ethics inquiry into abuse of power as Alaska's governor. At times Ms. Palin has been a serious political leader and at times the mother of a personality on *Dancing with the Stars*. A mere kaleidoscope pales in comparison to the former governor of Alaska.

Given this complexity, it is not surprising that everyone has an opinion about her. One Website—www.SarahPalinIsAnIdiot.com—is offset by another—www.AmericaNeedsSarahPalin.blogspot.com—and both contain voluptuous opinions. Some people hate Palin's rustic provincialism while others respect her Western forthrightness. Some find it treasonous that John McCain let her get so close to the reins of power and some can't wait for her to become the first female chief executive. Some find her to be pedantic in the extreme, woefully uneducated, while others discover deep truths in even her offhand comments. Men ogle her and women want to become her. She is detested—truly detested—by people who cannot say why. She is adored—genuinely adored—by people who can't put their thoughts into words. Each day, Sarah Palin makes people mute.

One thing remains true, however: Both friend and foe substantiate their claims by pointing to Palin's speech patterns, often concentrating on their pedestrian qualities:

- My wife said it best: Palin sounds like me, like ordinary women everywhere. (Auzenne, 2008)
- Just because Palin speaks like a regular American (educated at public schools and universities), people want to label her as a hick. (Penhen, 2008)
- Openly mocking someone for their grammar is elitist. Why do you think so-called "grammar Nazis" are so unpopular on forums and comment sections across this great Internet? It's not because they're wrong, it's because they're jerks. (Svandoren, 2009)
- To most Americans, Mrs. Palin sounds real and truthful. Mr. Obama sounds uh.. uh..uh..like he's lying or hiding something . . . uh . . . uh..or trying not to slipup and say the wrong thing. (Lil Rascal, 2008)

When defending Ms. Palin, the bloggers are also defending themselves, of course, as well as a cultural heritage prizing plain speech. One detects class sensitivity here, perhaps even some Babbitry and anti-intellectualism. Nonetheless, Palin's speech is seen as an instantiation of the way things ought to be. For her detractors, on the other hand, Palin's speech is the truest sign of her unsuitability for political office—and for much else:

- Condoleezza Rice is taken seriously. Maybe Palin is not respected because she is unable to form a coherent sentence. (Knight Templar, 2010)
- I think she's a phony. Whenever she speaks, I'm reminded of someone who didn't prepare at all for her job interview because she incorrectly believed she was smart enough to BS her way through it. (Just Sayin, 2009)
- It's because she talks like a woman. Almost all women in the public sphere have learned to some extent to adopt a masculine way of speaking; it's why they can get taken seriously. But Sarah Palin has never had to. (Masculinist, 2010)

- Sarah needs to step back and get educated on the issues (and educated in general). I don't believe the left "hate" her, I think they are in awe of her absolute stupidity. (Frishman, 2009)

Here, too, is American sociology writ large—a nation still feeling the need to imitate its European forebears; a nation prizing thoroughness and scientific precision; a nation believing powerfully in the bootstraps of formal education. Poor Sarah Palin, caught in the cultural crossfire.

But there is more, much more, for Sarah Palin is ambitious, exceptionally ambitious. Sarah Palin, who did not hesitate for a moment when asked to run for vice president (Seelye, 2008). Sarah Palin, who made $7 million on her first book (Allan, 2010), a book that was "crafted politically, with every single detail of the narrative honed carefully for specific constituencies" (Sullivan, 2009, para. 2). Sarah Palin, who made a movie about Alaska about Sarah Palin and who was described as a "lightweight opportunist" as a result (Hinckley, 2010, para. 2). Sarah Palin, who went into the "Sarah Palin Across America business" (Carr, 2010) and who was dubbed "alley-cat smart" by another former governor of Alaska (Green, 2011, section 2, para. 11). In short, Palin is ambitious, but ambitious in a particularly unfocused way.[1]

This chapter examines the linguistic toll that ambition takes. Our data are narrow in scope but broad in implication. Our claim is that Sarah Palin wanders when she speaks. Habitually, she starts down one path and then goes off in another direction, commenting on the grand things—and the everyday things—she notices. Polar bears, Russia, Obamacare, family values, whitewater rafting, the First Dude, commonsense constitutionalism, prayer warriors, Joe the Plumber, going rogue, death panels, the Wasilla Bible Church. All are distinct Palin properties. All are offered up constantly, partial ideas in search of larger thematics. The themes rarely appear, however, which makes the *saying*, not the said, the source of her rhetorical power. "Anyone who can think all these thoughts at the same time," Palin seems to be saying, "is worthy of your attention." The playwright Wilson Mizner sums up the rhetorical consequences of ambition: "A slave has but one master. An ambitious man has as many as there are people who helped him get his fortune" (Deni, 2003, para. 19).

DICTION measures discursive breadth with the variable of Insistence, an indicator of rhetorical focus and agenda control. Its assumption is that repeating key terms constantly reveals a speaker's preference for a limited, orderly world intended to keep an audience on a short leash. To calculate this score, DICTION identifies all nouns and noun-derived adjectives and then performs this calculation: [Number of Eligible Words × Sum of their Occurrences] ÷ 10. The Insistence score is highly sensitive to text length, so DICTION extrapolates all passages analyzed to a 500-word standard for this and all other variables. The average 500-word passage registers 59.3 on Insistence, but most politicians do not score this high (averaging 45.6), no doubt because they are constantly seeking "room to maneuver." Sarah Palin is even more exploratory, averaging only 28.2. Sarah Palin does not insist; she deflects.

Why? What makes her so different from other politicians? Why does she not stay on-topic and get her business done? Does she lack the depth to pursue public policy intensively or is she choosing instead to be "emergent" for her listeners, letting them meander through the issues with her? Is this a political strategy on her part, or does she lack the mental ability to concentrate her thoughts? Would her Insistence scores naturally rise if she someday takes the "point" in a national presidential run, or would they stay genially low as she chats her way through the morning talk shows? One woman, one variable, many questions.

We surmise that it is Sarah Palin's ambition, her jejune and kaleidoscopic ambition, that makes her so itinerant. Ambition, what social scientists define as a strategic response to an opportunity structure (Stone & Maisel, 2003), defines Palin. Research shows that political ambition attracts those having a heightened sense of political efficacy and high status needs; it also increases when people face sudden changes in their lifestyles and when they are aggressively recruited to serve (Fox & Lawless, 2011). People who monitor others' feelings are also likely to be ambitious (Maestas, 2003), as are those with an inherent (vs. an occasional) interest in public policy (Gaddie, 2004). While all politicians are ambitious, Sarah Palin is driven in these ways. She evidences that when speaking.

Palin's Perambulations

Figure 9.1 shows how Insistence scores are distributed generally. Usually, serious people doing serious things—lawyers, scientists, corporate executives, journalists—score high on this variable. Those in the creative fields—dramatists, performers, bloggers, and TV entertainers—are far less insistent. Messages at the "focused" end of the chart are more technical, more likely to be written than oral, more formal than informal, while

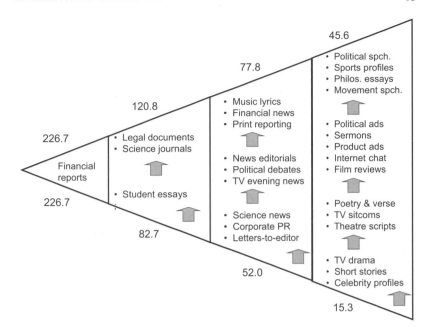

FIGURE 9.1 *Insistence* scores by rhetorical genre (*n* = 28,189).

texts scoring low on Insistence are transactional rather than monologi-
cal, spontaneous rather than planned, and they resemble natural human
speech rather than crafted prose.

Genre scoring in the midrange on Insistence include serious matters
gone popular, which obviously includes all things political. Our data show
that politicians dance between the technical and the fashionable because,
even though they must deal with complex issues like nuclear arms nego-
tiations and airline security each day, they must also find a "delivery system" for making these matters understandable to a diverse electorate. It
is inevitable, then, that the rhetorical features to which politicians are intuitively attracted—metaphors, examples, analogies, and digressions—are
the very things that degrade Insistence scores (even though they make
things interesting for voters).

Financial reports, on the other hand, are rarely lively. They hew to the
bottom line, drilling ever deeper into a topic until the subject matter (and
sometimes the reader) are exhausted. We see these features on display in
the following passage, which scores a 65.5 on Insistence and whose repeti-
tions are so numerous as to use up the available orthographic indicators:

Sales and **earnings** set records. **Earnings** per share rose **19** *percent* and return on equity reached **20.8** *percent*. Seven of our nine *businesses* had **earnings** higher than last YEAR, and for six the INCREASES were double-digit. Overall, we continued to move toward realizing the full long-term potential of our leadership *businesses*. Operating **earnings** of the *businesses* INCREASED **28** *percent* and for the period **2002** to **2005** our **earnings** per share have INCREASED at an average annual rate of about **17** *percent*. We also continued the accelerating change in the composition of our company. For fiscal **2005**, commercial and international sales were up **30** *percent* from last YEAR, and now comprise **72 percent** of total sales. That compares with **65** *percent* in **2004** and only **39** *percent* a decade ago. (Rockwell, 1995; emphasis added)

Consider, in contrast, a much more athletic use of language. The following passage is breathy in the extreme, with each sentence taking up a new topic—a frisky dog, a recent film, someone's eyeglasses, a personal trainer. Nothing being discussed here is important but all of it is digestible. Upon finishing the passage, one feels embarrassed for having wasted one's time. And yet *People* magazine delivers such pap up to 3.5 million readers each month. Not surprisingly, the storylet scores only a 7.5 on Insistence. Not a repetition in sight, but such a good read:

Jennifer Aniston should be on easy street, but at the moment—late for a date with a movie camera on a sweltering Manhattan morning—she's stuck in traffic on Hudson Street. Her personal trainer turned up late for an exercise session at Aniston's two-bedroom West Village sublet. Which left her little time to get ready for work. Which led to her crunching her glasses underfoot. Which made it tough to inspect the gunk her 7-month-old Australian shepherd mix puppy, Enzo, threw up on the rug. As the van ferrying her and Enzo to the film's Lower East Side location creeps past six pallbearers carrying a casket, Aniston frowns: "Geezuz, I hope that's not some sort of omen." (Miller, 1997)

Given Sarah Palin's unique biography—beauty queen turned mother turned governor turned vice-presidential candidate turned media celebrity—she is an inviting case study for DICTION. The Insistence variable measures how a speaker balances interiority and exteriority, steadfastness and exploration, tensions that are central to the Palin story line: Why can't she stay on-track? Why doesn't that bother her supporters? What matters will she *not* discuss in public? Which inquiries are too impertinent to make of her? Why is she likely to respond anyway? Because Palin is so open about so many things, she constantly invites surveillance. In contrast, when running for the Republican nomination in 2008, the former governor of Massachusetts, Mitt Romney, talked of taxes and health care and little else. He was judged a one-trick pony as a result, while Palin was seen by the press as an ever-expanding universe.

With regard to the media, Palin gives the lie to certain well-established norms. Researchers have shown, for example, that female candidates typically receive less coverage than men (see Kahn, 1994; Heldman, Carroll & Olson, 2005), but that is clearly untrue for Sarah Palin. Also, studies show that reporters focus more heavily on the electoral viability of women than men (E. Falk, 2010), but the press could not stop talking about the "Palin juggernaut" when 2011 rolled around. During the 2008 campaign, Palin received more news coverage than her running mate, John McCain, and got *both* more "negative visibility" *and* "positive visibility" than her VP-rival, Joe Biden (Miller & Peake, 2010). Not surprisingly, Palin attracted a great deal of "novelty" coverage from the press, even when compared to Barack Obama (Meeks, 2010). Palin also received more "maternal" commentary than prior female candidates (Harp, Loke & Bachmann, 2010), which may explain why her coverage in local newspapers was more positive than that in national outlets (Miller & Peake, 2010).

For the press, Sarah Palin was a bonanza, an outcome she invited. We reached that conclusion by analyzing 31 of her public statements between October 15, 2007 (a TV interview with Charlie Rose), and June 27, 2010, when she delivered a controversial speech at California State University–Stanislaus, where her speaking fee became a cause célèbre. Included in this sample (which amounted to 173 verbal passages) were media interviews during the 2008 campaign, stump speeches before and after that election, presentations at Tea Party rallies and to conservative interest groups, and a medley of other appearances, including her resignation as governor, a foreign policy speech in Hong Kong, remarks at a Gridiron Dinner in Washington, and a monologue she delivered on Jay Leno's television program.[2]

Interestingly, her Insistence scores during chats with the mainstream media and the conservative cable channels were virtually identical. Also, her partisan speeches did not differ on Insistence from her remarks at more general gatherings. She surpassed the political mean for Insistence only on three major occasions—during an endorsement speech for Texas governor Rick Perry in 2010, during a similar event for John McCain that same year, and when receiving the key to the city of Peoria in April 2010. On all other occasions, she wandered across the political landscape.

Figure 9.2 puts this in historical perspective. Palin has one of the lowest average Insistence scores of any politicians studied to date.[3] Many of the candidates are bunched tightly in figure 9.2, with neither (1) era, (2) party, (3) topic, nor (4) speech setting distinguishing sharply among them. Standing apart from the pack are Dwight Eisenhower, John Anderson, and Sarah Palin, the only candidates averaging less than 30 on Insistence. Why these three? Perhaps it is because they were introduced to the American electorate (and to the norms of mass campaigning) quite suddenly, a condition that includes Ross Perot as well. All four were politically unaligned for the most part; all four had little campaign experience; all had unclear positions on most issues; and all were, in their own ways, ambitious. Absent a well-worked-out platform, absent a set of abiding principles, Insistence scores are likely to be low.

When do such scores rise? Taking a strong ideological position can do the trick, which may explain Harry Truman's high score when running for reelection in 1948, although Barry Goldwater presents a counterexample

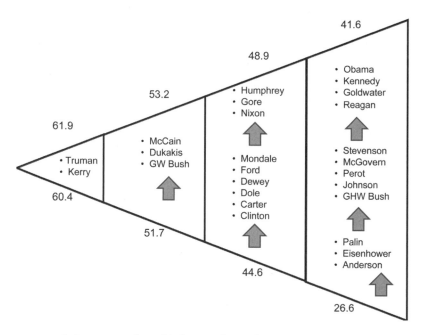

FIGURE 9.2 *Insistence* scores by political personality: 1948–2010.

by hovering near the mean in 1964. Inexperience too may cause candidates to compensate by narrowing their focus (e.g., Kerry, McCain, Dukakis, and George W. Bush), although Obama, McGovern, and the elder Bush did not take that option. Our researches suggest other possibilities. Candidates' Insistence scores increase: (1) among those with long-standing party affiliations,[4] (2) for those running in the general election (where greater clash demands greater focus) as opposed to the primaries,[5] and, ironically, (3) among those waging a losing campaign (in 2008, both Barack Obama and John McCain had much lower Insistence scores than did their primary rivals, perhaps because they were trying to build broad coalitions).[6]

A speech's subject matter may also be important. For George W. Bush, at least, technical topics—e.g., the economy and the environment—called forth greater Insistence than did values-based subjects (patriotism, religion, etc.).[7] For similar reasons, Mr. Bush increased his Insistence scores during formal briefings but lowered them when addressing party members.[8] He also embraced a narrower agenda when confronting the press than when speaking to friendly audiences.[9] Mostly, though, with a mean of 60.0 and a standard deviation of 50.0 (for some 30,000 texts), Insistence is a varying variable, a complex function of personality, situation, genre, topic, and modality. Except when it comes to Sarah Palin. What makes her so distinctive? We address that question in the remainder of this chapter.

Palin's Parataxis

Technically, Sarah Palin employs parataxis, a tone, as defined in the *Oxford Dictionary of Literary Terms*, "marked by the juxtaposition of clauses or sentences, without the use of connecting words [which] has the effect of abruptness because the relationship between one statement and the next is not made explicit." It is "common in orature (oral literature) and in fast-moving prose, especially if intended for young listeners or readers" (*Concise Oxford Companion to the English Language*). Hemingway is the scion of parataxis; he makes a reader tumble forward, always unsure but constantly intrigued: "The sun was coming over the hills. A bass jumped, making a circle in the water. Nick trailed his hand in the water. It felt warm in the sharp chill of the morning" (Hemingway, 1966, p. 95). Julius Caesar also used parataxis—"I came. I saw. I conquered."—as have Homer, Beckett, Raymond Carver, and the Gospel of Mark. Because its connective tissues are so thin, a paratactic message creates what Richard Lanham (1983, p. 29) calls a kind of "semantic democracy."

Consider, for example, the introduction to one of Sarah Palin's speeches, the one given to the student body at Cal State–Stanislaus. As we see below, her clauses are linked by what one writer calls "the noncommittal connective *and*" (Abrams, 1992, p. 304–5), which makes her audience feel a kind of "experience in process," a "piling up" and swiftness" (Sturm, 2010, para. 4):

> **And** then though, you know, I was expecting quite a few protests, protesters. I thought that, you know, I'd get a little bit of the Ann Coulterism **and** I thought, hey, that would be cool. I love Ann Coulter **and** more power to her as she goes on college campuses **and** she talks about America and American values and principles **and** what it means to be an American **and** I expected a little bit of that. But it's been nothing but absolute loveliness here in this part of California **and** I so appreciate the hospitality **and,** again, I do appreciate your boldness.

One can forgive Ms. Palin for her run-on introduction. She was excited to be on the campus after many weeks of controversy, controversy that ultimately went viral. Also, her audience was enthusiastic and anticipatory. Parataxis signals a speaker's "urgency . . . to express" themselves (Sandefur, 2003, p. 120) and builds "instant identification and empathy" with an audience (Reed, 1973, p. 43). With Palin's speech, however, the running-on never stopped. Even when getting to the meat of her talk, she implies that everything is of equal importance:[10]

> **And** we must celebrate our relentless sunny optimism. Remember: that's what Reagan was known for. That had to have come from California, that sunny optimism. **And** that pioneering spirit that built this country. It inspired us to cross oceans **and** carve out a life in the wilderness **and** by the sweat of our brow to create and contribute and to build a better life in America. We must embrace our entrepreneurial drive to build **and** to produce **and** to innovate **and** allow America to remain the world's standard-bearer for excellence. **And** we must affirm our willingness to stand up for people across the globe who are yearning to be free. They look to us; we are that beacon of hope for what it means to be free. **And** truly that is nothing to apologize for.

As we see here, parataxis features a "list mentality" (Lanham, 1983, p. 32) that rejects the focused "hypotactic" tone loved by bankers and bureaucrats. One linguist relates parataxis to "emotionality" and "women's language" (Coates, 1985, p. 25), while another finds it "highly applauded by blacks" but "exasperating to whites who wish you'd be direct and hurry up and get to the point" (Smitherman, 1977, p. 148). So why does Sarah Palin use such a tone and why do her audiences respond well to it? Figure 9.3 hints at the answers by tracing the flow of her Stanislaus speech. It shows Palin waxing and waning, occasionally achieving focus (in segments 2, 4, and 7–8) but never sustaining it. With Sarah Palin, it really is one damn thing after another.

Figure 9.4 provides more texture, with the unshaded (paratactic) portions of the chart becoming a lesson in miscellany: apostles and fish swim together while Glenn Beck and Adolph Hitler consort conspiratorially. But by backing away a bit, one easily gets the speech's overall sensibility—an arc of freedom that embraces both capitalism and education, the expression of ideas and their militant defense, as well as individual initiative and collective resolve. As Smitherman (1977, p. 148) says of African-American sermonizing, "like the flow of nature's rivers and streams, it all eventually leads back to the source." While some may doubt

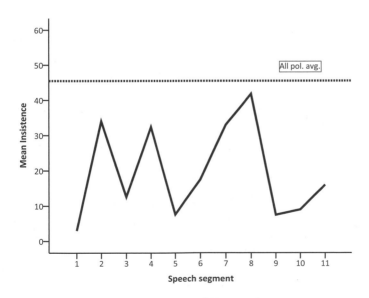

FIGURE 9.3 *Insistence* scores during Cal State–Stanislaus speech.

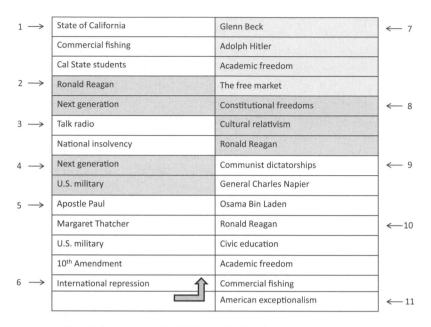

FIGURE 9.4 Topical dispersion for the Cal State–Stanislaus speech.

that Palin's speech warranted a $75,000 speaking fee, the emotional flow of her thoughts comes through quite clearly.

Still, many are appalled by Palin's aimlessness. Joe McGinnis (2011), for one, finds Palin to be poorly educated, arrogant, and lazy—and also manipulative—and would be unsurprised by her apparent aimlessness. Hence, McGinnis would be delighted by *Vanity Fair*'s line editing of her resignation speech as governor, a speech that drifted as predictably as the Alaskan snows ("Palin's Resignation," 2009). Figure 9.5 depicts the damage they did. To get a more empirical estimation of the alterations, the original and amended versions of the speech were passed through DICTION. As we see in figure 9.6, the *Vanity Fair* editors did what editors do, removing digressions and overstatements, increasing use of the active voice, and, notably, increasing her Insistence score fourfold. The result was a crisp and businesslike speech. Gone were the gratuitous asides and personal reminiscences. Gone too were the redundancies and clichés. But gone, especially, was the speech's sweet indolence. *Vanity Fair* took the Palin out of Palin.

Did that improve things? Should Palin use speechwriters more regularly? Would she be a better leader if she were more hypotactic? And if

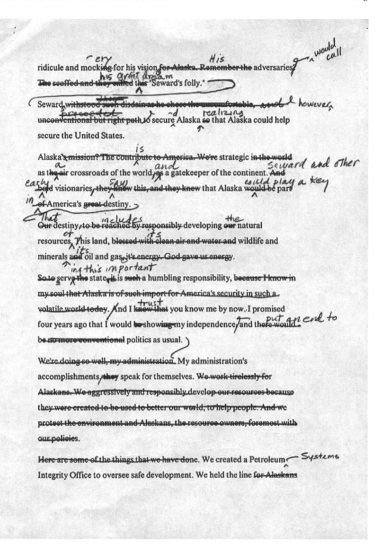

FIGURE 9.5 Palin's resignation speech as edited by *Vanity Fair.*

she made such changes, would her adoring public still embrace her, or would they sense a cheat, suspecting she had suddenly "gone D.C."? Tone, after all, is not only a message quality but also a message itself. Palin's parataxis tells her audiences that she trusts them, that she has little to hide, that she is open to their ideas. Many Americans have responded well to these invitations. We need to ask why.

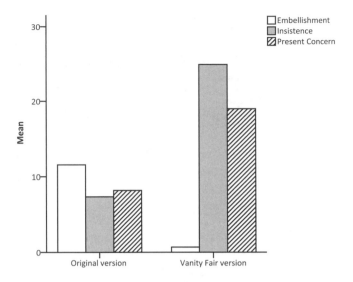

FIGURE 9.6 Lexical features of Palin's resignation speech: original vs. *Vanity Fair* version.

Palin's Polymorphism

To our way of thinking, Sarah Palin's tone results from how her personal ambition blends with powerful aspects of American culture itself. Palin is, after all, a woman in a male-dominated occupation, a westerner confronting an eastern establishment, a religious person in an increasingly secular society, a Republican in a party-challenged era, and, always, an outsider to much of what has preceded her. Her attempt to bridge these divides and remain whole is not uncourageous. Added to this is her own psychological complexity: one who goes to church but admits to having inhaled; a person who preaches family values but who became a grandmother out of wedlock; a union wife in corporatist clothing; a knockout who wants to be taken seriously. When she awakes each day, Sarah Palin becomes a case study in the aporia of meaning.

Palin's parataxis results from all of this. She is "accessible, ordinary, unpretentious," says *The New Republic* columnist and linguist John McWhorter (2010, para. 21), but she is also plagued by "utter subjectivity." That is, says McWhorter, "she speaks very much from the inside of her head." McWhorter (2010, para. 13) also notes that "part of why Palin speaks the way she does is that she has grown up squarely within a period of American history when the old-fashioned sense of speech as a carefully planned recitation, and public pronouncements as performative oratory, has been quite obsolete." The result, says *New York Times* essayist Robert Draper (2010, p. 46), is that Palin's "improvisatory ethic" makes her "erratic and short on self-discipline," but also confers on her an "aura of authenticity." Ordinary people, after all, constantly wander around in their conversations, rarely looking over their shoulders at the grammarians. Not surprisingly, then, Palin has become a devotee of new media technologies that also prize spontaneity. "I just Tweet; that's just the way I roll," says Palin (Draper, 2010, p. 47).

These same instincts feed a hungry press corps. During the 2008 campaign, Herbst (2010, p. 38) reports, Palin's "rallies produced a strong air of unpredictability," which "ratcheted up the intensity and the subsequent media scrutiny." As a result, journalists constantly "conveyed a sense that 'anything could happen' at a Palin rally" and that expectation, in turn, kept the nation's eyeballs glued to her. Teachers of oratory from the earliest times have instructed their charges to convey a "vivid sense of the moment" when speaking, a lesson that Palin has learned brilliantly. Her low Insistence scores produce "a searching kind of expression" that emphasizes "preliminary thought but that nonetheless feels existentially authoritative" (McWhorter, 2010, para. 28). A speaker like Palin easily shares the moment with her listeners (often in call-response fashion), and that endears them to her. Such a "chatty" tone is also appealing to talk television, on which Palin has become a staple (Stevenson, 2010). Spontaneity, reciprocity, self-disclosure, exploration, trust. Sarah Palin is a person of her times.

She is also a woman, and that is a fascinating aspect of her story. Palin apparently aspires to everything promised by first- and second-wave feminism (Daum, 2010), but that can be uncomfortable for a conservative ... and so she wanders. Some scholars (Strolovitch et al., 2010) predicted that Palin would garner support from "gender-conscious" Republicans if she ran for high office in 2012, but they also noted that female delegates at the 2008 Republican convention liked John McCain more than her. Palin's image among Republican men is equally complex. They are attracted to her "masculine displays of toughness," while her feminine qualities make her "palatable rather than threatening" (Edwards, 2010, p. 35). White working-class men find her especially appealing, reports Healey (2010), but other scholars find only confusion in the Palin Complex of Selves: "[She] combines the extremes of femininity (pretty, fertile, and youthful) with the extremes of masculinity (macho, fearless, self-sufficient). Her half-flirtatious, half-defiant tone thus radically renovates the prevailing idea of what it means to be an iconic woman attempting to 'break the glass ceiling'" (Kahl & Edwards, 2009, p. 272).

Stereotypes associated with female speech change only glacially, and Palin's low Insistence scores play to the regnant prejudices. Studies show that men are more concerned with topic control than women (Bell, Mc-Carthy & McNamara, 2012; Payne & Cangemi, 1997; Liao & Tseng, 1997) and are more likely to venture an answer to a question when confronted by uncertain conditions (Giuliano et al., 1998). Men also move expeditiously when speaking, reports Deborah Tannen (1994), while women tend to "drift" from topic to topic and get irritated when men try to redirect things. Men are also more likely to "hijack" a conversation via topic control (Hawisher & Sullivan, 1998) and are not averse to using interruptions to do so (Holmes, 1995).

But there is also an upside to the Palin approach: It is perfectly adapted to the electronic media, a fact that Palin makes stunningly obvious. According to Jamieson (1988, p. 84), "television invites a personal, self-disclosing style that draws public discourse out of a private self and comfortably reduces the complex world to dramatic narratives. Because it encompasses these characteristics, the once spurned womanly style is now the style of preference" in an electronic age. Parataxis, of course, is only one weapon available to women, and it has an obvious downside: it can seem weak and deferential, an approach suited to women unsure of who they are or what they believe. And so we are left with a truly contemporary dilemma: the irrefutable fact of gender wrapped in the enigma of changing social stereotypes. That complexity produces both advantages and disadvantages for Sarah Palin.

One popular charge against the paratactic tone is that its users shift from topic to topic because they do not know where they are going, that they are philosophically bankrupt. Charges like these have been lodged against Sarah Palin from the minute she appeared on the national scene. Tina Fey of *Saturday Night Live* (2008) was particularly devastating in this regard. Note, for example, how she uses exaggerated parataxis to lampoon the recently named vice-presidential candidate's ill-fated interview with CBS's Katie Couric:

> Like every American I'm speaking with, we're all about this. We're saying, "Hey, why bail out Fannie and Freddie and not me?" But ultimately what the bailout does is, help those that are concerned about the healthcare reform that

is needed to help shore up our economy to help . . . uh . . . it's gotta be all about job creation, too. Also, too, shoring up our economy and putting Fannie and Freddie back on the right track and so healthcare reform and reducing taxes and reining in spending . . . 'cause Barack Obama, y'know . . . has got to accompany tax reductions and tax relief for Americans, also, having a dollar value meal at restaurants. That's gonna help. But one in five jobs being created today under the umbrella of job creation. That, you know . . . Also . . . (Fey, 2008)

The words spoken by Fey as Palin make no sense or, better, they make only one kind of sense: they reveal a woman who doesn't know much about the issues of the day but who is delightfully plucky. Even against a backdrop of sardonic relief, however, another message comes through: Palin rejects airy intellectualism because she cares about ordinary Americans.[11] Her supporters sense that, sorting through the bafflegab and finding someone just like them. As Morris (2011) says, Palin's rhetoric helps constitute "imaginary communities" through "narcissistic identification," which is an academic way of saying that people see themselves in the former governor. Sarah Palin might ask: "Is that a federal crime? Don't all politicians bond with their constituents? Barack Obama is nerdy, George W. Bush clumsy, and Joe Biden windy. Is being ditzy inherently worse?"

It can be when it plays to gender stereotypes, some argue. According to Susan Douglas, Palin's approach "perpetuates the notion that women don't know anything and they don't have to know anything. They can just bat their eyelashes . . . They can just flirt their way to the top" (Lee & Wen, 2009, p. 96). Sam Harris (2008, para. 1) takes a more psychiatric view of Palin's incoherency when declaring, "Here, finally, was a performer who—being maternal, wounded, righteous and sexy—could stride past the frontal cortex of every American and plant a three-inch heel directly on that limbic circuit that ceaselessly intones 'God and country.'"

Palin is particularly mystifying to members of the press whose reportage, as we saw in chapter 2, is invariably Insistent. But Palin is more than mystifying to them, she is galling. Says Toby Harnden (2009, para. 7) of the *Daily Telegraph*: "[Palin] has rendered herself a joke, playing right into the hand of the opponents of the Republican party by fulfilling the stereotype of her as an intellectually idle, self-absorbed, overweeningly ambitious empty vessel who thinks she can just wing it to the White House." From a patrician perspective, Harnden is right, but Sarah Palin also comes from *somewhere*, and her sense of place is important. Palin comes from a small town that prizes hard work more than an elite education (Morris,

2011). She comes from the west, with its weak party system and political fluidity (Marcy, 2010). And she comes from Alaska, what Robert Mason (2010, p. 186) calls a "settler society" that authorizes "a credible message of social renewal and political differentiation." It is this differentiation, says Mason, that gives Palin her moral authenticity, her instinct to go it alone and think in the moment. Back east things are too connected, too systemic. Palin's parataxis thumbs its nose at those conventions.

Palin's tone also sends a special message to the Republican oligarchy: "I am willing to make new friends and build new bridges." "That's fine," the party responds, "but what about the old friends and old bridges?" Traditionalists are naturally suspicious of modernity, but postmodernity scares them silly. What is a party to do with a celebrity conservative who embraces a populist fable (Smith, 2010, p. vii), an attack dog with a folksy lexicon (Purnell, Raimy & Salmons, 2009), an outsider who wants to be her own kind of insider (Benoit & Henson, 2009), a woman with credibility but no gravitas (Rae, 2010), a media personality with political reach but no political responsibility (Lawrence & Schafer, 2010)? For traditional Republicans, Sarah Palin is just too complex to imagine. And yet she exists.[12]

Traditional Republicans would discount Sarah Palin if she were just one crazy paratactic woman, but she is not. She has friends and they drink tea. Together, they created a bloc of fifty or so House members on the eve of the 112th Congress. What would they do once in office? What wouldn't they do? Earmarks, taxes, housing, the Fed, health care, immigration—they were all on the line. Despite her unique rhetorical tone, Sarah Palin helped launch a political movement. That movement, in turn, further explains why Palin speaks as she does.

Palin's Partners

The orderliness found among hypotactic speakers stems from two factors: (1) they know where they have been and (2) they know where they are going. Lawyers are informed by precedent, scientists by prior research, corporate executives by the rules of finance. These histories guide how they say what they say. Third parties, even faux third parties like the Tea Party, have few such advantages and, as a result, are often quixotic. As a result, say Rosenstone, Behr, and Lazarus (1996, pp. 11–12), they rarely survive their founder's passing. But they can do mischief in the meantime. Research finds that legislators with strong local ties and individual bases of support can undermine party unity once in office (Tavits, 2009). They "affect the content and range of political discourse, and ultimately public policy, by raising issues and opinions that the two major parties have ignored" (Rosenstone et al., 1996, p. 8). The parties usually react by incorporating the dissidents' views into their own platforms (Chamberlain, 2010), but the "dystopia of factionalism that Madison feared in Federalist #10" threatens the political establishment in the interim (Schneck, 2001, p. 144).

Third parties give citizens "the opportunity to vent their hostility, anger, or extreme beliefs within the electoral arena" (Mazmanian, 1991, p. 1105), and that can be a palliative for a troubled electorate. The downside is that such parties typically ride on the coattails of a charismatic figure rather than depend on retrospective judgments—"How is the nation doing?"—or partisan orientations—"Where does absolute truth lie?" (Luks, Miller & Jacobs, 2003). From a rhetorical perspective, then, third parties cannot depend on tradition, and that has advantages and disadvantages. Inventing things in situ makes political discourse unpredictable and often newsworthy. On the other hand, it can make one sound daffy or dangerous to traditional voters.

What does DICTION discover when examining Tea Party rhetoric? It finds Sarah Palin writ large. Fifteen public statements (46 passages) were run through the program and, as we see in figure 9.7, most were just as paratactic as Palin and several had even lower Insistence scores.[13] They were reactive as well: When the Republican tone (R-tone) and Democratic tone (D-tone) (see chapter 3) were computed for Tea Party members and compared to those of major party candidates, the Tea Partiers differed significantly on both dimensions. Figure 9.8 shows them to have less R-tone than the Republicans and far less D-tone than the Democrats. The fact that the Tea Party's R-tone scores lagged those of traditional Republicans is especially noteworthy for the elections of 2012 and beyond.[14]

Some observers might find these results surprising, since the Tea Party is so often seen as a subset of the Republican Party. Tea Party members themselves, however, would be less surprised, seeing themselves as politically unaffiliated (Patrakis, 2011, September 22) and joined only by a virulent Constitutionalism. Kohn (2011, November 10) agrees, describing Tea Partyers as postparty activists whose revulsion with the D.C. establishment even makes them comrades-in-part with the Occupy Wall Street protestors (Phelan, 2011, November 9). One especially observant Tea Party member complains that both the right and the left are trying to either co-opt the Tea Party or frame it as the source of all evil:

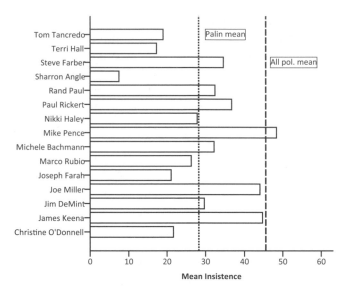

FIGURE 9.7 Insistence scores for Tea Partiers (vs. Palin and mainstream politicians).

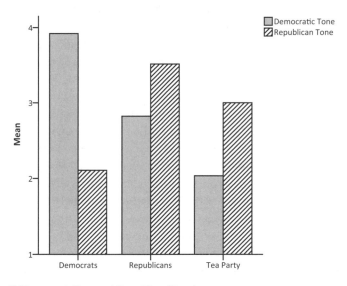

FIGURE 9.8 Democratic Tone and Republican Tone by party.

> You know something is afoot when forces of the elites of left and right begin to
> unite, with Bill O'Reilly, and his recent mini-me, Laura Ingraham, along with
> all the other usual suspects, aligning with such leftist jackals as Maureen Dowd,
> who today compare the Tea Party members of Congress to suicide bombers.
> (America, 2011, July 21)

Because third parties are so often personality centered rather than philosophically based, they often flag and fail during competitive races. As Gregory Schneider (2010, p. B11) notes, a candidate like Ron Paul, for example, "sparked some of the deepest attachments, yet thinnest support" in the 2008 presidential primaries. In addition, says Schneider, ideological coherence is something to worry about:

> The conservative movement contains more factions than Joseph's dream coat
> contains colors. Much of the time the factions disagree on policy, further com-
> plicating the efforts of those in power to bring about the desired change sought
> by the electorate. Some of the time they disagree about principle: What should
> be emphasized, economic or social issues. During the Reagan administration,
> which should have been a moment of unity for the conservative movement,
> every faction carped about Reagan's failure to address its concerns. (Schneider,
> 2010, p. B10)

Because it is philosophically disparate, Tea Party rhetoric is also cumbersome (as shown by its low Insistence scores). To achieve rhetorical lift, it must resort to a smorgasbord of concerns that makes it sound listlike. Because it is a "bumper sticker movement," says Richard Geldard (2010), the Tea Party has "no heart and thus no poetry." It wanders around, citing a plethora of concerns before espying a solution. It also produces a meta-rhetoric, dilating on matters of definition. Because it is constantly clearing away the brush rather than setting out on a grand trek, its prose becomes leaden. It often uses the ancient trope of expeditio, the "method of residues," serially dismissing options until one grand solution is found:

- Trying to define the Tea Party is a difficult task, and it should be. It's rough
  around the edges and it's mostly not definable. (Lerner, 2010)
- I can tell you it is not about materialism. It is not simply about economics. And
  it is a mistake to assume it can be explained by polls on the most important
  issues from menus devised by tea-party leaders. (Farah, 2010).

- The Tea Party is not an extension of the organized Republican Party nor is it a Conservative movement. It is more complex than this. (OC Tross, n.d.)
- Who belongs to the tea party? Most of us have never been involved in politics, other than voting. We are just concerned citizens that see Washington destroying our nation. We are not affiliated with any political party. (Roanoke Tea Party, n.d.)
- [The Tea Party] is not a political party. It's not a "shadow government." It's not a lobbyist. It's not a think tank. It's not any particular state, national or even local organization. This means there are things the movement is *not capable of doing*. (McHugh, 2010)

Sarah Palin is rarely this pedantic. Her rhetorical gifts include the ability to meander deftly. When she presents a list of concerns, she interrupts it with cozy digressions or clever potshots at her opponents. Guided by her own insatiable ambition, Palin is comfortable within her own skin and hence willing to make direct, personal contact with her audience. She lingers with them, making her points but letting audiences view her as a flesh-and-blood person. As a result, her spontaneity has become her rhetorical signature. One of the few truly insistent speeches she has made was a heavily scripted (and heavily staffed) presentation in Hong Kong just after resigning as governor, ostensibly in an attempt to burnish her international credentials. The speech made a few headlines but not nearly as many as the off-the-cuff (low-insistent) comments she made on November 8, 2010, when attacking Fed chair Ben Bernanke for buying up treasuries. Her remarks on that occasion gave a political cast to normally antiseptic matters and spawned controversy as a result. Wanderer though she may be, Sarah Palin often wanders productively.

Conclusion

Sarah Palin is largely known for being known. She was an undistinguished governor of a non-populous state and then ran for vice-president unimpressively. She has, to be sure, shown remarkable ability to attract the attention of the nation's press and to fill up a lecture hall. Her main accomplishment has been to associate herself with several Tea Party members who ascended to high office in the off-year elections of 2010, including Rand Paul, Pat Toomey, Kelly Ayotte, Marco Rubio, and Nikki Haley. But a number of her endorsees—Christine O'Donnell, John Raese, Tim

Burns, Sharron Angle, and, most embarrassingly, Joe Miller of Alaska—went down in defeat. It remains to be seen if Ms. Palin herself has a political future.

If she runs for national office again someday, she will have to address her paratactic problem. There are several reasons why mainstream politicians score twenty or more points higher on Insistence than she does: (1) they have something programmatic to say, (2) they are accustomed to being in the spotlight, and (3) they know they will be scrutinized by the press and the bloggers. Sarah Palin is learning these lessons, but her gaffes have mostly occurred when she wandered into uncharted terrains: "We believe that the best of America is in these small towns that we get to visit, and in these wonderful little pockets of what I call the real America, being here with all of you hard working very patriotic, um, very, um, pro-America areas of this great nation" (quoted in Stein, 2008, October 17).

Whatever her future might hold, Sarah Palin has lessons to teach. Her "dollop here, dollop there" approach has garnered attention, much of it positive, although she remains a polarizing political figure. She has become a national symbol but a dialectical one—a retrograde woman with postfeminist tendencies; a frontierswoman who can mix it up with urban know-it-alls; a magnet for legacy media but one also able to exploit the new media for personal advantage; a classic Republican but only when she wants to be. Given this mixture, Sarah Palin is now a suitable topic for discussion at any cocktail party in the United States.

When all is said and done, though, parataxis is not a formula for political success and extreme ambition alone cannot sustain a career. Making things up on the spot (Palin often uses her own palm as a teleprompter) and turning asides into headlines ultimately lead to trouble. That is especially true when one goes negative. According to *The New Republic*'s Michelle Cottle (2010, p. 6), Palin, Michele Bachmann, and Lynne Cheney "stand out for their ability to rant, rave, name-call, finger-point and peddle the most outrageous distortions in service to their cause," while scholar Janis Edwards (2010, p. 36) notes that Palin's success "depends largely on balancing extremes of feminine and masculine tendencies." Exaggeration combined with serendipity does not sustainability make.

Nevertheless, Sarah Palin has added a distinctive voice to the national discussion and become a welcome relief from hidebound ways of engaging the electorate. Rightly or wrongly, she has given a voice to people who felt unheard, and that is an unalloyed good in a large and heterogeneous nation. Sarah Palin is young and feisty like Barack Obama, but she is not him. She is traditional and charismatic like Ronald Reagan, but she is not him either. Both men were, in different ways, hypotactic and both men were, in different ways, strong leaders. If Sarah Palin is to follow their lead, she must blend her opportunism with good judgment. Rhetorically, she must also tighten things up . . . but not excessively.

PART IV

Beyond Language

CHAPTER TEN

The Possibilities of Political Tone

If a law were passed prohibiting the American people from discussing political tone, they would become mute. They prove that each day and, especially, each quadrennium. Take, for example, the Republican debate held in Goffstown, New Hampshire, on June 13, 2011. Seven stalwart souls assembled that evening, touting their life stories and philosophical instincts. Mostly, they sounded the same: Barack Obama was a failure and they, in contrast, were made of sterner stuff. Mitt Romney, Newt Gingrich, Herman Cain, Tim Pawlenty, Michele Bachmann, Rick Santorum, and Ron Paul showed up for the debate, chatted among themselves for two hours, and then repaired to the spin room.

What can be said about a debate scheduled seventeen months before an election? The party's ultimate candidates were unknown at the time, no real money had been raised, the campaign's issues were still embryonic, and a thousand events and disclosures—the very things that would turn the tide of the election—had yet to surface. And yet the New Hampshire debate was held and it elicited reactions. Potential voters responded from the head, they responded from the gut, and they responded, especially, to political tone. Although just beginning to sort things out, they were, in the words of Maurice Merleau-Ponty (1962), "condemned to meaning":

- Mitt Romney: "pandering, slick, and about as genuine as Dukakis in a Tank"
- Michele Bachmann: "a brighter, better spoken version of Palin"
- Herman Cain: "needs more refined answers"
- Ron Paul: "clearly brilliant, if a little daffy"
- Tim Pawlenty: "too many generalities ... made him look weak and shallow" (reader responses to Cillizza, 2011).

What precisely do these people mean? It is hard to say. What gives them their confidence? Even harder to say. But they are intelligent in the ways that all people are intelligent: They hear what they hear, they compare it to what they have heard before, and then make their call. They know nothing of literary or semantic theory and they would think it daft to be called walking-around phenomenologists. But that is what they are— hard-working processors of lexical and syntactic data, persons who sense what they sense even if they cannot say how or why. When watching the New Hampshire debate, they drew on their entire beings—their memories, their expectations, their imaginations, their abiding prejudices—and formed their impressions. They are sages, these Americans, and they get political tone.

Your authors know tone differently, more scientifically and less intuitively. We have identified eight language effects in this book—the Balanced Tone, the Urgent Tone, the Resilient Tone, etc.—and linked them to eight abiding challenges—partisanship, institutionalization, ambition, etc. We are confident that the tones we have identified are verifiable, although our interpretations can surely be questioned. Unlike the citizens in New Hampshire, however, we know *how* we know what we know, and that gives us a certain confidence.

Admittedly, our approach is not perfect. In identifying word choice as central to political tone, we have not explained everything that make politics politics. We have not, for example, looked at syntax, imagery, phonology, dialect, morphology, and the other factors involved in encoding and decoding. We have tried, however, to bring our data to life by quoting extensively from the texts analyzed, thereby combining close inspection with what Franco Moretti calls "distant reading." At his Literary Laboratory at Stanford University, Moretti is using computer-aided text analysis to see, among other things, how genre came to be constructed across the ages and how novelists built "plots" into the structures of their novels (Williams, 2011). Literature, says Moretti is "a collective system that should be grasped as such," that we cannot understand a nation's literature until we stand back and see how its components relate to one another (Schulz, 2011). We have taken a similar approach here but have also made a stronger claim: That standing back is what ordinary voters do when processing a text, using what they have previously seen and heard to understand each new stimulus.

Research techniques like ours are increasingly being put into practice. One corporation, Lymbix, for example, is performing "tone checks" of email prior to issuance to keep senders from being embarrassed by what they have written. Another company, Thompson-Reuters, is using "sentiment sensitive" software to see if media reportage accurately predicts the performance of stock portfolios (Bowley, 2010). Yet another company, Achievement Metrics, is analyzing the speech patterns of star college football players for NFL teams to see if they have the "conceptual complexity," "need for power," and "deliberativeness" required in professional football (Agger, 2011).

More impressively, the Google Books Project is spawning considerable research in the humanities, examining how words and their meanings have changed over the centuries. For example, the word "lifestyle" first appeared in 1915 but did not become commonplace until the 1970s (Nunberg, 2010). Examining these language trajectories, such scholars reason, helps us appreciate the witnessed but unseen, the very kinds of patterns discussed throughout this book. "The objective study of subjectivity," says Brian Knutson (2010, para. 1), "will transform the academy and the world beyond." A strong claim, but something new is surely happening when *Science* devotes an entire issue to corpus analytics and when the new director of MIT's Media Lab urges scholars to "break traditional academic frameworks and think about science's view of art, say, or think about art from a mathematical perspective" (quoted in Young, 2011, para. 14).

One prominent anthropologist, Greg Urban (2010, p. 123), has spent considerable time identifying the linguistic effect of catalytic events, "crucial junctures in the flow of culture through time." Urban identifies three variables that affect how human messages are produced: (1) the law of transmission, which says that we learn our speech patterns from one another; (2) the law of inertia, which holds that we will continue speaking as we do until something "disruptive" happens, and (3) the law of force, which says that things will change proportionate to the amount of external force applied to it. We have seen all three effects in this book: members of the same political party echo their forebears; political scandal overturns long-standing rhetorical habits; economic factors change a campaign's dialectic. While computers can be ham-handed when processing a text, they can sort through large amounts of language and become a repository for lexical norms. These text-against-text comparisons help us see patterns we could not otherwise see, an enterprise that pays homage to C. P. Snow's two cultures.

If nothing else, the studies pursued in this book make one thing clear— leaders use tone to get things done that would be otherwise hard to do. A deft tone can help a nation establish its identity and bridge its ideological divides. Tone helps some leaders cope with sweeping cultural shifts and others with institutional inertia. Words have let one man turn war into a campaign cudgel and let another make history for his racial group. Words have also helped one leader cope with the stresses of impeachment and another transfix the nation in a whirlwind of vague locutions. Tone—a universal tonic for that which ails a body politic.

While powerful, tone is also subtle (and just as frequently misunderstood), which is why many of the questions pursued in this book have been basic ones: Can politicians be truly distinguished from nonpoliticians? Why would anyone bother speaking on a Saturday morning? Other issues have been more ephemeral but intriguing: Why does Sarah Palin produce such bimodal reactions? Is the Tea Party really a party? While computers are handy for generating answers, their real value lies in the questions they raise, some of which are conceptual and others applied. We turn to them in that order.

Tone: An Abiding Concept

Tone is an impertinent thing. From a social scientific perspective, it ought not to exist. People who use the word *tone* often do not know precisely what they are saying. It is not uncommon for them to rub their thumb, index, and middle fingers together to describe a particular tone, a sure sign they are in conceptual trouble. Tone might even be thought of as an urban myth . . . until something important happens: A U.S. congresswoman is shot in Arizona and suddenly every newspaper in the nation screams about tone in seventy-two-point font:

- Obama is Seeking Right Time, Tone for Speech (*The Washington Post*)
- After Shooting Spree in Tucson, Time to Tone Down the Vitriol (*USA Today*)
- Ailes Tells Fox Anchors to "Tone it Down" (*The New York Times*)
- Democratic Leader: Cool the Political Rhetoric (*Associated Press Online*)
- Advertisers Finally Have to Tone Down TV Commercials (*Lancaster Sunday News*)
- Ugly Rhetoric also Spilling into Sports (*The Lexington Herald Leader*)

The Gabrielle Giffords case shows that tone registers with people. Similarly, when Newt Gingrich accused Barack Obama of having a "Kenyan colonial mindset," or when Sarah Palin exhorted her supporters with the command "Don't retreat. Reload," or when Michele Bachmann rallied her troops against the "gangster government" in Washington, alarm bells went off and not just in Democratic households. After the Giffords tragedy, everyone seemed to agree that politics had become unacceptably coarse in the U.S. Although tone can be hard to define, it is not hard to hear, a point made by Mark Lilla (2011, p. 14): "History doesn't happen when a leader makes an argument, or even strikes a pose. It happens when he strikes a chord."

Tone is also a meta-message, a way of saying something about one's relationships. Thus, when politicians hit the wrong note, voters sometimes take it personally: "Why would he say such a thing in my presence?" Even a practiced pol like Newt Gingrich can stub his toe, as he did in May 2011 when arguing that "right-wing social engineering" was no more desirable than "left-wing social engineering" (Allen, 2011). Some Republicans called these remarks treasonous, but what really happened was that Gingrich had gotten the tone wrong. His remarks said something untoward about (1) his self-understanding ("the smartest guy in the room"), (2) his view of his audience ("they're hanging on my every word"), and (3) his view of his own party ("they're grown-ups; they can handle it").

Throughout this book, we have stressed how intimately tone is connected to cultural forces. Culture precedes speech—mostly without our knowing it—and speech, in turn, reinforces cultural norms. For example, no matter what their political beliefs, people knew that Newt Gingrich was too big for his britches when he sounded off in May 2011. Even though modesty of speech is hard to find in politics, it remains an aspirational quality. This is true even for those addicted to the banalities of reality TV. Viewers take in the pontifications on these shows as if they were watching a train wreck. The tone of such shows titillates them but it also makes them vaguely apprehensive. Ultimately, reality TV reminds viewers who they are not.

Tone, we believe, is omni-functional. It conditions or qualifies what is being said and thus permits a kind of double-messaging: "We face hard times but we shall prevail"; "I have erred on this occasion but will do better in the future." Because it is multilayered, tone can perform impressive feats: helping us forget Monica Lewinsky; emboldening us for a war on terror; building bridges across partisan divides. Tone sometimes embodies our anxieties (the Urgent Tone) and sometimes reminds us what we all value (the Balanced Tone). Politicians seek out certain venues to sound a particular note; graduation ceremonies are good for that, as are athletic events and shuttle launches. Tone can also serve as a mnemonic device, reminding us of cherished values: sobriety at Arlington National Cemetery, stateliness at the United Nations. An energetic tone can hearten people during troubled times, a didactic tone can explain the country's financial outlook. Getting the tone wrong, on the other hand, often leads to editorializing:

- Arguments for locating the train station have taken on a modern day political tone—emotion and unsound logic rather than analysis and common sense. (Burmeister, 2010, March 21)
- The best thing that happened to me was moving into a county where progress and growth were the political tone, not that mess called Richmond County politics. (Moyer, 2001, July 22)
- San Jose Mayor Chuck Reed's biennial ethics review has taken on an unfortunate political tone. (San Jose mayor's proposed ethics reforms, 2009, December 11)
- A Euclid city councilman . . . showed evidence of a tin ear for political tone Monday night. (Cheers & Jeers, 2002, June 21)

Our prior expectations about tone are sometimes confirmed but, equally often, tone surprises us. For example, most Americans who watched Bill Clinton's failed apology to the nation on August 17, 1998, knew he had lawyered up, and they were right. Most Americans also sense that Republicans and Democrats sound different from one another, and they are correct about that as well. Those who find the Tea Party to be rather chaotic are also right, as are those who find politicians to be cheerier than others. It is also not surprising that elected officials in the U.S. lard their speeches with religious refrains or that they take refuge in traditional American values when the pressure is on.

But we found the unexpected as well: Despite their protestations of being transpartisan, Tea Party members sound more Republican than anything else. We also discovered that, contrary to popular opinion, Barack Obama was less distinguished by his optimism in 2008 than by his group spirit. Other of our data found a rather restrained George W. Bush, a finding that opens up an entirely new way of viewing the Bush presidency. Speaking of ideology, we also found that cable TV "ranters" were not partisan in the traditional sense but were, instead, circus performers of the first order. Perhaps most surprising of all, we found ardent Republicans and Democrats often opting for a blended tone, a sign that cultural forces are still powerful in U.S. politics.

Certain of our findings have been reassuring and others unsettling. Some will be disturbed, for example, to learn that a comparatively aimless person like Sarah Palin can command the attention of an entire nation. Others will be offended that George W. Bush wrapped himself in the American flag when running for reelection only to shift his tone immediately thereafter. On the other hand, Bush apologists will be disturbed that commentators have distorted what the president said and how he said it. It will be problematic to still others that Ronald Reagan's Saturday morning interchanges have become a political sideshow where everyone talks to everyone but where no one talks—directly—to anyone.

Other findings in this book are more heartening. Pluralists, for example, will be pleased to learn that independents running for the presidency have a distinctive political tone, speaking neither like Democrats nor Republicans. It is also comforting to know that, despite the brickbats thrown at them, U.S. politicians are more pragmatic than hortatory. Also, they rarely refer to one another by name, leaving that job to the nation's press. Given the economic difficulties facing the American people in 2008, it was also encouraging to learn that candidates Obama and McCain avoided high-blown rhetoric, concentrating instead on the facts of the day and then identifying solutions lying within the electorate (for Obama) or in visionary leadership (for McCain).

Throughout this book, we have concentrated more heavily on culture than personality, but biographical studies of tone can be interesting. It will not be shocking to learn, for example, that Jimmy Carter had the highest Embellishment scores ever recorded in our studies, a fact that points to his preachy, rather avuncular tone. Barry Goldwater, in contrast, was pugnacious in the extreme, scoring highest on both Liberation terms ("don't tread on me") and Exclusion terms ("not in my back yard"). The patrician John Kerrey used Cognitive words more often, and the publican Gerald Ford less often, than anyone else. It also stands to reason that John McCain scored highest on Aggression, Bob Dole on Ambivalence, and George McGovern on Blame (he was antiwar, after all). These are incidental facts, but collectively they say something interesting: The American people seem to listen for linguistic oddities and punish candidates who stray too far from the mean. So, for example, Ross Perot scored higher on Tenacity and Denial and lower on Human Interest and Cooperation than anyone who has run for the presidency during the last sixty years.

Perot knew exactly what he wanted to say; getting elected seemed an afterthought to him.

Facts like these prove the value of looking at politics through a rhetorical lens. Rhetoric is not just a behavioral entity—speeches, advertisements, interviews—but also a way of thinking. To think rhetorically is to hold out hope that just the right touch can offset trouble. Words are not exactly cheap but they are plentiful—inexhaustible, really. To believe in word solutions is to believe that everything is possible. This is an outrageous notion but it comes naturally to politicians.

While economists feature rational actors calculating marginal utilities, rhetoric acknowledges a world of imponderables. That is why politicians are so often condemned to metaphor: "It is really not this, but rather something like that." The sociological model of politics is different still, looking to demography to explain political outcomes. Rhetoric also features people but it treats them more dynamically, as creatures who can be "hailed" in different ways. So, for example, John Kerry could not bring out the inner-city vote in 2004 but his comrade-in-arms, Barack Obama, did so quite magically in 2008. Rhetoric alone did not account for such differences, but it was part of the mix.

There are other models of politics as well: the psychological model featuring people's deep-seated needs, the historical model focusing on the great cycles of social change. Rhetoric seems small in the presence of such grand forces, but rhetoric is also a *behavioral* thing, a way of doing something when other options have been foreclosed. Tone, a tool people use (sometimes unwittingly) to create distinct social impressions via differential word choice, can reinscribe old truths in fresh ways and offer up entirely new considerations for the political agenda. Tone is natural to politics because it is centered in human relationships. Thinking carefully before saying something can forestall contentiousness, a fact that all diplomats learn sooner or later.

Looking at the world from a rhetorical vantage point lets us rethink age-old issues. Take, for example, the much-lamented "disconnect" between government and the governed in the United States. Authors who have studied such matters argue that growing economic gaps have marginalized the nation's poor (McCarty, Poole & Rosenthal, 2006), while others see a racial element in that disaffection (Kinder & Sanders, 1996). Scholars have also identified a growing gap between the well-informed and those who find politics a bore (Delli Carpini & Keeter, 1997). There are other explanations as well: Today's leaders are a cut below their predecessors (Lim, 2008); growing partisanship has made it hard to pass legislation (Fiorina & Abrams, 2009); politicians sell out to Big Business when taking office (Boggs, 2001); government has gotten so large that the average citizen has gotten lost (Stigler, 1975); and the mass media, once considered a linchpin between people and their leaders, have turned the former against the latter (Patterson, 1993).

All of these explanations for political disaffection are plausible, but rhetorical forces are at work as well. Consider, for example, the contrary slopes in figure 10.1. Here we see that politicians have increasingly focused on their own values and experiences over time and excused the electorate from their discussions. These lexical shifts have been subtle but steady. Politics has also become more technical, emphasizing global warming, credit default swaps, nuclear throw weights, and the like. As a result, politics now seems too specialized for many, and so they pull away. Despite these trends, however, politicians have also kept up a steady stream of happy talk (*celebrate, amazing, inspire, protect*). This odd mixture of go-away/come-hither might be contributing to voters' cynicism.[1]

Political tone is a small thing and American politics a very large thing indeed. But it makes little sense, we reason, to dismiss rhetorical facts out of hand. Our data are based on observable human behavior produced by multiple actors in a variety of social settings. Our evidence is based on "mere words," but that phrase too must be deconstructed. Why do so many of us feel we are more than our words? Why do we treat words as flotsam and jetsam lying atop tides that we alone control? Would it not be better to turn our words into questions, to wonder grandly, openly, about the secrets they hold? We will now try to do just that.

Tone: A Beckoning Concept

It is said, quite unscientifically, that birds sing sweetest at the edge of the forest. That has been our assumption as well. Scholarly work in interstitial areas—the spaces between disciplines, the spaces between methodologies and epistemologies—opens up ideas in especially provocative ways. Using a computer to study language patterns is only one such example. We have embraced that approach not because it provides definitive answers but because it opens up new vistas. Tone, a concept frequently discussed in literary studies but only rarely in the social sciences, deserves additional study. Our study leads us to identify seven domains that seem especially inviting.

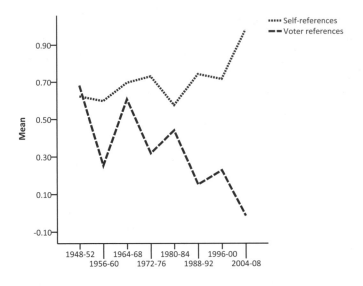

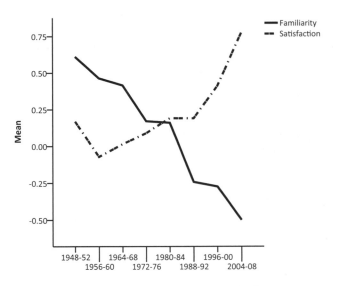

FIGURE 10.1 Tonal shifts in American politics: 1948–2008 (*n* = 5,529).

Tonal evolution

Language habits come from somewhere—from mother's knee, from ethnic or regional influences, from educational and religious training, from membership in voluntary societies. Language is Darwinian, constantly adjusting to new opportunities, new vicissitudes. Tracing a given verbal tone over time can therefore put new ideas on the table. We have found, for example, that Certainty has declined over the years. Why? Do politicians no longer have the strength of their convictions? Are they overwhelmed by a confusing, ever-changing world? Similarly, Mark Smith (2007) finds that economistic premises now dominate the discourses of both political parties (but for different reasons). Why do such tropes "chain out" over time? When is that good or bad?

Like anything Darwinian, some things come but other things go. For example, many women are now outraged that conservatives like Sarah Palin and Michele Bachmann draw on liberationist themes—self-determination, equal opportunity, etc.—to advance policies anathema to '60s feminists. Why do some of these hegemonic discourses loosen up over time and why do some maintain their edge? Why do once-radical mantras (Gandhi's "do or die" or the Black Panthers' "power to the people") become clichés in another era? Conversely, why do some linguistic constructions find instant acceptance—the Clinton campaign's "It's the economy, stupid" or Ronald Reagan's "morning in America"—despite their sometimes odd relationships to the facts?

Tonal strength

Political leadership depends on rhetoric—hardly a novel thought. But the devil is in the details. By definition, politicians are "boundary spanners," persons attempting to accommodate opposing groups. Yet as Pfau (2005) reports, it is a constant challenge for centrist leaders to reach right, then left, without losing their balance. How can we determine when they have gone too far? Banaszak's (2010) study of feminists working within the federal bureaucracy is a fascinating case in point, but she leaves us with several unanswered questions: How do state actors frame policies grounded in nonstate premises? What is the linguistic cost of bureaucratic involvement or, conversely, of adherence to a narrow political ideology? How can one lead without pandering, include without overincluding? All leaders face questions like these sooner or later.

This book has shown several ways in which language and leadership intersect, but more work needs to be done. Brandice Canes-Wrone (2005) argues that U.S. leaders often stake out bold policy positions, that they are not panderers and louts. But what does leadership actually *sound like* across cases? Leading requires rhetorical sensitivity (Hart & Burks, 1972), the ability to push for a mandate without inciting overreactions. This is delicate work. For leadership to take hold, abstract ideas (e.g., justice, equity, prudence) must be humanized, the logical intertwined with the emotional. As Hanmer (2009) observes, it takes more than structural reforms to advance voter recruitment, for example; it takes motivational reform as well. Exogenous forces like a nation's economy are undeniably powerful, says Vavreck (2009), but linguistic skill is required of our leaders to "handle" the economy appropriately. Tone is not everything but it is also not nothing.

Tonal equivalence

Leaders do not live alone. They live with a great many of their fellow citizens, and we need to know more about them as well. Public opinion surveys are helpful in that regard, and in a web-based world they are surely plentiful. But surveys cannot get at the assumptions underlying people's beliefs, nor at their latent values. Fortunately, wonderful work has been done by Walsh (2003), Lindquist (2002), Bryan (2003), and others, scholars brave enough to listen—carefully and on-site—to what the American people are saying. We need more such studies because, as Myers (2004) argues, opinions are really produced *between* people during their interactions with one another. At all other times, says Myers, attitudes are theoretical, not empirical, constructs.

Do voters learn from their leaders? Leaders from voters? Will the advent of the New Media increase the flow of information across the lay/ elite divide? Will leaders respond in kind or treat Twitter and Facebook as propaganda devices? The stakes here are real. A leader who cannot hear is ultimately a leader who cannot be heard, a fate amply proven in the Arab Spring of 2011. Grill's (2007) findings are crucial in this regard. He notes that governments are frequently responsive to public concerns but are often not seen as sufficiently involved. How to offset such perceptions? Find new ways of sharing, says Grill, because voters are largely proceduralists, people who want to be part of the action but who have less need to control actual outcomes.

heteroglossal

Tonal contagion

We now live in a world of intermediation where all messages mix and mingle, a world that drives originalists crazy. A question like "Who said that?" is now hard to answer. A question like "Who originally said that?" is impossible to answer. In such a world, tones become commodities easily appropriated by others. Suburban whites speak Urban Funk; country music plays well in Buffalo; valley girls are found in Des Moines. Politics produces these ventriloquistic effects as well. For example, Domke (2004) finds politicians borrowing religious refrains for patently sectarian adventures (like a war in the Middle East). Similarly, the genius of Fox News lies not so much in ideology as in the language of outrage it has popularized, a tone that begins with *Fox and Friends* in the morning and ends with Bill O'Reilly at night. The Fox Tone taps a cluster of attitudes— the world is unjust, conspiracies abound, the righteous are doomed—and hence packs a political punch.

Political messages also draw on the entertainment world: Sarah Palin makes a self-serving documentary about Alaska; Fred Thompson announces his presidential candidacy on the Leno show; all candidates worth their salt now have a YouTube channel. Admittedly, politics is meant to be a popular art, but at what cost? Do such free-wheeling messages advance leadership or degrade it? Take the example of former Congressman Anthony Wiener of New York. It was Twitter, we suggest, even more than sex, that seduced Wiener the seducer. Twitter made a public man feel private in public. The Twitter Tone—"It's just you and me"; "I'm not who I purport to be"; "We're alone together."—proved the congressman's undoing. Powerful stuff, that.

Tonal reach

A large and diverse democracy must continually ask if it is speaking a common language. As Kenneth Burke (1950) has said, to identify with another is to take that person's identity as your own, at least in part, at least for a while. Language is the magic that lets that happen, and so we must ask: Are leaders responding quickly enough to the nation's changing demographics? Are young people being brought into the fold? women? African-Americans? How does an aging white male give such people a sense of inclusion? And what of Hispanics and Asians, increasingly large constituencies with little or no mainstream political heritage? When engaging them politically, what should one say and how?

There is another side to this same coin—the danger of being dominated by factional interests. During the lead-up to the 2012 election, for example, former Senator Rick Santorum of Pennsylvania found it hard to be heard on economic issues because of his prior right-to-life rhetoric. Partisan loyalties must be continuously re-earned, says Nardulli (2005), but doing so can make one claustrophobic. Hillygus and Shields (2008) say that "bridge issues" can help leaders avoid such traps, but how does one reach out to new groups and maintain a sense of self? How can one speak another's language without seeming larcenous (Cosgrove, 2007)? Such questions will not go away in a growing heterogeneous nation like the United States.

Tonal rivalries

Studies of political reporting are popular but the results are often unsettling. Scholars find, for example, that voters often pick up the language of the press when talking about candidates (Kim & McCombs, 2007), a particular danger since reportage is often unspecific (Arnold, 2004) and profoundly cynical (Hart, 1994). Also, news coverage is breathless, particularly during election season. Campaign reports feature horse races and pugilistics, making deliberative democracy seem inertial in comparison. These tonalities may explain why Americans are typically dissatisfied with 434 members of the U.S. House, the only exception being their own local representative.

Bennett, Lawrence, and Livingston (2007) argue that reporters frequently tell the story that political leaders want told, but the reverse is also true: Politicians are dragged into the press's strategy-based discussions, which accomplish very little. Our studies, though, find a sharp difference between the tone of the average news story and the average political speech, and we find those results heartening. Given the overweening power of the First and Fourth Estates, these linguistic separations advance the cause of pluralism. No matter how persistent the press might be, a democracy is often best served when a politician says, "I'm not going there. Next question." In a nation prizing press freedoms, there will always be a next question.

Tone is not everything, but it is important. This is especially true in governance, where the difference between political positions is often slight. It is even truer in the United States, which tends to morselize things so that diverse constituencies can be obliged. Once the debates have ended and the laws written, tone takes over: "A shocking betrayal of basic American values," declares the right. "An outrageous betrayal of the people's will," responds the left. These are the sounds of political compromise.

But sometimes only one tone can be heard. On the stump, the candidates may scream and the candidates may bellow, but often the electorate just yawns, sensing that tone alone separates the candidates, that accommodationism reigns supreme. Voters complain about this uni-tone, turning to Lewis Carroll for help with their arguments:

1996: It is exceedingly distasteful to write this letter, but the facts won't blink away. We have two uninspiring candidates for president. Tweedle-dum and Tweedle-dee? (Dole stuck in the past, 1996)

2000: The site's prognosis is that Big Money has bought off the democratic process by funding the election, making it a contest between Tweedle-dum and Tweedle-dee, and choking the electorate by cutting off the oxygen of democracy. (Elton, 2000)

2004: Refraining from participation shouldn't be an option. The choice is clear—hold my nose and vote for Bush or Kerry. It will be a decision between Tweedle-dee and Tweedle-dum. How depressing! (Neither candidate is worthy, 2004)

2008: Many voters are sick and tired of voting for Tweedle-dee, the Democrat, or Tweedle-dumb, the Republican. Passionate, dedicated independents could take out the do-nothing politicians from the two major parties. (Brandenburg, 2008)

2011: Rand Paul and Paul Ryan have become the Tweedle-dee and Tweedle-dum of the GOP. These two guys were supposed to be the "deep thinkers" of the Republican Party, supposedly the Gingriches for our times, if you ever considered Newt one. (Death of the GOP?, 2011)

Tonal source

Most citizens, and many historians, treat leaders' public remarks as indices of their essential beings. There is something natural about this assumption—words as a window into the soul—and many intriguing psychobiographies have been written based in part on this premise (McAdams, 2010; A. Falk, 2010). But even a moment's reflection reveals that national-level politicians body forth others' words as well—those of their speechwriters—and so the route from verbalization to the Self is serpentine at best. For all practical purposes, claim Campbell and Jamieson (2008), an American president is a "corporate entity" who speaks the views of a syndicate of professional writers and policy wonks. While a chief executive may be involved in the creative process, and while good speechwriters adjust their lexicons and cadences to the "chief's" preferences and capacities, most speechmaking these days is a corporate product.[2]

And speechmaking is only part of the mix. A political administration is now a complex thing that includes traditional genres—position papers, press conferences, proclamations, declarations, announcements, signing statements—but also blogs, websites, streaming videos, and Twitter feeds. Can such a symphony contain a synchrony? Can a singular worldview develop across all these message platforms? If so, who or what produces that rhetorical discipline? If not, what do the disjunctions tell us? Do the continuities, or the discontinuities, best point up the special demands placed on a given politician or administration? And how many roles can a leader play without seeming distended or feckless? Can person and persona still be joined together, or has that become impossible in a busy media-centric age? Questions like these invite the use of tools like DICTION, tools that can patiently track, and remember, the *patterns* of political stimuli today's citizens are being asked to understand and appreciate.

Conclusion

Political tone is a funny thing. No, really. Without tone, humor would be impossible: "Yeah, Obama is cool. He is so cool that I feel like sometimes he must be on Xanax" (Maher quoted by Woods, 2009, para. 6). Without tone, the following statement would make no sense: "It's weird watching President Bush struggle with excuses for why we went to war. As he struggles, it reminds us all what a terrific liar Bill Clinton really was" (Kilborn, 2011). Without tone, even TV's Dana Carvey could not have channeled the nation's forty-second president: "I just wasn't funny as Clinton at the time; I had no hook in him. Later on, I got into my own rhythm with Clinton, where he does these throwaway digressions that are kind of self-congratulatory" (Heisler, 2009, para 49).

Tone is important not because it gives comedians a job but because it blends politics with humanity. Politicians can walk away from their spouses, their parties, and even their ideals but they cannot walk away from their tones, at least not easily. This is not to say that tones are appropriated at birth and returned in the afterlife. Instead, tones merge and morph, pushed about by cultural and personal forces. Because tones are also relational, they send out important signals: "I am one of you." "I am superior to you." "We are better together."

Throughout this book, we have asked embarrassingly basic questions—When people form impressions based on political tone, to what are they reacting? What, specifically, are they hearing? We have also asked: What makes politics political? Have campaigns changed? Do Republicans differ from Democrats? Why are political ads compelling? What distinguishes the news? The book has also touched on some of the knottiest choices facing the U.S.: A powerful but not-too-powerful chief executive; an active citizenry but one that acts judiciously; a watchdog press whose ministrations help rather than hinder governance; political arm twisting between Congress and the executive branch; debates that dramatize policy options or turn politics into a sideshow. Without tone, the political world would be opaque, or so we have argued here.

We have tried in this book to walk a tightrope between scientific description and thoughtful interpretations of voters' inchoate feelings. Tone is not an easy thing to describe but it is an easy thing to sense; connecting these experiences has been our job. When looking at tone, we have confronted questions of national identity, changing cultural dynamics, and both institutional and psychological pressures. Because it is a subtle thing, tone makes us suspicious but that does not mean it can be dismissed. Each day, people become upset by tone, crave new versions of it, admire it, savage it. Tone is mysterious, and it is unsettling because it is mysterious. Tone is a message about a message—that which is implied by that which is said. We have tried to read these messages carefully throughout this book. Still, a thousand questions beckon.

Notes

Chapter One

1. These and other popular refrains can be found in http://www.brainyquote .com/

2. For more playful works in this vein see Open Court Publishers' series on the philosophical dimensions of popular culture: http://www.opencourtbooks.com/ categories/pcp.htm. A more scholarly set of studies can be found in Routledge's series on the philosophical aspects of contemporary film: http://www.routledge .com/books/series/philosophers_on_film_PHILFILM/.

3. Portions of the following have been extracted and revised from Hart (2001b) and Hart (2000).

4. There are exceptions to the rule, of course, the most notable of whom is Mr. Frank Luntz, a political consultant who listens carefully and perceptively to what voters and politicians are saying. While Luntz has hardly produced a "grand theory" of political discourse, his observations are uncannily wise, often providing rich hypotheses that serious scholars might well explore further. See Luntz (2010) and Luntz (2006).

5. For a detailed description of DICTION's variables see Hart (2000), pp. 245–251.

6. These cities, regionally distributed throughout the United States and including a cross-section of political attitudes and demographic characteristics, are Fall River, Massachusetts; Utica, New York; Trenton, New Jersey; Roanoke, Virginia; Lake Charles, Louisiana; Wichita Falls, Texas; Springfield, Ohio; St. Joseph, Missouri; Duluth, Minnesota; Provo, Utah; Billings, Montana; and Salinas, California. Each has a population of approximately 100,000 persons.

Chapter Two

1. Clinton, acceptance speech at the Democratic National Convention, New York (July 16, 1992); Carter, address to the AFL-CIO at Dearborn, Mich. (September 15, 1976); Bush, campaign speech (October 30, 2000); Goldwater, nation-

ally broadcast speech on ABC-TV (October 9, 1964); Anderson, speech at the New York Liberal Party dinner, New York (October 9, 1980).

2. For more on these matters see Hart (1994).

3. The following scores are listed from highest Normality score to lowest within each genre. *Public dialogue*: political debates = 148.278; internet chat = 138.470; group discussion = 135.643; theater scripts = 133.337; phone conversations = 120.185. F [4, 958] = 81.827, *p* < .001. *Formal speechmaking*: political campaigns = 159.120; social movements = 158.372; White House = 157.809; mainstream religion = 151.146, corporate public relations = 149.822. F [4, 2437] = 44.137, *p* < .001. *Print news*: campaign news = 158.257; science reporting = 151.576; technology news = 146.882; financial news = 145.762. F [4, 7653] = 45.859, *p* < .001. *Television fare*: political news = 158.907; prime time drama = 133.911; prime time sitcoms = 133.133; product ads = 106.046. F [3, 1546] = 399.520, *p* < .001. *Personal expression*: letters to the editor = 142.270; poetry = 128.062; email = 127.797; song lyrics = 118.228. F [3, 6399] = 151.968, *p* < .001. *Professional commentary*: newspaper editorials = 144.277; polemical essays = 142.178; legal briefs = 134.667; annual reports = 118.400. F [3, 420] = 56.600, *p* < .001. *blogs*: political = 160.533; technological = 154.827; entertainment = 154.200; corporate = 153.387; personal = 148.480. F [4, 365] = 17.601, *p* < .001.

4. Maurizio Viroli has interesting things to say about how traditional politics changed (both operationally and rhetorically) when the State gained prominence in Western history. See Viroli (1992).

5. *Realism* for politicians = 52.1160; press = 47.8638; citizens = 49.5899. F [2, 23062] = 3020.477, *p* < .001.

6. *Optimism* for politicians = 50.9561; press = 49.0088; citizens = 49.0200. F [2, 23062] = 689.847, *p* < .001. *Certainty* for politicians = 49.2288; press = 48.1973; citizens = 48.2090. F [2, 23602] = 143.071, *p* < .001.

7. See Hansen, Kanthak & Victor, (2011) and Seligman (1998). We have also replicated these findings: *Optimism* for winning candidates = 50.9900, for losing candidates = 50.1743. F [1, 5604] = 73.012, *p* < .001.

8. *Commonality* for politicians = 49.808; press = 49.448; citizens = 49.408. F [2, 27673] = 43.566, *p* < .001. *Voter References* for politicians = 5.106; press = 3.872; citizens = 5.225. F [2, 27673] = 333.697, *p* < .001. *Self-references* for politicians = 12.870; press = 3.032; citizens = 7.057. F [2, 27673] = 3966.929, *p* < .001. *Party references* for politicians = 0.614; press = 2.253; citizens = 1.775. F [2, 27673] = 619.795, *p* < .001. *Leader references* for politicians = 3.073; press = 12.635; citizens = 6.308. F [2, 27673] = 3966.929, *p* < .001.

9. *Activity* for politicians = 50.385; press = 52.920; citizens = 49.175. F [2, 27673] = 1784.793, *p* < .001.

10. *Insistence* for politicians = 46.249; press = 70.292; citizens = 52.066. F [2, 27673] = 635.391, *p* < .001. *Religious references* for politicians = 12.870; press = 3.032; citizens = 7.057. F [2, 27673] = 3966.929, *p* < .001. *Patriotic references*

for politicians = 3.160; press = 1.039; citizens = 2.028. F [2, 27673] = 1051.635, $p < .001$.

Chapter Three

1. The authors deeply appreciate the help of Ms. Keri Thompson, who helped collect data for this chapter and who made useful theoretical suggestions as well.

2. *D-tone* for Democrats' speeches = 2.8574; for Republicans' speeches = 1.1954. F [1, 3695] = 121.665, $p < .001$. *R-tone* for Democrats' speeches = 1.9053; for Republicans' speeches = 3.6731. F [1, 3695] = 367.771, $p < .001$.

3. *D-tone* for Democrats' debates = 1.9421; for Republicans' debates = 1.0745 F [1, 847] = 21.205, $p < .001$. *R-tone* for Democrats' debates = 2.5860; for Republicans' debates = 3.3182. F [1, 3695] = 12.134, $p < .001$. *D-tone* for Democrats' ads = 3.5849; for Republicans' ads = 1.7743. F [1, 678] = 25.658, $p < .001$. *R-tone* for Democrats' ads = 1.3132; for Republicans' ads = 2.6378. F [1, 678] = 12.741, $p < .001$.

4. *RDD* for victorious Democrats = 1.5420; for losing Democrats = 2.3933. F [1, 1684] = 18.141, $p < .001$. *RDD* for victorious Republicans = 5.0766; for losing Republicans = 4.2150. F [1, 1684] = 19.186, $p < .001$.

5. *R-tone* for Republican incumbents = 3.9373; for challengers = 2.9649. F [1, 2358] = 51.178, $p < .001$. *D-tone* for Democratic incumbents = 3.1242; for challengers = 2.7259. F [1, 2298] = 8.201, $p < .004$.

6. For more on the party branding issue see Jarvis (2005).

7. For a listing of the speeches analyzed in this section see chapter 9 note 13.

8. *D-tone* for Democrats' speeches = 3.0606; for conventional Republicans' speeches = 2.4897; for independents' speeches = 1.0467; for Tea Party speeches = 2.0357. F [3, 1392] = 15.929, $p < .001$. *R-tone* for Democrats' speeches = −1.2442; for conventional Republicans' speeches = 0.3732; for independents' speeches = −0.7649; for Tea Party speeches = .0029. F [3, 1392] = 26.617, $p < .001$.

9. *RDD* for Democrats' speeches = 1.9380; for Republicans' speeches = 4.7678; for political rants = −0.4358. F [2, 3975] = 315.168, $p < .001$.

10. *D-tone* for Democrats' speeches = 2.8412; for Republicans' speeches = 1.9942; for religious sermons = 0.0830; for corporate speeches = 0.4254; for protest speeches = 2.0332. F [4, 4737] = 85.050, $p < .001$. *R-tone* for Democrats' speeches =1.7562; for Republicans' speeches = 3.4938; for religious sermons = 4.6164; for corporate speeches = 0.4820; for protest speeches = 0.4243. F [4, 4737] = 144.423, $p < .001$.

11. *R-tone* for Republican debates = 3.3182; for ads = 2.6378; for speeches = 3.6731. F [2, 2687] = 11.312, $p < .001$. *D-tone* for Republican debates = 1.0745; for ads = 1.7743; for speeches = 1.9053. F [2, 2687] = 16.632, $p < .001$. *R-tone* for Democratic debates = 2.5860; for ads = 1.3132; for speeches = 1.7954. F [2, 2533] = 28.848,

$p < .001$. *D-tone* for Democratic debates = 1.9421; for ads = 3.5849; for speeches = 2.8574. F [2, 2533] = 19.193, $p < .001$.

Chapter Four

1. Portions of this chapter have been drawn from Hart & Lim (2011).

2. In our sample, Spatial terms ranged from 0 to 90, with a standard deviation of 6.9. For Temporal terms, the range was 0 to 125 and the standard deviation was 8.6.

3. These epochal changes are most apparent for the press, followed by politicians and letter writers. *Time-space ratio* for press: 1940s = −.4526; 1950s = −.0452; 1960s = −.2995; 1970s = −.0288; 1980s = .2960; 1990s = .4712; 2000s = .1866. F [6, 24233] = 87.749, $p < .001$. For politicians: 1940s = −.3492; 1950s = .0354; 1960s = −.4155; 1970s = −.1525; 1980s = .0290; 1990s = .2318; 2000s = −.1691. F [6, 5100] = 19.548, $p < .001$. For letter writers: 1940s = −.3714; 1950s = −.1246; 1960s = −.2761; 1970s = −.3149; 1980s = −.1300; 1990s = −.0983; 2000s = −.3067. F [6, 7512] = 5.152, $p < .001$.

4. Given this study's large N, it is not surprising that an effect for the time-space ratio was found. But the sheer magnitude of that effect is truly impressive: *Time-space ratio* for print reportage = .0472; for broadcast news = .7022. F [1, 13407] = 445.257, $p < .001$.

5. *Time-space ratio* for debates = −.3491; for ads = .2583; for speeches = −.0156. F [2, 5526] = 37.899, $p < .001$.

6. There is considerable statistical difference in the time-space ratios for the three voices examined here: letter writers = −.2071; politicians = −.0399; press = .1630. F [2, 27159] = 175.918, $p < .001$.

7. *Time-space ratio* when campaigning = .0595; when governing = .4257. F [1, 1254] = 38.984, $p < .001$.

8. *Time-space ratio* for during the main campaign = .−.1116; during the last 2 weeks = .1343. F [1, 3714] = 31.199, $p < .001$.

9. *Time-space ratio* for Republicans = −.2150; for Democrats = .1862. F [1, 3695] = 92.732, $p < .001$.

10. *Time-space ratio* for Obama = .4881; for McCain = −.2229. F [1,512] = 39.392, $p < .001$.

11. *Time-space ratio* for Bush in 2000 campaign = .0830; for Bush in 2004 campaign = −.5337. F [1, 962] = 33.202, $p < .001$.

Chapter Five

1. These general subjects included a variety of subtopics. These included: (1) foreign affairs: terrorism, defense spending, homeland defense, regional conflicts, disarmament treaties, foreign aid, war crimes, and trade embargoes; (2) domestic economy: taxation, unemployment, spending priorities, inflation, deficit reduction, economic stimulus, and interest rates; (3) international trade: trade agreements, protectionism, environmental treaties, trade imbalances, loss of jobs and

job retraining, free vs. fair trade; (4) domestic problems: immigration and border protection, Social Security, health care reform, welfare reform, school prayer, farm policy, energy policy, veterans benefits, environmental protection, property rights, education, drug policy, domestic violence; (5) human values: memorials, eulogies, holiday well-wishes, anniversaries; voluntarism; (6) partisan politics: political scandal, candidate or party endorsements, administration defenses and apologies, judicial controversies, the congressional agenda.

2. Our coding rules were quite straightforward. *References to the president* were taken literally, thereby excluding references to the chief executive's party (e.g., "Republicans") but including references to "the president," the "administration," and "the White House." During lame-duck presidencies, it was common for the respondent to engage the president-elect and not the sitting president. In these instances, we stuck with the literal coding rule of "no reference."

Because the speeches were all quite short and inevitably on a single subject, there was little ambiguity about the *President's topical focus*. Occasionally, we confronted cases where the president and the respondent addressed the same general topic (e.g., "the economy") but took it in totally different directions (e.g., "lower taxes" vs. "more jobs"). In those cases, we coded it as a "different topic." In speeches described as *No reference/multiple topics*, an uninformed audience would be unable to tell from the text that the speech had been given as a response to the president.

3. For *Insistence*: policy speeches = 40.5100; campaign speeches = 44.9504; radio addresses = 57.2953. $F[2, 2208] = 29.190, p < .001$.

4. For *Insistence*: presidents = 57.1521; respondents = 66.9340. $F[1, 1090] = 11.335, p < .001$.

5. For *Commonality*: policy speech = 50.1058; campaign speech = 50.2268; weekend address = 51.0249. $F[2, 2208] = 22.485, p < .001$. For *Optimism*: policy speech = 50.6922; campaign speech = 51.1700; weekend address = 52.1417. $F[2, 2208] = 58.337, p < .001$.

6. For *Realism*: policy speech = 51.2036; campaign speech = 52.5223; weekend address = 51.0249. $F[2, 2208] = 48.013, p < .001$. For *Personal narrative*: policy speech = 1.2577; campaign speech = 2.3467; weekend address = 1.0693. $F[2, 2208] = 97.035, p < .001$. *Personal narrative* is a composite measure built from several of DICTION's individual variables. Personal narratives were defined as a speaker's descriptions of social activities occurring at some particular time and place. After standardization, the following variables were combined to produce this index: Self-references + Human Interest + Temporal terms + Motion + Spatial terms. For a more robust explication of this construct see Hart & Lind (2011).

7. George W. Bush, surprisingly, was the most Optimistic (Reagan = 50.8272; Clinton = 51.8370; Bush43 = 53.4722. $F[2, 516] = 14.158, p < .001$), while Bill Clinton was higher on Commonality (Reagan = 50.4180; Clinton = 51.7142; Bush43 = 50.6854. $F[2, 516] = 8.160, p < .001$) and especially on Realism (Reagan = 50.0575;

Clinton = 52.7623; Bush43 = 50.8331. F[2, 516] = 42.290, p < .001). Mostly, though, the crisp, upbeat tone of the weekend addresses remained the same across presidencies and during the individual chief executives' tenures in office as well.

8. For *Optimism*: presidents = 52.5183; respondents = 51.0964. F [1, 1088] = 9.945, p < .001. For *Personal Narrative*: presidents = 1.0989; respondents = 0.3441. F [1, 1088] = 22.092, p < .001.

Chapter Six

1. Portions of this chapter have been drawn from Hart & Sawyer (2003).

2. *Realism* score for Truman = 51.4788; Eisenhower = 51.9350; Kennedy = 52.9772; Johnson = 52.5697; Nixon = 53.4109; Ford = 52.6618; Carter = 50.4556; Reagan = 51.1703; Bush Sr. = 50.8216; Clinton = 53.4508; GWBush = 51.6758; Obama = 51.6730. F [11, 2659] = 12.523, p < .001. *Commonality* score for Truman = 50.4031; Eisenhower = 49.8323; Kennedy = 49.8657; Johnson = 49.4025; Nixon = 49.3897; Ford = 50.0651; Carter = 49.9030; Reagan = 49.7911; Bush Sr. = 49.2875; Clinton = 50.3041; GWBush = 49.4638; Obama = 50.6146. F [11, 2659] = 24.083, p < .001.

3. In a few important ways, Clinton's "impeachment speeches" differed from a random sampling of his policy addresses, although the August 17 speech was by far the most exceptional. The following data for DICTION's master variables show the kinds of adaptations he was forced to make when addressing the Lewinsky situation: *Realism* score for crisis speeches = 44.6606; policy speeches = 53.0567. F [1, 61] = 87.838, p < .001. *Certainty* for crisis speeches = 46.2311; policy speeches = 49.8647. F [1, 61] = 35.594, p < .001. *Commonality* for crisis speeches = 49.7128; policy speeches = 50.1618. F [1, 61] = 0.472, p < .495. *Activity* for crisis speeches = 49.1489; policy speeches = 50.3180. F [1, 61] = 2.805, p < .001. *Optimism* for crisis speeches = 44.6328; policy speeches = 51.2487. F [1, 61] = 3.968, p < .050.

Chapter Seven

1. Bush's topical breakdown for his 2,228 speeches was as follows: education (3.1%), national defense (26.5%), human values (25.4%), law & order (5.4%), health & science (9.1%), economy (24.4%), and other topics (6.1%).

2. The data reported here include campaign speeches (n = 2,511), televised ads (n = 655), and campaign debates (n = 820).

3. DICTION amply captured these differences: *Hortatory Tone* for 2000 campaign = −1.2449; 2004 campaign = 0.5891. F [1, 289] = 65.429, p < .001.

4. *Hortatory Tone* for briefings = −1.1244, rallies = 1.0636, ceremonies = −.0516, [2, 1636] = 90.607, p < .001. This caution on Bush's part can also be seen in his avoidance of overstatements in pluralistic settings: *Hortatory Tone* for governmental audiences = 0.1530, national audiences = −1.1599, local or invited audiences = 0.7806, [2, 2,225] = 127.286, p < .001.

5. In addition to the foregoing, the other critiques of Bush analyzed in this

study include Merskin (2004), Parry-Giles (2008), Smith (2008), Spring & Packer (2009), and Zarefsky (2004).

6. F [1, 297] = 130.896, $p < .001$.

7. *Optimism* for Original Bush = 48.6882; Excerpted Bush = 54.8186. F [1, 297] = 19.128, $p < .001$. *Commonality* for Original Bush = 47.4955; Excerpted Bush = 51.2420. F [1, 297] = 16.042, $p < .001$.

8. From Winokur (1990, pp. 89–109).

9. When Mr. Bush's "most important" speeches are contrasted to the overall Bush dataset, we find that the former are significantly more hortatory than the latter, thereby suggesting that both scholars and the press have been generalizing too hastily when describing Mr. Bush's rhetorical habits. *Hortatory Tone* for important speeches = 2.7996, for all other speeches = –.0473, [1, 2,226] = 33.935, $p < .001$.

Chapter Eight

1. The comparisons presented here result from the overall dataset for the Campaign Mapping Project described in chapter 1. *Optimism* for 1948–2004: print coverage = 49.0159; political speeches = 51.0603. F [1, 13228] = 1707.365, $p < .001$. For 2008 only: print coverage = 48.9575; political speeches = 49.9395. F [1, 1708] = 30.671, $p < .001$.

2. *Hortatory tone* for Democrats: predecessors = .8505; Obama = –.7884. F [1, 1673] = 18.065, $p < .001$. For Republicans: predecessors = 1.3293; McCain = –.1557. F [1, 1708] = 24.686, $p < .001$.

3. *Realism* for Obama: primary = 50.6970; general = 53.2248. F [1, 300] = 44.417, $p < .001$. For McCain: primary = 48.8475; general = 52.0738. F [1, 172] = 44.530, $p < .001$.

4. *Insistence* for Obama: primary = 20.2703; general = 41.6417. F [1, 300] = 24.775, $p < .001$. For McCain: Primary = 27.8737; General = 53.2420, F [1, 172] = 16.283, $p < .001$).

5. *Time-space ratio* for Obama: primary = –1.1661; general = .6171. F [1, 300] = 87.401, $p < .001$. For McCain: primary = –1.2238; general = –.1144. F [1, 172] = 36.496, $p < .001$.

6. *Realism*: prior Ds = 52.4902; Obama = 53.2248. F [1, 1684] = 12.804, $p < .001$. *Optimism*: prior Ds = 50.7801; Obama = 49.7412. F [1, 1684] = 20.624, $p < .001$. *Commonality*: prior Ds = 50.1226; Obama = 51.1208. F [1, 1684] = 34.913, $p < .001$. *Hortatory Tone*: prior Ds = –1.8096; Obama = –.0377. F [1, 1684] = 115.153, $p < .001$.

7. *Embellishment*: prior Ds = .5921; Obama = .3863. F [1, 1684] = 212.699, $p < .001$.

8. *Embellishment*: McCain = 1.1293; Obama = .3863. F [1, 512] = 11.957, $p < .001$.

9. *Self-references*: McCain = 17.0737; Obama = 12.8088. F [1, 512] = 29.587, $p < .001$.

10. *Hortatory Tone* for Obama: campaign speeches = –.9945; governing

speeches = .8096. F [1, 671] = 122.661, p < .001. *Realism*: campaign speeches = 52.7483; governing speeches = 50.8166. F [1, 665] = 77.345, p < .001.

11. *Optimism* for Obama: campaign speeches = 49.7539; governing speeches = 51.4441. F [1, 665] = 31.651, p < .001.

12. *Self-references* for Obama: campaign speeches = 12.8022; governing speeches = 9.1731. F [1, 665] = 29.760, p < .001. *Embellishment*: campaign speeches = .4099; governing speeches = .5698. F [1, 665] = 43.085, p < .001.

13. *Hortatory Tone* for earlier presidents: campaign speeches = .9998; governing speeches = 1.3240. F [1, 1254] = 7.635, p < .006. *Self-references*: campaign speeches = 12.2530; governing speeches = 8.3732. F [1, 1254] = 75.487, p < .001. *Embellishment*: campaign speeches = .5882; governing speeches = .6860. F [1, 1254] = 8.835, p < .003. *Realism*: campaign speeches = 52.6835; governing speeches = 51.2036. F [1, 1254] = 94.458, p < .006.

14. *Commonality* for Obama: campaign speeches = 50.8588; governing speeches = 50.4134. F [1, 665] = 7.824, p < .005.

15. Obama's drop in urgency was barely noticeable. Still, it may have registered on some as a sign of slight disengagement from the issues. For *time-space ratio*: campaign speeches = .1245; governing speeches = –.1014. F [1, 671] = 3.809, p < .05.

Chapter Nine

1. For additional commentary on how Palin's ambition leads her astray see Egan (2010), Dunn (2011), Tanenhaus (2009), Goldstein & Shear (2008), Miller (2010), and Sirota (2011).

2. Sources for the Palin texts analyzed are as follows: See http://www.palintv .com for Women of Joy speech, Louisville, 4/10/10; remarks for McCain senatorial campaign, Tucson, 3/26/10; key to the city speech, Peoria, 4/21/10; speech on behalf of Rick Perry, Houston, 2/7/10; Memorial Day remarks, Fairbanks, 2/13/10; Right to Life address, Evansville, 1/11/10; Tea Party rally, Searchlight, Nevada, 3/27/10; Seward House address, Auburn, New York, 6/6/09; Michael Reagan intro, Anchorage, 6/3/09. See http://www.lexisnexis.com for Charlie Rose interview, 10/12/07; VP candidate debut, Dayton, 8/29/08; campaign speech in Clearwater, Florida, 10/6/08. See http://www.c-spanvideo.org for Restoring Honor Rally with Glenn Beck, 8/27/10; speech to the Southern Republican Leadership Conference, New Orleans, 4/9/10; Tea Party speech, Nashville, 2/6/10. See http://www.foxnews.com for Glenn Beck interview, 1/13/10; Chris Wallace interview, 2/7/10; Sean Hannity interview, 4/27/10. See http://elections.nytimes.com/ for RNC nomination acceptance speech, 9/3/08. See http://www.standardnewswire.com/news for weekly radio address, 9/8/08. See http://abcnews.go.com/Politics/Vote2008 for Charles Gibson interview, 9/13/08. See http://www.cbsnews.com/stories for Katie Couric interview, 9/24/08. See http://www.hughhewitt.com/transcripts for Hugh Hewitt interview, 9/30/08. See http://www.debates.org for vice-presidential debate, 10/3/08. See http://www.canada.com/calgaryherald/story.htm for Nicholas Sarkozy prank call,

11/1/08. See http://www.americanrhetoric.com/speeches for Governors Association address, Miami, 11/15/08. See http://transcripts.cnn.com for Wolf Blitzer interview, CNN, 6/12/2009.

3. *Insistence* for Democrats = 46.272; prior Republicans = 46.307; Palin = 28.260. $F [2, 3504] = 23.074, p < .001$.

4. *Insistence* for Democrats = 46.272; for Republicans = 46.307; for independents = 34.070. $F [2, 3537] = 12.440, p < .001$.

5. *Insistence* during primaries = 23.769; during general election = 45.540. $F [1, 474] = 36.543, p < .001$.

6. *Insistence* for victors in primary = 23.769; for losers in primary = 34.833. $F [1, 295] = 12.886, p < .001$.

7. *Insistence* for George W. Bush on technical topics = 65.192; on axiological topics = 56.051. $F [1, 2089] = 26.693, p < .001$.

8. *Insistence* for George W. Bush in briefings = 64.755; in rallies = 58.357. $F [1, 1923] = 13.654, p < .001$.

9. *Insistence* for George W. Bush in press conferences = 65.730; in invited addresses = 58.520. $F [1, 1994] = 17.132, p < .001$.

10. Daniel Kies (1990, p. 243) notes that parataxis usually implies an "equality of the information foci" on the part of the speaker.

11. One is reminded in this context of Richard Hofstadter's (1966) observation that many Americans have an anti-intellectual strain that makes people like Sarah Palin appealing precisely because she confesses to none of the scholarly mysteries.

12. Being raised in an era of constant technological disruptions, rapidly shifting sources of authority, changing aesthetic standards, and a cultural willingness to try ever-new things, Sarah Palin is a postmodern child or, as Zygmunt Bauman would have it, a child of liquid modernity. Says Bauman (2005, p. 2): "Liquid life is a precarious life, lived under conditions of constant uncertainty. The most acute and stubborn worries that haunt such a life are the fears of being caught napping, of failing to catch up with fast-moving events, of being left behind, of overlooking 'use by' dates, of being saddled with possessions that are no longer desirable, of missing the moment that calls for a change of tack before crossing the point of no return. Liquid life is a succession of new beginnings—yet precisely for that reason it is the swift and painless endings, without which new beginnings would be unthinkable." Out of all this we get Sarah Palin (and much else).

13. The speeches analyzed in this portion of the study include the following: Sharron Angle, speech in Gardnerville, Nevada, October 10, 2010; Michele Bachmann, speech at Living Word Christian Center, Minneapolis, October 14, 2006; Jim DeMint, CPAC speech in Washington, February 18, 2010; Joseph Farah, *The Tea Party Manifesto*, March 18, 2010; Steve Farber, *The Tea Party Revolution: A Manifesto*, December 5, 2009; Nikki Haley, Fox TV, *On the Record*, June 23, 2010; Terri Hall, address to the San Antonio Tea Party, San Antonio, April 15, 2009; James Keena, speech at a Tea Party rally in Kellogg Park, Plymouth, MI, April 22, 2009;

Joe Miller, CNN interview with John King, October 19, 2010; Christine O'Donnell, concession speech in Delaware, November 2, 2010; Rand Paul, victory speech in Kentucky, November 2, 2010; Mike Pence, Taxpayer March on Washington, September 14, 2009; Paul Rickert, Tax Day speech, April 15, 2009; Marco Rubio, CPAC speech in Washington, February 18, 2010; and Tom Tancredo, Tea Party speech in Nashville, February 5, 2009. URLs for these texts can be obtained from the authors upon request.

14. *Democratic tone* for Democrats = 3.9215; for Republicans = 2.8236; for Tea Party = 2.0357. F [2, 2670] = 34.752, $p < .001$. *Republican tone* for Democrats = 2.1082; for Republicans = 3.5164; for Tea Party = 3.0092. F [2, 2670] = 61.881, $p < .001$.

Chapter Ten

1. *Familiarity* for 1948–52 = 0.611; for 1956–60 = 0.464; for 1964–68 = 0.415; for 1972–76 = 0.171; for 1980–84 = 0.160; for 1988–92 = –0.241; for 1996–2000 = –0.273; for 2004–8 = –0.499. F [7, 5521] = 116.836, $p < .001$. *Satisfaction* for 1948–52 = 0.169; for 1956–60 = –0.071; for 1964–68 = 0.154; for 1972–76 = 0.090; for 1980–84 = 0.191; for 1988–92 = 0.191; for 1996–2000 = 0.411; for 2004–8 = 0.774. F [7, 5521] = 41.481, $p < .001$. *Self-references* for 1948–52 = 0.623; for 1956–60 = 0.652; for 1964–68 = 0.696; for 1972–76 = 0.726; for 1980–84 = 0.661; for 1988–92 = 1.050; for 1996–2000 = 0.858; for 2004–8 = 1.013. F [7, 5521] = 13.651, $p < .001$. *Voter references* for 1948–52 = 0.682; for 1956–60 = 0.252; for 1964–68 = 0.607; for 1972–76 = 0.319; for 1980–84 = 0.441; for 1988–92 = 0.152; for 1996–2000 = 0.228; for 2004–8 = –0.014. F [7, 4614] = 27.288, $p < .001$.

2. For more on these matters see Medhurst (2003).

References

Aberbach, J. D., & Rockman, B. A. (1999). Hard times for presidential leadership? (And how would we know?). *Presidential Studies Quarterly, 29,* 757–777.

Abrams, M. H. (1992). *A glossary of literary terms* (6th ed.). Fort Worth: Harcourt Brace.

Achter, P. J. (2000). Narrative, intertextuality, and apologia in contemporary political scandals. *Southern Communication Journal, 65,* 318–333.

Ackland, R. (2005). *Mapping the U.S. political blogosphere: Are conservative bloggers more prominent?* Paper presented at BlogTalk Downunder 2005, Sydney. Retrieved from http://voson.anu.edu.au/papers/polblogs.pdf

Adam, B. (1995). *TimeWatch: The social analysis of time.* Cambridge: Polity Press.

Adams, H. (1952). *Democracy: An American novel.* New York: Farrar, Strauss & Young, Inc.

Agger, M. (2011, April 27). Turning words into touchdowns: Does a player's speech predict how he'll perform in the NFL? *Slate.* Retrieved from http://www.slate.com/id/2292312/

Alexander, L. (2009, April 25). Response to the president's radio address. *Federal News Service.* Retrieved from http://www.fnsg.com/transcript.htm?id=20090425t1374&nquery=&query=alexander&from=

Allan, N. (2010, March 1). What is Sarah Palin worth? *Atlantic.* Retrieved from http://www.theatlantic.com/business/archive/2010/03/what-is-sarah-palin-worth/36814//

Allen, J. (2011, May 21). The Gingrich "gaffe." *Huffington Post.* Retrieved from http://www.huffingtonpost.com/jodie-allen/the-gingrich-gaffe_b_864931.html

Allen, M. (2002, September 6). On the campaign trail, Bush boosts his domestic policies. *The Washington Post,* p. A5.

Allison, J. R., & Hunter, S. D. (2006). The feasibility of improving patent quality one technology at a time: The case of business methods. *Berkeley Technical Law Journal, 21,* 729–794.

Alter, J. (1998, September 21). Spinning out of sinning. *Newsweek, 132,* 45.

Alter, J. (2010). *The promise: President Obama, year one*. New York: Simon & Schuster.

America, M. (2011, July 21). Bi-partisan war on the Tea Party and Sarah Palin [Web log post]. Retrieved from http://markamerica.com/2011/07/31/bi-partisan -war-on-the-tea-party-and-sarah-palin/

Anderson, B. (1983). *Imagined communities: Reflections on the origin and spread of nationalism*. New York: Verso.

Anderson, J. (1980, September 11). Address to employers and employees. Redondo Beach, California. Housed in the Campaign Mapping database at http://keywords.communication.utexas.edu/keywords

Anderson, R. D. (2007). Discourse and the export of democracy. *St. Antony's International Review, 2*, 18–34.

Andreeva, N. (2009, September 4). Will Obama get big four support for health care speech?. *Adweek*. Retrieved from http://www.adweek.com/news/television/will -obama-get-big-four-support-health-care-speech-113381

Ansolabehere, S., & Iyengar, S. (1995). *Going negative: How attack ads shrink and polarize the electorate*. New York: Free Press.

Appel, E. C. (2003). Rush to judgment: Burlesque, tragedy, and hierarchal alchemy in the rhetoric of America's foremost political talkshow host. *Southern Communication Journal, 68*(3), 217.

Arnold, R. D. (2004). *Congress, the press, and political accountability*. Princeton: Princeton University Press.

Auletta, K. (2010, January 25). Non-stop news: With cable, the Web, and tweets, can the president—or the press—still control the story? *New Yorker,* 38.

Auzenne, M. (2008, September 9). Palin's appeal (blog post). *Democracy for America*. Retrieved from https://secure.democracyforamerica.com/blog_posts /26659-palins-appeal

Bai, M. (2010a, May 20). Voter insurrection turns mainstream, creating new rules. *New York Times*, p. A13.

Bai, M. (2010b, June 8). Democrat in Chief? *New York Times Magazine*. 34ff.

Baker, P. (2008, August 31). Storm politics present risks and rewards. *New York Times*. Retrieved from http://www.nytimes.com/2008/09/01/world /americas/01iht-01memo.15782144.html .

Balz, D. (2010, January 10). For Obama, a tough year to get the message out. *Washington Post*. Retrived from http://www.washingtonpost.com/wp-dyn/content /article/2010/01/09/AR2010010902198.html

Banaszak, L. A. (2010). *The women's movement inside and outside the state*. Cambridge: Cambridge University Press.

Barber, J .D. (1992). *The presidential character: Predicting performance in the White House* (4th ed.). Englewood Cliffs, N.J.: Prentice Hall.

Barnhart, A. (2001, November 26). The little picture: Bush no match for "must see TV"—maybe president should have checked listings. *Electronic Media*, 9.

Bashor, H. (2004). Content analysis of short, structured texts: The need for multi-faceted strategies. *Journal of Diplomatic Language, 1*(4), 1–13.

Bastedo, R. W., & Lodge, M. (1980). The meaning of party labels. *Political Behavior, 2*(3), 287–308.

Bauman, Z. (2005). *Liquid Life*. Malden, Mass.: Polity Press.

Baumer, D. C., & Gold, H. J. (1995). Party images and the American electorate. *American Politics Quarterly, 23*(1), 33–61.

Beasley, V. B. (2004). *You, the people: American national identity in presidential rhetoric*. College Station: Texas A&M University Press.

Beem, C. (1999). *The necessity of politics: Reclaiming American public life*. Chicago: University of Chicago Press.

Bell, C. M., McCarthy, P. M., & McNamara, D. S. (2012). Using LIWC and Coh-Metrix to investigate gender differences in linguistic styles. In McCarthy, P. M., & Boonthum-Deneche, C. (Eds.). *Applied natural language processing: Identification, investigation, and resolution*. Hershey, PA: Information Science Reference.

Bellah, R. N. (1992). *The broken covenant: American civil religion in time of trial* (2nd ed.). Chicago: University of Chicago Press.

Bellah, R. N., Madsen, R., Sullivan, W. M., Swidler, A., & Tipton, S. M. (1991). *The good society*. New York: Knopf.

Benedict, R. (1989). *Patterns of culture*. Boston: Houghton Mifflin, c. 1934.

Bennett, W. L., Lawrence, R. G., & Livingston, S. (2007). *When the press fails: Political power and the news media from Iraq to Katrina*. Chicago: University of Chicago Press.

Benoit, K., Laver, M., & Mikhaylov, S. (2009). Treating words as data with error: Uncertainty in text statements of policy positions. *American Journal of Political Science, 53*(2), 495–513.

Benoit, W. L. (1995). *Accounts, excuses, and apologies: A theory of image restoration strategies*. Albany: State University of New York Press.

Benoit, W. L. (2004). Political party affiliation and presidential campaign discourse. *Communication Quarterly 52*(2), 81–97.

Benoit, W. L., & Henson, J. R. (2009). A functional analysis of the 2008 vice presidential debate: Biden versus Palin. *Argumentation and Advocacy, 46*(1), 39–50.

Benoit, W. L., & McHale, J. P. (1999). Kenneth Starr's image repair discourse viewed in 20/20. *Communication Quarterly, 4*, 265–280.

Black, E. (1978). The sentimental style as escapism, or the devil with Dan'l Webster." In K. K. Campbell & K. H. Jamieson (Eds.), *Form and genre* (pp. 75–86). Washington: National Communication Association.

Bligh, M. C., Kohles, J. C., & Meindl, J. R. (2004). Charisma under crisis: Presidential leadership, rhetoric, and media responses before and after the September 11th terrorist attacks. *Leadership Quarterly, 15*, 211–239.

Boder, D. P. (1940). The adjective-verb quotient: a contribution to the psychology of language. *Psychological Record, 3*, 310–343.

Boggs, C. (2001). *The end of politics: Corporate power and the decline of the public sphere.* New York: Guildford Press.

Borchert, J., & Zeiss, J. (2004). *The political class in advanced democracies.* New York: Oxford University Press.

Boskin, J. (1997). American political humor: Touchables and taboos. In J. Boskin (Ed.), *The humor prism in twentieth century America* (pp. 71–84). Detroit: Wayne State University Press.

Bostdorff, D. M. (2003). George W. Bush's post–September 11 rhetoric of covenant renewal: Upholding the faith of the greatest generation. *Quarterly Journal of Speech, 89*(4), 293–319.

Bowden, G. (2010). Obama, Palin, and Weber: Charisma and social change in the 2008 U.S. election. *Canadian Review of Sociology, 47*, 171–190.

Bowley, G. (2010, December 22). Computers that trade on the news. *New York Times.* Retrieved from http://dealbook.nytimes.com/2010/12/23/computers -that-trade-on-the-news/

Boyarin, J. (1994). Space, time, and the politics of memory." In J. Boyarin (ed.), *Remapping memory: The politics of TimeSpace* (pp. 1–38). Minneapolis: University of Minnesota Press.

Boyer, P. J. (1988, February 3). Networks refuse to broadcast Reagan's plea. *New York Times,* p. 10. Retrieved from http://www.lexisnexis.com

Boynton, G. R., & Lodge, M. (1994). Voters' images of candidates. In A. Miller & B. Gronbeck (Eds.), *Presidential campaigns and American self-images* (pp. 176–189). Boulder, CO: Westview.

Bradley, W. (1982, October 16). Response to the President's radio address. United Press International. Retrieved from http://www.lexisnexis.com

Brainerd, C. J., & Reyna, V. F. (1993). Memory independence and memory interference in cognitive development. *Psychological Review, 100*, 42–67.

Brandenburg, L. H. (2008, September 17). A winning third-party strategy should target U.S. House [opinion]. *San Jose Mercury News.* Retrieved from http://www.lexisnexis.com

Brewer, M. D. (2005). The rise of partisanship and the expansion of partisan conflict within the American electorate. *Political Research Quarterly, 58,* 219–229.

Brewer, M. D. (2009). *Party images in the American electorate.* New York: Routledge.

Brewer, M. D., & Stonecash, J. (2009). *Dynamics of American political parties.* New York: Cambridge University Press.

Broder, D. (2008, November 2). The amazing race. *Washington Post.* Retrieved from http://www.lexisnexis.com

Bromwich, D. (2010, November 25). The rebel germ. *New York Review of Books,*

57(18). Retreived from http://www.nybooks.com/articles/archives/2010/nov/25/rebel-germ/

Brooks, D. (2007, August 17). The ascent of a common man. *New York Times*, A23.

Brovero, A. F. (2000). 13 angry men: Dale Bumper's ad hominem impeachment trial of President Clinton. *Argumentation and Advocacy, 36*, 218–226.

Brummett, B. (2008). *A rhetoric of style*. Carbondale: Southern Illinois University Press.

Brunschwig, K. (2009). *How did John McCain and Barack Obama run their campaign in 2008 compared to Franklin Roosevelt and Herbert Hoover in 1932 in the same context of economic crisis?* Paper presented at the annual meeting of the Midwest Political Science Association, Chicago.

Bryan, F. (2003). *Real democracy: The New England town meeting and how it works*. Chicago: University of Chicago Press.

Bucy, E. P., & Grabe, M. E. (2007). Taking television seriously: A sound and image bite analysis of presidential campaign coverage, 1992–2004. *Journal of Communication, 57*, 652–675.

Burke, K. (1966). *Language as symbolic action*. Berkeley: University of California Press.

Burke, K. (1967). *The philosophy of literary form*. Baton Rouge: Louisiana State University Press.

Burke, K. (1950). *A rhetoric of motives*. Berkeley: University of California Press.

Burmeister, W. (2010, March 21). Focus: High speed rail station [letter to the editor]. *Wisconsin State Journal*, p. B2. Retrieved from http://www.lexisnexis.com

Burnett, D. (2003). Mapping time: chronometry on top of the world. *Daedalus, 132*(2), 5–19.

Burroway, J., & Stuckey-French, E. (2007). *Writing fiction: A guide to narrative craft* (7th ed.). New York: Pearson.

Busby, R. (2001). *Defending the American presidency: Clinton and the Lewinsky scandal*. New York: Palgrave.

Bush, G. W. (2000, June 13). Social security [advertisement video file]. Retrieved from http://pcl.stanford.edu/campaigns/2000/bush/index.html

Bush, G.W. (2000, July 10). Speech at the NAACP annual convention, Baltimore, MD. Retrieved from http://www.washingtonpost.com/wp-srv/onpolitics/elections/bushtext071000.htm

Bush, G. W. (2000, July 20). New Americans [advertisement video file]. Retrieved from http://pcl.stanford.edu/campaigns/2000/bush/index.html

Bush, G. W. (2000, September 9). How about you? [advertisement video file]. Retrieved from http://pcl.stanford.edu/campaigns/2000/bush/index.html

Bush, G. W. (2000, September 26). Education recession [advertisement video file]. Retrieved from http://pcl.stanford.edu/campaigns/2000/bush/index.html

Bush, G. W. (2004, January 20). State of the Union Address, Washington, D.C.

Retrieved from http://www.washingtonpost.com/wp-srv/politics/transcripts/bushtext_012004.html

Bush, G. W. (2004, March 2). Speech on homeland security, Washington, D.C. Retrieved from http://www.politicallibrary.net/library/B/Bush%20George%20W/Bush_GW_2004_03_02.htm

Bush, G. W. (2004, August 26). Speech at Farmington, New Mexico, rally. Retrieved from http://georgewbush-whitehouse.archives.gov/news/releases/2004/08/20040826-10.html.

Bush, G. W. (2004, September 17). Campaign speech in Charlotte, NC. Retrieved from http://www.presidentialrhetoric.com/campaign/speeches/bush_sept17.html

Bush, G. W. (2004, October 2). Remarks in Columbus, Ohio. Retrieved from http://www.allamericanpatriots.com/2003565

Bush, G. W. (2004, October 18). Homeland security and the presidential agenda. Speech in Marlton, NJ. Retrieved from http://www.presidentialrhetoric.com/campaign/speeches/bush_oct18.html

Bush, G. W. (2004, October 21). Campaign speech in Hershey, PA. Retrieved from http://www.presidentialrhetoric.com/campaign/speeches/bush_oct21.html

Bush, G. W. (2005, January 20). Inaugural address. Washington, D.C. Retrieved from http://www.bartleby.com/124/pres67.html

Bush, G. W. (2005, August 30). President commemorates 60th anniversary of V-J Day. Retrieved from http://www.whitehouse.gov/news/releases/2005/08/20050830-1.html.

Bush, G. W. (2008, February 7). Speech to the 2008 Conservative Political Action Conference, Retrieved from http://www.conservative.org/cpac/

Cahoone, L. (2001). *Locale and progress.* Paper presented at the annual meeting of the American Political Science Association, San Francisco.

Cameron, C. M. (2002). Studying the polarized presidency. *Presidential Studies Quarterly, 32*(4), 647–663.

Campbell, J. E. (2005). Why Bush won the presidential election of 2004: Incumbency, ideology, terrorism, and turnout. *Political Science Quarterly. 120*(2), 219–241.

Campbell, K. K. (1989). *Man cannot speak for her.* Westport, CT: Praeger.

Campbell, K. K., & Burkhoder, T. R. (1997). *Critiques of contemporary rhetoric* (2nd ed.). Belmont, CA: Wadsworth Publishers.

Campbell, K. K., & Jamieson, K. H. (2008). *Presidents creating the presidency: Deeds done in words.* Chicago: University of Chicago Press.

Canes-Wrone, B. (2005). *Who leads whom? Presidents, policy, and the public.* Chicago: University of Chicago Press.

Cannon, C. W. (1998, September 14). The survival strategy. *National Journal, 28,* 6–12.

Carr, D. (2010, April 4). How Sarah Palin became a brand. *New York Times.*

Retrieved from http://www.nytimes.com/2010/04/05/business/media/05carr .html?ref=business

Carson, J., Koger, G., Lebo, M., & Young, E. (2010). The electoral costs of party loyalty in Congress. *American Journal of Political Science 53*(3), 598–616.

Carter, S. (1994). On American time: Mythopoesis and the marketplace. *Journal of American Culture, 17*(2), 35–39.

Chafets, Z. (2008, July 6). Late-period Limbaugh. *New York Times Magazine.* Retrieved from http://www.nytimes.com/2008/07/06/magazine/06Limbaugh-t .html?_rD1&

Chamberlain, A. (2010). An inside-outsider or an outside-insider? The Republican primary campaign of Ron Paul from a third-party perspective. *Politics & Policy, 38*, 97–116.

Cheers & Jeers (2002, June 21). *Plain Dealer*, p. B8. Retrieved from http://www .lexisnexis.com

Cho, J. M., Boyle, M. P., Keum, H., Shevy, M. D., McLeod, D. M., Shah, D. V., & Pan, Z. (2003). Media, terrorism, and emotionality: Emotional differences in media content and public reactions to the September 11th terrorist attacks. *Journal of Broadcasting and Electronic Media, 47*, 309–327.

Cillizza, C. (2008, December 14). Obama makes a point of speaking of the people, to the people. *The Washington Post,* p. A05. Retrieved from http://www.lexis nexis.com

Cillizza, C. (2011, June 13). New Hampshire Republican debate: Winners and losers. *Washington Post.* Retrieved from http://www.washingtonpost.com/blogs /the-fix/post/new-hampshire-republican-debate-winners-and-losers/2011/06/13 /AGZCqsTH_blog.html

Clark, G. (2004). *Rhetorical landscapes in America: Variations on a theme from Kenneth Burke.* Columbia: University of South Carolina Press.

Clayman, S. E., Elliott, M. N., Heritage, J., & Beckett, M. K. (2010). A watershed in White House journalism: Explaining the post-1968 rise of aggressive presidential news. *Political Communication, 27*(3), 229–247.

Clayman, S. E., Elliott, M. N., Heritage, J., & McDonald, L. L. (2006). Historical trends in questioning presidents, 1953–2000. *Presidential Studies Quarterly, 36*(4), 561–583.

Clinton, W. J. (1994, February 5). Weekly radio address to the nation. Retrieved from *The American Presidency Project*: http://www.presidency.ucsb.edu/ws /index.php?pid= 49331

Clinton, W. J. (1994, April 23). Weekly radio address to the nation. Retrieved from *The American Presidency Project*: http://www.presidency.ucsb.edu/ws/index .php?pid= 50255

Clinton, W. J. (1995, July 15). Weekly radio address to the nation. Retrieved from *The American Presidency Project*: http://www.presidency.ucsb.edu/ws/index .php?pid=51624

Clinton, W. J. (1996, October 6). The first Clinton-Dole presidential debate. Retrieved from http://www.debates.org/index.php?page=october-6-1996-debate-transcript

Clinton, W. J. (1996, October 16). The second Clinton-Dole presidential debate. Retrieved from http://www.debates.org/index.php?page=october-16-1996-debate-transcript

Clinton, W. J. (1998, March 7). Weekly radio address to the nation. Retrieved from *The American Presidency Project*: http://www.presidency.ucsb.edu/ws/index.php?pid=55592

Clinton, W. J. (1998, August 17). Statement by the president. National Archives and Records Administration. Retrieved from http://clinton6.nara.gov/1998/08/1998-08-17-statement-by-the-president.html

Clinton, W. J. (1998, August 28). Remarks of the president in commemoration of the 35th anniversary of the March on Washington. National Archives and Records Administration. Retrieved from http://clinton6.nara.gov/1998/08/1998-08-28-remarks-by-president-in-commemoration-of-mlk-march.html

Clinton, W. J. (1998, September 9). Remarks by the president to the Florida Democratic Party. National Archives and Records Administration. Retrieved from http://clinton6.nara.gov/1998/09/1998-09-09-remarks-by-the-president-to-the-florida-democratic-party.html

Clinton, W. J. (1998, September 11). Remarks by the president at religious leaders breakfast. National Archives and Records Administration. Retrieved from http://clinton6.nara.gov/1998/09/1998-09-11-remarks-of-the-president-at-religious-leaders-breakfast-a.html

Clinton, W. J. (1998, September 16). Press conference of President Clinton with President Vaclav Havel of Czech Republic. National Archives and Records Administration. Retrieved from http://clinton6.nara.gov/1998/09/1998-09-16-joint-press-conference-with-president-havel-a.html

Clinton, W. J. (1998, September 24). Remarks by the president on income and poverty report. National Archives and Records Administration. Retrieved from http://clinton6.nara.gov/1998/09/1998-09-24-remarks-by-the-president-on-poverty-and-income-report.html

Clinton, W. J. (1998, October 30). Remarks by the president on the economy. National Archives and Records Administration. Retrieved from http://clinton6.nara.gov/1998/10/1998-10-30-remarks-by-the-president-on-the-economy.html

Clinton, W. J. (1998, November 2). Interview of the president by BET. National Archives and Records Administration. Retrieved from http://clinton6.nara.gov/1998/11/1998-11-02-interview-of-the-president-by-bet.html

Clinton, W. J. (1998, December 11). Statement by the president. National Archives and Records Administration. Retrieved from http://clinton6.nara.gov/1998/12/1998-12-11-statement-by-the-president.html

Clinton, W. J. (1998, December 19). Statements by the president, the vice president, Congressman Richard Gephardt, and chief of staff John Podesta. National Archives and Records Administration. Retrieved from http://clinton6 .nara.gov/1998/12/1998-12-19-statement-by-president-vice-president-gephardt -podesta.html

Clinton, W. J. (2000, May 6). Weekly radio address to the nation. Retrieved from *The American Presidency Project*: http://www.presidency.ucsb.edu/ws/index .php?pid=58446

Clinton, W. J. (2004). *My life.* New York: Knopf.

Cloud, D. L. (2011). *We are the union: Democratic unionism and dissent at Boeing.* Champaign: University of Illinois Press.

Coates, J. (1985). *Women, men, and language: A sociolinguistic account of sex differences in language.* London: Longman.

Coe, K., Domke, D., Graham, E. S., John, S. L., & Pickard, V. W. (2004). No shades of gray: the binary discourse of George W. Bush and an echoing press. *Journal of Communication, 54,* 234–252.

Coe, K., & Neumann, R. (2011). The major addresses of modern presidents: Parameters of a data set. *Presidential Studies Quarterly 41,* 727–751.

Coffey, D. (2004). *Variation in state party agendas: A computer-assisted analysis of state party platforms.* Paper presented at the annual meeting of the Southern Political Science Association, New Orleans.

Cohen, J. E. (2010). *Going local: Presidential leadership in the post-broadcast age.* Cambridge, U.K.: Cambridge University Press.

Collier, K. (2006). *Battle lines: Reconsidering power within the White House by tracking prose.* Paper presented at the annual convention of the American Political Science Association, Philadelphia. Retrieved from http://www.ken collier.org/research/CollierAPSA2006Paper.pdf

Collins, J., Kaufer, D., Vlachos, P., Butler , B., & Ishizaki, S. (2004). Detecting collaborations in text: Comparing the authors' rhetorical language choices in the Federalist Papers. *Computers and the Humanities, 38*(1), 15–36.

Collins, M., & Vinicius, L. (2009). Computer-mediated communication and the role of adolescence in language development. *Internet Journal of Biological Anthropology, 3*(1). Retrieved from http://www.ispub.com/journal/the-internet -journal-of-biological-anthropology/volume-3-number-1/computer-mediated -communication-and-the-role-of-adolescence-in-language-development.html

Conley, D. (2008). Virtuoso. *Communication and Critical/Cultural Studies, 5,* 307–311.

Connolly, W. E. (2008). *Capitalism and Christianity, American style.* Durham, NC: Duke University Press.

Cordingley, K. (2010). *One nation: American collective identity in major presidential speeches.* Paper presented at the 96th Annual Convention of the National Communication Association, San Francisco.

Cosgrove, K. M. (2007). *Branded conservatives: How the brand brought the right from the fringes to the center of American politics.* Oxford: Lang.

Cotter, C. P., & Hennessy, B. C. (1964). *Politics without power: The national party committees.* New York: Atherton.

Cottle, M. (2010). Pink elephants. *New Republic, 241*(7), 5–6.

Courser, Z. (2010). The Tea Party at the election. *Forum, 8*(4), article 5.

Creadick, A. G. (2010). *Perfectly average: The pursuit of normality in postwar America.* Amherst: University of Massachusetts Press.

Crew, R. E., & Lewis, C. (2011). Verbal style, gubernatorial strategies, and legislative success. *Political Psychology, 32*(4), 623–642.

Crockett, D. A. (2003). George W. Bush and the unrhetorical rhetorical presidency. *Rhetoric and Public Affairs, 6*(3), 465–486.

Dalton, R. (2004). *Democratic challenges, democratic choices: The erosion of political support in advanced industrial democracies.* New York: Oxford University Press.

Danner, M. (2005, January 13). How Bush really won. *New York Review of Books. 52*(1). Retrieved from http://www.nybooks.com/articles/archives/2005/jan/13/how-bush-really-won/

Datta, M. N. (2007). The legacy of George W. Bush: The good, the bad, and the ugly. *Bad Subjects, 77.* Retrieved from http://bad.eserver.org/issues/2007/77/datta.html.

Daum, M. (2010, May 20) Sarah Palin, feminist. *Los Angeles Times.* Retrieved from http://articles.latimes.com/2010/may/20/opinion/la-oe-0520-daum-fword-20100520.

Davidson, R. H. (2009). The presidency and congressional time. In J. A. Thurber (Ed.), *Rivals for power: Presidential-congressional relations* (4th ed.). Lanham, MA: Rowman & Littlefield.

Death of the GOP?, (2011, May 2). *Washington Times.* Retrieved from http://communities.washingtontimes.com/neighborhood/ad-lib/2011/may/2/death-gop/

Deering, C. J., & Maltzman, F. (1999). The politics of executive orders: Legislative constraints on presidential power. *Political Research Quarterly, 52*(4), 767.

DeFrank, T. M. (1983, April 18). An overused "weapon"? *Newsweek,* 22.

Delanty, G. (2000). The resurgence of the city in Europe?: The spaces of European citizenship. In E. Isin (Ed.), *Democracy, Citizenship, and the Global City* (pp. 79–92). London: Routledge.

Delli Carpini, M. X., & Keeter, S. (1997). *What Americans know about politics and why it matters.* New Haven: Yale University Press.

de Moraes, L. (2002, October 8). Bush talks, but networks speechless. *Washington Post,* p. C01. Retrieved from http://lexisnexis.com

Deni, L. (2003, June 29). Broadway to Vegas. Retrieved from http://www.broadwaytovegas.com-June29,2003.html

Densmore, L. B. (1997). *The sound of leadership: An update.* Unpublished M.A. thesis, University of Texas at Austin.

Denton, H. H. (1982, April 4). Before the mike; Reagan turns to a medium he knows to deliver his message to the nation. *Washington Post*, A1.

Dewey, J. (1954). *The public and its problems.* Chicago: Swallow Press.

Dickinson, G., Blair, C., & Ott, B. L. (Eds.). (2010). *Places of public memory: The rhetoric of museums and memorials.* Tuscaloosa: University of Alabama Press.

Diermeier, D., Godbout, J. F., Yu, B., & Kaufmann, S. (2007). *Language and ideology in Congress.* Paper presented at the annual meeting of the Midwest Political Science Association, Chicago.

Dionne, E. J., Jr. (2009, January 15). Mysterious intellect. *New Republic.* Retrieved from http://www.tnr.com/article/politics/mysterious-intellect

Ditonto, T. (2009). *The outsider and the presidency: Framing Clinton and Obama in the 2008 Democratic presidential primary race.* Paper presented at the annual meeting of the Midwest Political Science Association, Chicago.

Doerfel, M. L., & Connaughton, S. L. (2009). Semantic networks and competition: Election year winners and losers in U.S. televised presidential debates, 1960–2004. *Journal of the American Society for Information Science and Technology*, 60(1), 201–218.

Dole, R. (1996, October 22). Campaign speech in Grand Blanc, MI. Housed in the Campaign Mapping database at http://keywords.communication.utexas.edu/keywords/

Dole stuck in the past. (1996, November 4). *Tampa Tribune*, p. 10. Retrieved from http://www.lexisnexis.com

Domke, D. (2004). *God willing? Political fundamentalism in the White House, the "war on terror," and the echoing press.* Ann Arbor: Pluto Press.

Domke, D., & Coe, K. (2007). *The God strategy: How religion became a political weapon in America.* New York: Oxford University Press.

Dowd, M. (2009, January 17). The long, lame goodbye. *New York Times.* Retrieved from http://www.nytimes.com/2009/01/18/opinion/18iht-eddowd.1.19460244.html

Draper, R. (2010, November 21). The rogue room: A who's who and what's what of Sarah Palin's inner circle. *New York Times Magazine*, 41–49, 60–62.

Dreier, P., Mollenkopf, J., & Swanstrom, T. (2001). *Place matters: Metropolitics for the twenty-first century.* Lawrence: University of Kansas Press.

Druckman, J. N., & Holmes J. W. (2004). Does presidential rhetoric matter? Priming and presidential approval. *Presidential Studies Quarterly*, 34(4), 755–778.

Druckman, J. N., Kifer, M. J., & Parkin, M. (2010). Timeless strategy meets new medium: Going negative on congressional campaign web sites, 2002–2006. *Political Communication*, 27, 88–103.

Dumm, T. L. (2008). Barack Obama and the souls of white folk. *Communication and Critical/Cultural Studies*, 5, 317–320.

Dunn, G. (2011). *The lies of Sarah Palin: The untold story behind her relentless quest for power.* New York: St. Martin's.

Edwards, G. C. (2003). *On deaf ears: The limits of the bully pulpit*. New Haven: Yale University Press.

Edwards, J. L. (2010). Symbolic womanhood and Sarah Palin: Running against the feminist grain. In J. Robert E. Denton (Ed.), *Studies of identity in the 2008 presidential campaign* (pp. 25–39). Lanham, MA: Rowman and Littlefield.

Egan, T. 2010, Dec 4. The junkie and the atheist. *New York Times*, A23.

Eidenmuller, M. E. (2002). American evangelicalism, democracy, and civic piety: A computer-based stylistic analysis of Promise Keepers' stadium event and Washington D.C. rally discourses. *Journal of Communication and Religion, 25*, 64–85.

Eisenhower, D. (1956, October 12). The people ask the president [television broadcast]. Retrieved from http://www.presidency.ucsb.edu/ws/?pid=10640

Eitmann, A. (2009). *Fighting words: How Barack Obama's campaign uses oratory to trespass on Republican-owned issues*. Paper presented at the annual meeting of the Southern Political Science Association, New Orleans.

Elder, L., & Greene, S. (2009). *The politics of parenthood and the 2008 electoral campaign: The use of parent and family themes in party appeals and election coverage*. Paper presented at the annual meeting of the Midwest Political Science Association, Chicago.

Elton, S. (2000, November 5). Bore, Gush fuel electoral malaise. *Toronto Star*. Retrieved from http://www.lexisnexis.com

Emler, N., & Frazer, E. (1999). Politics: The education effect. *Oxford Review of Education. 25*(1&2): 252–273.

Eriksen, T. H. (2001). *Tyranny of the moment: Fast and slow time in the information age*. London: Pluto Press.

Eshbaugh-Soha, M. (2010). The tone of local presidential news coverage. *Political Communication, 27*, 121–140.

Eshbaugh-Soha, M., & Peake, J. S. (2008). The presidency and local media: Local newspaper coverage of President George W. Bush. *Presidential Studies Quarterly, 38*(4), 609–630.

Esser, F. (2008). Dimensions of political news cultures: Sound bite and image bite news in France, Germany, Great Britain, and the United States. *International Journal of Press/Politics, 13*, 401–428.

Etzioni, A. (1993). *The spirit of community: Rights, responsibilities, and the communitarian agenda*. New York: Crown Publishers.

Fahnestock, J. (2011). *Rhetorical style: The uses of language in persuasion*. New York: Oxford University Press.

Falk, A. (2010). *The riddle of Barack Obama: A psychobiography*. New York: Praeger.

Falk, E. (2010). *Women for president: Media bias in nine campaigns* (2nd ed.). Urbana: University of Illinois Press.

Fallows, J. (2008, September). Rhetorical questions. *Atlantic, 302*. Retrieved from http://www.theatlantic.com/magazine/archive/2008/09/rhetorical-questions/6943/

Farah, J. (2010, March 18). *The Tea Party manifesto*. Retrieved from http://www.wnd.com/index.php?pageId=128541

Farrell, K. (2011). *Berserk style in American culture*. New York: Palgrave Macmillan.

Feather, N. (1985). Attitudes, values, and attributions: Explanations of unemployment. *Journal of Personality and Social Psychology, 48*, 876–889.

Fenn, R. K. (2001). *Time exposure: The personal experience of time in secular societies*. New York: Oxford University Press.

Feste, K. (2011). *America responds to terrorism: Conflict resolution strategies of Clinton, Bush, and Obama*. New York: Palgrave/Macmillan.

Fey, T. (2008, October 2). Tina Fey as Sarah Palin. *Saturday Night Live*. Retrieved from https://billcreswell.wordpress.com/2008/10/02/tina-fey-as-sarah-palin-katie-couric-snl-skit-video-transcript/

Fineman, H. (2009, November 30). Channeling the Gipper. *Newsweek, 154*(22), 23.

Finkelstein, S. (1997). Inter-industry merger patterns and resource dependence: A replication and extension of Pfeffer (1972). *Strategic Management Journal, 18*, 787–810.

Fiorina, M. P., & Abrams, S. J. (2008). Political polarization in the American public. *Annual Review of Political Science.* 11:563–588.

Fiorina, M. P., & Abrams, S. J. (2009). *Disconnect: The breakdown of representation in American politics*. Norman: University of Oklahoma Press.

Fish, S. (2002, March 29). Is everything political? *Chronicle of Higher Education*. Retrieved from http://chronicle.com/article/Is-Everything-Political-/45993

Fleisher, R., & Bond, J. R. (1996). The president in a more partisan legislative arena. *Political Research Quarterly, 49*(4), 729.

Foote, J. S. (1990). *Television access and political power: The networks, the presidency, and the "loyal opposition."* New York, NY: Praeger.

Foucault, M. (1986). Of other spaces. *Diacritics, 16*, 22–27.

Fox, R. L., & Lawless, J. L. (2011). Gaining and losing interest in running for public office: The concept of dynamic political ambition. *Journal of Politics, 73*(2), 443–462.

Freeman, J. (1986). The political culture of the Democratic and Republican parties. *Political Science Quarterly, 101*, 327–356.

Freie, J. (2009). *The postmodern campaign for the presidency: Obama versus McCain*. Paper presented at the annual meeting of the Western Political Science Association, Vancouver, BC.

Frishman, M. A. (2009, November 11). Sarah Palin: Why some love her and others hate her (blog post). *Mary's Christianity Blog*. Retrieved from http://christianity.about.com/b/2009/07/08/sarah-palin-why-some-love-her-and-others-hate-her.htm

Gaddie, R. K. (2004). *Born to run: Origins of the political career*. Lanham, MD: Rowman and Littlefield.

Galvin, D. (2010). *Presidential party building*. Princeton: Princeton University Press.

Gastil, J. (2008). *Political Communication and Deliberation*. Thousand Oaks, CA: Sage Publications.

Gartner, J. D. (2008). *In search of Bill Clinton: A psychological biography*. New York: St. Martin's Press.

Geldard, R. (2010). Why the Tea Party has no poets. *Huffington Post*. Retrieved from http://www.huffingtonpost.com/richard-geldard/why-the-tea-party-has -no_b_632658.html?view=print

Gelzinis, P. (2010). A new political tone in Southie. *Boston Herald*, September 13. p. 10. Retrieved from http://www.lexisnexis.com.

Gergen, D. (1998, August 31). Can he save his presidency? *U.S. News & World Report, 125*, 36.

Gergen, D., & Zelleke, A. (2008, July 17). What kind of leader would McCain or Obama be? *Christian Science Monitor*, A9.

Gerhardt, M. J. (2001). Impeachment defanged and other institutional ramifications of the Clinton scandals. *William and Mary Law Review, 60*: 59–96.

Gerhardt, M. J. (2008). *The power of precedent*. New York: Oxford University Press.

Gerring, J. (1998). *Party ideologies in America, 1828–1996*. Cambridge, UK: Cambridge University Press.

Gerson, M. (2010, September 10). As midterms loom, Obama has lost his rhetorical touch. *Washington Post*. Retrieved from http://www.washingtonpost.com /wp-dyn/content/article/2010/09/08/AR2010090805912.html

Gibbs, N., & Duffy, M. (1998, August 31). I misled people. *Time, 152*, 27–35.

Gibson, R., & Rommele, A. (2001). Changing campaign communications: A party-centered theory of professionalized campaigning. *International Journal of Press and Politics, 6*(4), 31–43.

Gibson, W. (1966). *Tough, sweet, and stuffy: An essay on modern American prose styles*. Bloomington: Indiana University Press.

Giddens, A., & Pierson, C. (1998). *Conversations with Anthony Giddens: Making sense of modernity*. Cambridge: Polity Press.

Gitlin, T. (1993, Spring). The rise of identity politics. *Dissent, 40*, 172–177.

Gitlin, T. (2007). *The bulldozer and the big tent: Blind Republicans, lame Democrats, and the recovery of American ideals*. Hoboken, NJ: John Wiley & Sons.

Giuliano, T. A., L. C. Barnes, S. E. Fiala, & D. M. Davis. (1998). *An empirical investigation of male answer syndrome*. Paper presented at Annual Convention of the Southwestern Psychological Association, New Orleans.

Goldstein, A., & Shear, M. D. (2008, August 30). Tenacious reformer's swift rise. *Washington Post*. A1.

Goldzwig, S. R., & Dionisopoulos, G. N. (1989). John F. Kennedy's civil rights discourse: The evolution from "principled bystander" to public advocate. *Communication Monographs, 56*, 179–198.

Goodstein, E. S. (2005). *Experience without qualities: Boredom and modernity.* Stanford: Stanford University Press.

Gore, A. (2000, August 17). Address accepting the presidential nomination at the Democratic National Convention in Los Angeles. Retrieved from http://www.presidency.ucsb.edu/ws/index.php?pid=25963

Gormley, K. (2010). *The death of American virtue: Clinton vs. Starr.* New York: Crown Publishers.

Gosnell, H. F. (1980). *Truman's crisis: A political biography of Harry S. Truman.* Santa Barbara: Greenwood.

Gould, L. L. (2003). *The modern American presidency.* Lawrence: University Press of Kansas.

Graddy, D. B. (2004). Gender and online discourse in the principles of economics. *Journal of Asynchronous Learning Networks, 8*(4), 3–14.

Grafton, A. (2003). Dating history: The Renaissance and the reformation of chronology. *Daedalus, 103*, 74–85.

Green, J. (2011, June). The tragedy of Sarah Palin. *Atlantic.* Retrieved from http://www.theatlantic.com/magazine/archive/2011/06/the-tragedy-of-sarah-palin/8492/1/

Greenstein, F. I. (1998). There he goes again: The alternating performance style of Bill Clinton. *PS: Political Science and Politics, 31*, 178–181.

Greppi, M. (2009, January 5). Election keeps cable soaring. *Television Week, 28*(1), 9.

Grill, C. J. (2007). *The public side of representation: A study of citizens' views about representatives and the representative process.* Albany: State University of New York Press.

Gronbeck, B. (1997). Character, celebrity, and sexual innuendo in the mass-mediated presidency. In J. Lull & S. Hinerman (Eds.), *Media scandals: Morality and desire in the popular culture marketplace* (pp. 122–142). New York: Columbia University Press.

Gronke, P., & Newman, B. (2003). FDR to Clinton, Mueller to ?: A field essay on presidential approval. *Political Research Quarterly. 56*(4), 501–512.

Gunn, J. (2010). On speech and public release. *Rhetoric and Public Affairs, 13*, 1–41.

Gurian, P. (2009). *The impact of divisive primaries in the 2008 presidential campaign.* Paper presented at the annual meeting of the Western Political Science Association, Vancouver, BC.

Gutmann, A., & Thompson, D. (2004). *Why deliberative democracy?* Princeton: Princeton University Press.

Habermas, J. (1989). The public sphere: An encyclopedia article. In S. E. Browner & D. Kellner (Eds.). *Critical theory and society: A reader* (pp. 136–142). New York: Routledge.

Hall, M. (2009, January 20). Obama takes steps to change tone of D.C.; Early actions show an emphasis on openness, civility. *USA Today*, p. 4A.

Hallin, D. C. (1992). Sound bite news: Television coverage of elections, 1968–1988. *Journal of Communication, 42*(2), 5–24.

Hamilton, J. T. (2003). *All the news that's fit to sell: How the market transforms information into news*. Princeton: Princeton University Press.

Han, L. C. (2006). New strategies for an old medium: The weekly radio addresses of Reagan and Clinton. *Congress and the Presidency, 33*, 25–45.

Hanmer, M. J. (2009). *Discount voting: Voter registration reforms and their effects*. Cambridge: Cambridge University Press.

Hansen, S. B., Kanthak, K., & Victor, J. N. (2011). *Candidate traits, gender roles, and the 2008 vote*. Paper presented at the Research on Gender in Political Psychology Conference, Pittsburgh.

Hargittai, E., Gallo, J., & Kane, M. (2008). Cross-ideological discussions among conservative and liberal bloggers. *Public Choice, 134*: 67–86.

Hariman, R. (1995). *Political style: The artistry of power*. Chicago: University of Chicago Press.

Harnden, T. (2009, July 4). Sarah Palin is now the joke her opponents wanted her to be. *Telegraphcouk*. Retrieved from http://blogs.telegraph.co.uk/news/toby harnden/100002077/sarah-palin-is-now-the-joke-her-opponents-wanted-her -to-be/

Harp, D., Loke, J., & Bachmann, I. (2010). First impressions of Sarah Palin: Pit bulls, politics, gender performance, and a discursive media (re)contextualization. *Communication, Culture and Critique, 3*(3), 291–309.

Harris, C., Mayer, V., Saulino, C., & Schiller, D. (1996). The class politics of Rush Limbaugh. *Communication Review, 1*(4), 545–564.

Harris, J. F. (1995, April 19). Networks pass on president in prime time: White House couldn't improve on "Home." *Washington Post*, p. A20. Retrieved from http://www.lexisnexis.com

Harris, S. (2008, September 20). When atheists attack. *Newsweek*. Retrieved from http://www.newsweek.com/2008/09/19/when-atheists-attack.html

Harris, S. G., & Gresch, E. B. (2010). The emotions of change: merger sentiments, pleasure, and emotional expression. In N. M. Ashkanasy, W. J. Zerbe, & C. E. J. Härtel (Eds.) *Emotions and organizational dynamism* (pp. 189–220). Boston: Emerald Group Publishing Limited.

Hart, G. (1982, September 18). Response to the president's radio address. United Press International.

Hart, R. P. (1987). *The sound of leadership: Presidential communication in the modern age*. Chicago: University of Chicago Press.

Hart, R. P. (1994). *Seducing America: How television charms the modern voter*. New York: Oxford University Press.

Hart, R. P. (2000). *Campaign talk: Why elections are good for us*. Princeton: Princeton University Press.

Hart, R. P. (2001a). Citizen discourse and political participation: A survey. In L. Bennett & R. Entman (Eds.), *Mediated politics and the future of democracy* (pp. 407–432). New York: Cambridge University Press.

Hart, R. P. (2001b). Redeveloping DICTION: Theoretical considerations. In M. West (Ed.), *Theory, method, and practice of computer content analysis* (pp. 43–60). New York: Ablex.

Hart, R. P., & Burks, D. (1972). Rhetorical sensitivity and social interaction. *Communication Monographs, 39:* 75–91.

Hart, R., Jarvis, S., Smith-Howell, D., & Jennings, W. (2005). *Political keywords: Using language that uses us.* New York: Oxford University Press.

Hart, R. P., & Lim, E. T. (2011). Tracking the language of space and time: 1948–2008. *Journal of Contemporary History, 46,* 591–609.

Hart, R. P., & Lind, C. J. (2011). The rhetoric of Islamic activism: A DICTION study. *Dynamics of Asymmetric Conflict, 4,* 113–125.

Hart, R., & Pauley, J. (2004). *The political pulpit revisited.* West Lafayette, IN: Purdue University Press.

Hart, R., & Sawyer, K. (2003). Resurrecting the Clinton presidency: A linguistic profile. In R. Denton & R. Holloway (Eds.), *Images, scandal, and communication strategies of the Clinton presidency* (pp. 195–218). Westport, CT: Praeger.

Hart, S. (2001). *Cultural dilemmas of progressive politics: Styles of engagement among grassroots activists.* Chicago: University of Chicago Press.

Hartley, J. (2003). The frequencies of public writing: Tomb, tome, and time as technologies of the public. In H. Jenkins & D. Thorburn (Eds.), *Democracy and new media* (pp. 247–269). Cambridge, MA: MIT Press.

Hawisher, G. E., & Sullivan, P. (1998). Women on the networks: Searching for e-spaces of their own. In L. Worsham & S. C. Jarratt (Eds.), *Feminism and composition studies* (pp. 172–197). New York: MLA.

Hayden, K. (1998, August 18). Analysis: More apology, Mr. President, and less politics, please. *CNN: All Politics.* Retrieved from http://articles.cnn.com/1998 -08-18/politics/clinton.analysis_1_lewinsky-probe-clinton-independent -counsel-ken-starr?_s=PM:ALLPOLITICS

Hayes, D. (2005). Candidate qualities through a partisan lens: A theory of trait ownership. *American Journal of Political Science, 49*(4), 908–923.

Healey, K. (2010). For a culture and political economy of the prophetic: Critical scholarship and religious politics after the 2008 election. *Cultural Studies/ Critical Methodologies, 10*(2), 157–170.

Heclo, H. (2003). The political ethos of George W. Bush. In F. I. Greenstein (Ed.), *The George W. Bush presidency: an early assessment* (pp. 17–50). Baltimore: John Hopkins University Press.

Heisler, S. (2009, June 15). Interview: Dana Carvey and Robert Smigel. *AV Club.* Retrieved from http://www.avclub.com/articles/dana-carvey-and-robert -smigel,29184/

Heldman, C., Carroll, S.J., & Olson, S. (2005). "She brought only a skirt": Print media coverage of Elizabeth Dole's bid for the Republican presidential nomination. *Political Communication, 22*, 315–335.

Hemmingway, E. (1966). Indian camp. *The short stories of Ernest Hemingway*. New York: Charles Scribner's.

Herbst, S. (2010). *Rude democracy: Civility and incivility in American politics*. Philadelphia: Temple University Press.

Hetherington, M. J. (2009). Putting polarization in perspective. *British Journal of Political Science, 39*(2), 413–448.

Hillbruner, A. (1974). Archetype and signature: Nixon and the 1973 inaugural. *Central States Speech Journal, 25*, 69–181.

Hillygus, D. S., & Shields, T. G. (2008). *The persuadable voter: Wedge issues in presidential campaigns*. Princeton: Princeton University Press.

Hinckley, D. (2010, November 12). TLC show serves more as an infomercial for Sarah Palin than an inside look at Alaska. *New York Daily News*. Retrieved from http://articles.nydailynews.com/2010-11-12/entertainment/27080937_1 _sarah-palin-s-alaska-joe-mcginniss-palin-home

Hindman, M. (2008). *The myth of digital democracy*. Princeton: Princeton University Press.

Hofstadter, R. (1966). *Anti-intellectualism in American life*. New York: Vintage.

Holmes, J. (1995). *Women, men, and politeness*. London: Longman.

Holmes, S. (2008, November 19). Obama: Oratory and originality. *BBC*. Retrieved from http://news.bbc.co.uk/1/hi/world/americas/7735014.stm

Horvit, B., Schiffer, A. J., & Wright, M. (2008). The limits of presidential agenda setting: Predicting newspaper coverage of the weekly radio address. *International Journal of Press/Politics, 13*, 8–28.

Howard, P. N. (2005). *New media campaigns and the managed citizen*. New York: Cambridge University Press.

Huffaker, D. A., & Calvert, S. L. (2005). Gender, identity, and language use in teenage blogs. *Journal of Computer-Mediated Communication, 10*(2), article 1.

Hunter, M. L. (2005). *Race, gender, and the politics of skin tone*. New York: Routledge.

Huntington, S. P. (2004). *Who are we? The challenges to America's national identity*. New York: Simon & Schuster.

Ishizaki, S., & Kaufer, D. (2012). Computer-aided rhetorical analysis. In P. M. McCarthy & C. Boonthum-Deneche (Eds.). *Applied natural language processing: Identification, investigation, and resolution*. Hershey, PA: Information Science Reference.

Ivie, R. L., & Giner, O. (2007). Hunting the devil: Democracy's rhetorical impulse to war. *Presidential Studies Quarterly, 37*(4), 580–598.

Ivie, R. L., & Giner, O. (2009). American exceptionalism in a democratic idiom: Transacting the mythos of change in the 2008 presidential campaign. *Communication Studies, 60*(4), 359–375.

Iyer, V. (2005, December 28). Geldof to advise Tories on global poverty relief. *The Times*. Retrieved from http://www.timesonline.co.uk/tol/news/politics /article782978.ece

Jacobson, G. C. (2003). Partisan polarization in presidential support: The electoral connection. *Congress and the Presidency, 30*(1), 1–30.

Jacobson, G. C. (2008). *A divider, not a uniter: George W. Bush and the American people.* New York: Pearson Longman.

Jamieson, K. H. (1988). *Eloquence in an electronic age: The transformation of political speechmaking.* New York: Oxford University Press.

Jamieson, K. H., & Waldman, P. (2003). *The press effect: Politicians, journalists, and the stories that the shape the political world.* New York: Oxford University Press.

Jarratt, S. C. (2006). George W. Bush: Graduation speech at West Point. *Voice of Democracy 1*: 83–103.

Jarvis, S. (2005). *The talk of the party: Political labels, symbolic capital, and American life.* Lanham, MD: Rowman & Littlefield.

Jefferson, T. (2009). *The writings of Thomas Jefferson*, vol. 9: *1799–1803.* New York: Cosimo.

Jennings, S. (2006). *The new artist's manual: The complete guide to painting and drawing materials and techniques.* San Francisco: Chronicle Books.

Johnson, W. (1946). *People in quandaries: The semantics of personal adjustment.* New York: Harper.

Jost, J. T., Glaser, J., Kruglanski, A. W., & Sulloway, F. J. (2003). Political conservatism as motivated social cognition. *Psychological Bulletin, 129*, 339–375.

Just Sayin (2009, September 28). Comment to "Sarah Palin: Why some love her and others hate her" (comment to blog post). *Mary's Christianity Blog*. Retrieved from http://christianity.about.com/b/2009/07/08/sarah-palin-why-some-love -her-and-others-hate-her.htm

Kaid, L. L. (2004). Political advertising. In L. L. Kaid (Ed.), *Handbook of political communication research* (pp. 155–202). Mahwah, N.J.: Lawrence Erlbaum.

Kahl, M. L., & Edwards, J. L. (2009). An epistolary epilogue: Learning from Sarah Palin's vice presidential campaign. In J. L. Edwards (Ed.), *Gender and political communication in America: Rhetoric, representation, and display* (pp. 267–278). Lanham, MA: Rowman & Littlefield.

Kahn, K. F. (1994). The distorted mirror: Press coverage of women candidates for statewide office. *Journal of Politics, 56*, 154–66.

Kane, P., & Bacon, P. (2010, January 30). Obama talks to House Republicans in Baltimore in rare, televised debate. *Washington Post*. Retrieved from http://www .washingtonpost.com/wp-dyn/content/article/2010/01/29/AR2010012902401 .html

Kazin, M. (2005). The people, no. *Wilson Quarterly, 29*(3), 113–115.

Kelley, R. (1977). Ideology and political culture from Jefferson to Nixon. *American Historical Review, 82*, 531–562.

Kellner, D. (2007). Bushspeak and the politics of lying: Presidential rhetoric in the "war on terror." *Presidential Studies Quarterly. 37*(4), 622–645.

Kennedy, J. F. (2000 [1956]). *Profiles in courage.* New York: HarperPerennial.

Kenski, K., Hardy, B., & Jamieson, K. H. (2010). *The Obama victory: How media, money, and message shaped the 2008 election.* New York: Oxford University Press.

Kernell, S. (2007). *Going public: New strategies in presidential leadership.* (4th ed.). Washington: CQ Press.

Kies, D. (1990). Indeterminacy in Sentence Structure. *Linguistics and Education, 2,* 231–258.

Kidd, Q. (2008). The real (lack of) difference between Republicans and Democrats: A computer word score analysis of party platforms, 1996–2004. *PS: Political Science and Politics, 41,* 519–525

Kilborn, C. (2011). *Punchline.* Retrieved from http://www.loveburkeliving.com/Punchline.html

Kim, K., & McCombs, M. (2007). News story descriptions and the public's opinions of political candidates. *Journalism and Mass Communication Quarterly, 84*(2), 299–314.

Kinder, D. R., & Sanders, L. M. (1996). *Divided by color: Racial politics and democratic ideals.* Chicago: University of Chicago Press.

Kinsley, M. (2008). The leader we deserve. *Time.* October 27. Retrieved from http://www.time.com/time/magazine/article/0,9171,1851119,00.html

Kiousis, S. (2003). Job approval and favorability: The impact of media attention to the Monica Lewinsky scandal on public opinion of President Bill Clinton. *Mass Communication and Society, 6*(4), 435–451.

Klein, J. (2002). *The natural: The misunderstood presidency of Bill Clinton.* New York: Doubleday.

Klein, J. (2006). *Politics lost: How American democracy was trivialized by people who think you're stupid.* New York: Broadway Books.

Klein, J. (2007). The tone-deaf Democrats. *Time,* December 3, p. 35

Kluegel, J. R. (1990). Trends in whites' explanations of the black-white gap in socioeconomic status, 1977–1989. *American Sociological Review, 55,* 512–525.

Knight Templar. (2010, October 28). Wait a second? Thats [*sic*] in the First Amendment? (blog post). *The Escapist.* Retrieved from http://www.escapist magazine.com/forums/read/528.239778-Wait-a-Second-Thats-In-the-First-Amendment?page=2

Knutson, B. (2010, August 29). The objective study of subjectivism. *Chronicle of Higher Education.* Retrieved from http://chronicle.com/article/The-Objective-Study-of/124139

Koger, G., Masket, S., & Noel, H. (2010). Cooperative party factions in American politics. *American Politics Research, 38*(1), 33–53.

Kogl, A. (2002*). Place, capitalism, and democratic efficacy.* Paper presented at the annual meeting of the American Political Science Association, Boston.

Kohn, S. (2011, November 10). In 2011 vote, a post-partisan populism. *CNN*. Retrieved from http://www.cnn.com/2011/11/10/opinion/kohn-bipartisan -populism/index.html

Krause, G. A., & Cohen, J. E. (2000). Opportunity, constraints, and the development of the institutional presidency: The issuance of executive orders, 1939–96. *Journal of Politics, 62*(1), 88–114.

Krug, M. (2007). *An artist's handbook: Materials and techniques.* Abrams, NY: Abrams Studio.

Kupchan, C. A., & Trubowitz, P. L. (2007). Grand strategy for a divided America. *Foreign Affairs, 86*, 71–83.

Lacy, M. (2008). *Barack Obama's 2008 presidential campaign as a redemption drama.* Paper presented at the annual meeting of the National Communication Association, San Diego.

Lakoff, G. (2002). *Moral politics: How liberals and conservatives think* (2nd ed.). Chicago: University of Chicago Press.

Lakoff, G. (2009, February 24). The Obama code. *Huffington Post.* Retrieved from http://www.huffingtonpost.com/george-lakoff/the-obama-code_b_169580.html

Lane, R. (1962). *Political ideology: Why the American common man believes what he does.* New York: Free Press.

Lanham, R. (1983). *Analyzing prose.* New York: Scribners.

Lanham, R. (2007). *The economics of attention: Style and substance in the age of information.* Chicago: University of Chicago Press.

Lanoue, D. J., & Emmert, C. F. (1999). Voting in the glare of the spotlight: Representatives' votes on the impeachment of President Clinton. *Polity, 32*, 253–269.

Laver, M., Benoit, K., & Garry, J. (2003). Extracting policy positions from political texts using words as data. *American Political Science Review, 97*(2), 311–337.

Layman, G. C., Carsey, T. M., & Horowitz, J. (2006). Party polarization in American politics: Characteristics, causes, and consequences. *Annual Review of Political Science, 9*, 83–110.

Lawrence, R., & Bennett, W. L. (2001). Rethinking media politics and public opinion: Reactions to the Clinton-Lewinsky scandal. *Political Science Quarterly, 116*(3), 425–446.

Lawrence, R., & Schafer, M. L. (2010). *Debunking Sarah Palin: Mainstream news coverage of "death panels.".* Paper presented at the annual meeting of the Association for Education in Journalism and Mass Communication, Denver.

Lee, F. E. (2008). Dividers, not uniters: Presidential leadership and Senate partisanship, 1981–2004. *Journal of Politics, 70*(4), 914–928.

Lee, H. J., & Wen, H. (2009). Where the girls are in the age of new sexism: An interview with Susan Douglas. *Journal of Communication Inquiry, 33*, 93–103.

Lefebvre. H. (1991). *The production of space* (D. Nicholson-Smith, Trans.). Oxford: Blackwell. Original work published 1974.

Lerner, J. (2010, September 26). Defining the Tea Party. *Summit Daily.com*. Retrieved from http://www.allvoices.com

Lerner, M. (2009, September/October). Has President Obama abandoned you and his own vision of the caring society? *Tikkun Magazine*. Retrieved from http://www.tikkun.org/article.php/sept_oct_09_lerner_editorial

Levendusky, M. (2009). *The partisan sort: How liberals became Democrats and conservatives became Republicans*. Chicago: University of Chicago Press.

Lewis, D. E. (2003). *Presidents and the politics of agency design: Political insulation in the United States government bureaucracy, 1946–1997*. Stanford: Stanford University Press.

Liao, M-C., & Tseng, D. S. D. (1997). Conversational topic discontinuity markers in Taiwanese EFL classrooms. Retrieved from http://rnd2.ncue.edu.tw/ezcatfiles /b004/img/img/316/97-1-01paper.doc

Lichter, R., & Smith, T. (1996). Why elections are bad news: Media and candidate discourse in the 1996 presidential primaries. *Harvard International Journal of Press and Politics*, *1*, 15–35.

Light, P. C. (1995). *Thickening government: Federal hierarchy and the diffusion of accountability*. Washington: Brookings Institution.

Lilla, M. (2011, December 19). The president and the passions: Has Obama misunderstood the psychology of politics? *New York Times Magazine*, pp. 13–14.

Lil Rascal (2008, October 21). Jon Stewart to Sarah Palin: "F* you" (blog post). *Pop Rock Forum*. Retrieved from http://www.topix.com/forum/music/pop -rock/TA82HFJA6EKG50EMP/p41

Lim, E. T. (2003). The lion and the lamb: De-mythologizing Franklin Roosevelt's fireside chats. *Rhetoric and Public Affairs*, *3*, 437–464.

Lim, E. T. (2008). *The anti-intellectual presidency: The decline of presidential rhetoric from George Washington to George W. Bush*. New York: Oxford University Press.

Linder, S. B. (1970). *The harried leisure class*. New York: Columbia University Press.

Lindquist, J. (2002). *A place to stand: Politics and persuasion in a working-class bar*. New York: Oxford University Press.

Lucas, S. E., & Medhurst, M. J. (Eds.). (2008). *Words of a century: The top 100 American speeches, 1900–1999*. New York: Oxford University Press.

Luke, T. (1978). Culture and politics in the age of artificial negativity. *Telos, 35*, 55–72.

Luks, S., Miller, J. M., & Jacobs, L. R. (2003). Who wins? Campaigns and the third party vote. *Presidential Studies Quarterly*, *33*(1), 9–30.

Luntz, F. (2006). *Words that work: It's not what you say, it's what people hear*. New York: Hyperion.

Luntz, F. (2010). *What Americans really want . . . really: The truth about our hopes, dreams, and fears*. New York: Hyperion.

Maestas, C. (2003). The incentive to listen: Progressive ambition, resources, and opinion monitoring among state legislators. *Journal of Politics, 65*(2), 439–56.

Magnusson, W. (2001). *The search for political space.* Toronto: University of Toronto Press.

Marcy, M. B. (2010). Palin as prototype? Sarah Palin's career in the context of political women in the frontier west [electronic journal]. *Forum, 8*(2), 6ff.

Marietta, M. (2009). The absolutist advantage: Sacred rhetoric in contemporary presidential debate. *Political Communication, 26,* 388–411.

Marvell, A. (1994). To his coy mistress. In F. Kermode & K. Walker (Eds.), *Andrew Marvell* (pp. 22–23). New York: Oxford.

Masculinist (2010, April 18). Why Palin sounds dumb (blog post). *Derkeiler.com.* Retrieved from http://newsgroups.derkeiler.com/Archive/Soc/soc.men/2010 -04/msg00113.html

Mason, R. (2010). "Pitbulls" and populist politicians: Sarah Palin, Pauline Hanson and the use of gendered nostalgia in electoral campaigns. *Comparative American Studies, 8,* 185–199.

Mayhew, D. R. (2011). *Partisan balance: Why political parties don't kill the U.S. constitutional system.* Princeton: Princeton University Press.

Mazmanian, D. A. (1991). Third parties in American elections. In L. S. Maisel & C. Bassett (Eds.), *Political parties and elections in the United States: An encyclopedia* (vol. N–index, pp. 1105–1116). New York: Garland Publishing.

McAdams, D. P. (2010). *George W. Bush and the redemptive dream: A psychological portrait.* New York: Oxford University Press.

McAdams, D. P., Albaugh, M., Farber, E., Daniels, J., Logan, R. L., & Olson, B. (2008). Family metaphors and moral intuitions: How conservatives and liberals narrate their lives. *Journal of Personality and Social Psychology, 95*(4), 978–990.

McCain, J. (2008, September 5). Remarks in Cedarsburg, Wisconsin. Retrieved from http://www.youtube.com/watch?v=9HkKz901exQ

McCain, J. (2008, October 11). Weekly radio address by Senator John McCain (R-AZ), Republican presidential nominee. *Federal News Service.* Retrieved from http://lexisnexis.com

McCarty, J. A., & Hattwick, P. M. (1992). Cultural value orientations: A comparison of magazine advertisements from United States and Mexico. *Advances in Consumer Research, 19,* 34–38.

McCarty, N. M., Poole, K. T., & Rosenthal, H. (2006). *Polarized America: The dance of ideology and unequal riches.* Cambridge, MA: MIT Press.

McClosky, H. (1958). Conservatism and personality. *American Political Science Review, 52*(1), 27–45.

McCollam, D. (2010). A distant echo. *Columbia Journalism Review, 48,* 55–57.

McCurry, M. (2008). Memorandum to the president-elect. *Presidential Studies Quarterly, 38*(4), 700-706. doi:10.1111/j.1741-5705.2008.02672.x

McElhatton, J. (2011, May 4). Outsider hired for Obama speeches. *Washington*

Times. Retrieved from http://www.washingtontimes.com/news/2011/may/3/outsider-hired-for-obama-speeches/

McGinnis, J. (2011). *The rogue: Searching for the real Sarah Palin*. New York: Crown.

McGovern, G. (1972). *An American journey: The presidential campaign speeches of George McGovern*. New York: Random House.

McHugh, J. (2010, December 16). What the Tea Party is, is not, and its "core competence." *Michigan Capital Confidential*. Retrieved from http://www.mackinac.org/14194

McWhorter, J. (2010, April 6). What does Palinspeak mean? *New Republic*. Retrieved from http://www.tnr.com/blog/john-mcwhorter/what-does-palin speak-mean

Medhurst, M. J. (2003). Presidential speechwriting: Ten myths that plague modern scholarship. In K. Ritter & M. J. Medhurst (Eds.). *Presidential speech-writing: From the New Deal to the Reagan revolution and beyond* (pp. 3–20). College Station: Texas A&M University Press.

Meeks, L. (2010). *Is she man enough?: News coverage of male and females candidates at different levels of office*. Paper presented at the annual meeting of the Association for Education in Journalism and Mass Communication, Denver.

— Menand, L. (2001). *The metaphysical club*. New York: Farrar, Straus and Giroux.

Merleau-Ponty, M. (1962). *Phenomenology and perception* (Colin Smith, Trans.). New York: Routledge.

Merskin, D. (2004). The construction of Arabs as enemies: Post–September 11 discourse of George W. Bush. *Mass Communication and Society, 7*(2), 157–175.

Milkis, S. M. (2007). The rhetorical and administrative presidencies. *Critical Review, 19*(2–3), 379–401.

Milkis, S. M., & Rhodes, J. H. (2007). George W. Bush, the party system, and American federalism. *Publius: The Journal of Federalism, 37*(3), 478–503.

Miller, A. H. (1999). Sex, politics, and public opinion: What political scientists really learned from the Clinton-Lewinsky scandal. *PS: Political Science and Politics, 32*, 721–730.

Miller, L. (2010, June 21). Saint Sarah. *Newsweek, 155*, 32.

Miller, M. K., & Peake, J. S. (2010). *Rookie or rock star: Newspaper coverage of Sarah Palin's vice-presidential campaign*. Paper presented at the annual meeting of the American Political Science Association, Washington.

Miller, R. K. (1999). Presidential sanctuaries after the Clinton sex scandals. *Harvard Journal of Law and Public Policy, 22*, 647–734.

Miller, S. (1997, August 11). Jennifer's prime time. *People Magazine*. Retrieved from http://www.people.com/people/archive/article/0,,20122878,00.html

Mitchell. W. C. (1959). The ambivalent social status of the American politician. *Western Political Quarterly. 12*(3), 683–698.

Monteiro, G. (1998). Robert Frost's liberal imagination. *Iowa Review 28*(3), 104–127.

Mooney, A. (2008, November 11). Bush names his regrets, praises Obama. CNN Ticker. Available at http://politicalticker.blogs.cnn.com/2008/11/11/bush-names-his-regrets-praises-obama.

Moore, M. P. (1991). A rhetorical criticism of political myth: From Goldwater legend to Reagan mystique. *Communication Studies, 42*(3), 295–308.

Morris, M. (2011). The narcissistic style of American politics: Sarah Palin's rhetorical appeal. In B. Brummett (Ed.), *The politics of style and the style of politics* (pp. 47–58). Lanham, Md: Lexington Books.

Morris, M., Carranza, E., & Fox, C. (2008). Mistaken identity: Activating conservative political identities induces "conservative" financial decisions. *Psychological Science, 19*(11), 1154–1160.

Moyer, J. E. (2001, July 22). Blasts Richmond County government [letter to the editor]. *Augusta Chronicle*, p. A05. Retrieved from http://www.lexisnexis.com

Murphy, J. M. (2003). "Our mission and our moment": George W. Bush and September 11th. *Rhetoric and Public Affairs, 6*(4), 607–632.

Murphy, J. M. (2005). To form a more perfect union: Bill Clinton and the art of deliberation. *Rhetoric and Public Affairs, 8*(4), 657–678.

Murphy, J. M. (2009). Political economy and rhetorical matter. *Rhetoric and Public Affairs,* 12(2), 303–315.

Myers, G. (2004). *Matters of opinion: Talking about public issues.* Cambridge: Cambridge University Press.

Nagourney, A. (2009, May 13). G.O.P. worries about sounding a negative tone. *New York Times.* Retrieved from http://www.nytimes.com/2009/05/13/us/politics/12web-nagourney.html?_r=1

Namenwirth, J. Z, & Lasswell, H. D. (1970). *The changing language of American values: A computer study of selected party platforms.* Beverly Hills: Sage Publications.

Nardulli, P. F. (2005). *Popular efficacy in the democratic era: A reexamination of electoral accountability in the United States, 1828–2000.* Princeton: Princeton University Press.

Neither candidate is worthy (2004, September 4). *Oklahoman.* Retrieved from http://www.lexisnexis.com

Neustadt, R. (1990). *Presidential power and the modern presidents: The politics of leadership from Roosevelt to Reagan.* New York: Free Press.

Newport, F. (2010, October 14). Americans still trust own judgment more than politicians'. *Gallup.* http://www.gallup.com/poll/143675/americans-trust-own-judgment-politicians.aspx

Noonan, P. (1998, August 31). Why the speech will live in infamy. *Time, 152,* 36.

Norton, A. (1988). *Reflections on political identity.* Baltimore: Johns Hopkins University Press.

Nunberg, G. (2010, December 16). Counting on Google books. *Chronicle of Higher Education*. Retrieved from http://chronicle.com/article/Counting-on-Google-Books/125735/

Obama, B. (2006, November 20). Speech at Chicago Council on Global Affairs. Retrieved from http://www.thechicagocouncil.org/UserFiles/File/Obama%20 Remarks%20%20_11-20-06_.pdf

Obama, B. (2008, September 8). Remarks at North Farmington High School in Farmington Hills, Michigan. Retrieved from http://www.clickondetroit.com /video/17425800/index.html

Obama, B. (2008, September 9). A plan for education: Remarks in Dayton, Ohio. Retrieved from http://www.presidentialrhetoric.com/campaign2008 /obama/09.09.08.html

Obama, B. (2008, September 12). Remarks in Concord, New Hampshire. Retrieved from http://www.youtube.com/watch?feature=player_profilepage &v=uR1VruSYu7c

Obama, B. (2008, September 16). Remarks at the Colorado School of Mines, Golden, Colorado. Retrieved from http://www.presidentialrhetoric.com /campaign2008/obama/09.16.08.html

Obama, B. (2008, September 17). Remarks at Cashman Field in Las Vegas, Nevada. Retrieved from http://www.youtube.com/watch?v=CjoBuzuDXyE

Obama, B. (2008, October 7). Second presidential debate. Retrieved from http:// articles.cnn.com/2008-10-07/politics/presidential.debate.transcript

Obama, B. (2008, October 18). Remarks at the Gateway Arch in St. Louis, Missouri. Retrieved from http://www.presidentialrhetoric.com/campaign2008 /obama/10.18.08.html

Obama, B. (2008, October 20). Remarks in Tampa, Florida. Retrieved from http:// www.realclearpolitics.com/articles/2008/10/obamas_speech_in_tampa_florida .html

Obama, B. (2008, October 25). Remarks at the University of Nevada in Reno, Nevada. Retrieved from http://www.asksam.com/ebooks/releases.asp?file= Obama-Speeches.ask&dn=Remarks%20Reno%2c%20NV

Obama, B. (2008, November 2). Campaign speech at the statehouse in Columbus, Ohio. Retrieved from http://www.barackobama.com/2008/11/02/remarks_of _senator_barack_obam_153.php

Obama, B. (2009, January 20). Inaugural address. The nation's capital, Washington, D.C. Retrieved from http://abcnews.go.com/Politics/Inauguration/president -obama-inauguration-speech-transcript/story?id=6689022

Obama, B. (2009, July 22). Obama's news conference: President talks health care in his latest prime time news conference. Retrieved from http://www.cbsnews .com/stories/2009/07/23/politics/main5182101.shtml

Obama, B. (2010, September 9). Speech on the economy in Cleveland, Ohio. Retrieved from http://www.nytimes.com/2010/09/09/us/politics/09obama-text .html?_r=1&pagewanted=all

Obama, B. (2010, September 10). Speech in Cleveland, Ohio. Retrieved from http://
www.realclearpolitics.com/articles/2010/09/08/obamas_economic_speech_in_
cleveland_107070.html

Obama, B. (2011, January 13). President's speech on the Giffords incident.
Retrieved from http://www.suntimes.com/3288791-417/applause-gabby-hearts
-christina-lives.html

Obama, B. (2011, February 26). Weekly radio address to the nation. Retrieved
from http://www.whitehouse.gov/the-press-office/2011/02/26/weekly-address
-investments-education-innovation-and-infrastructure-are-e

Olbrys, S. G. (2005). *Seinfeld's* democratic vistas. *Critical Studies in Media Communication, 22*(5), 390–408.

O'Malley, M. (1990). *Keeping watch: A history of American time.* New York: Penguin.

Ong, W. J. (1982). *Orality and literacy: The technologizing of the word.* New York:
Routledge.

Osgood, C. E., Suci, G. J., & Tannenbaum. P. (1957). *The measurement of meaning.*
Urbana: University of Illinois Press.

Owen, D. (2000). Popular politics and the Clinton/Lewinsky affair: The implications for leadership. *Political Psychology, 21*, 161–177.

Owen, D., & Davis, R. (1998). *New media and American politics.* New York: Oxford
University Press.

Packer, G. (2004, July/August). Like a rock. *Mother Jones*, 28–41.

Palaima, T. (2009, April 2). The tools of power. *Times Higher Education.* Retrieved
from http://www.timeshighereducation.co.uk/story.asp?sectioncode=26&story
code=406001

Palin, S. (2011, January 12). Sarah Palin's speech on the Giffords incident.
Retrieved from http://deathby1000papercuts.com/2011/01/sarah-palin-blood
-libel-address-video-transcript/

Palin's resignation: The edited version (2009, July 20). *Vanity Fair.* Retrieved from
http://www.vanityfair.com/politics/features/2009/07/palin-speech-edit-200907

Parry-Giles, S. J. (2008). George W. Bush, second inaugural address. *Voices of
Democracy, 3*, 122–138.

Parry-Giles, S. J., & Parry-Giles, T. (2002). *Constructing Clinton: Hyperreality and
presidential image-making in postmodern politics.* New York: Peter Lang.

Patrakis, J. (2011, September 22). "The Tea Party does not equal Republican."
Andover Townsman Online [letter to the editor]. Retrieved from http://www
.andovertownsman.com/opinion/x1190856414/Letter-Tea-Party-does-not
-equal-Republican

Patrick, R., Prior, I., Smith, J. S., & Smith, AH. (1983). Relationship between blood
pressure and modernity among Ponapeans. *International Journal of Epidemiol-
ogy, 12*(1), 36–44.

Patterson, T. E. (1993). *Out of order.* New York: Vintage Books.

Patterson, T. E. (2002). *The vanishing voter: Public involvement in an age of uncertainty.* New York: Knopf.

Paul, N. C. (2004, May 4). For black ministers, political tone shifts. *Christian Science Monitor*, p. 2.

Payne, K., & Cangemi, J. (1997). Gender differences in leadership. *IFE Psychological: An International Journal*, 5(1), 22–43.

Penhen (2008, October 8). Comment on "Viewers left wanting more from debate" (comment on blog post). *Evansville Courier Press*. Retrieved from http://www.courierpress.com/comments/list/news/stories/138095/?comments_pages-1293582741=/comments/list/news/stories/138095/1/

Pennebaker, J. W. (2011). *The secret life of pronouns: What our words say about us.* New York: Bloomsbury Pres.

Perot, R. (1992). Speaking out [advertisement transcript]. Retrieved from http://campaignmapping.org/keywords/

Peters, C. (2010). No-spin zones. *Journalism Studies*, 11(6), 832–851.

Petrocik, J. R., Benoit, W. L., & Hansen, G. J. (2003). Issue ownership and presidential campaigning, 1952–2000. *Political Science Quarterly*, 118(4), 599–626.

Pew Research Center (2010). Distrust, discontent, anger, and partisan rancor. Retrieved from http://people-press.org/2010/04/18/distrust-discontent-anger-and-partisan-rancor

Pfau, M. W. (2005). *The political style of conspiracy: Chase, Sumner, and Lincoln.* East Lansing: Michigan State University Press.

Phelan, J. (2011, November 9). Six in 10 support policies addressing income inequality. *ABCNews*. Retrieved from http://abcnews.go.com/blogs/politics/2011/11/six-in-10-support-policies-addressing-income-inequality/

Piaget, J. (1954). *The construction of reality in the child.* New York: Basic Books.

Piper, K. (2002). *Cartographic fictions: Maps, race, and identity.* New Brunswick: Rutgers University Press.

Podhoretz, J. (2004, August 29). Not a bad place; why the prez comes to town with a good chance to romp. *New York Post*, p. 25.

Postrel, V. (2003). *The substance of style: How the rise of aesthetic value is remaking commerce, culture, and consciousness.* New York: HarperCollins.

Powell, C. (2010, September 19). Colin Powell critical of President Obama. *Politico*. Retrieved from http://www.politico.com/news/stories/0910/42381.html#ixzz10ZbNX0se

Puig, C. (2010). Don't be a 'Stranger,' Woody; Allen's latest is a disappointing ensemble effort. *USA Today*, September 22, p. 4D.

Purnell, T., Raimy, E., & Salmons, J. (2009). Defining dialect, perceiving dialect, and new dialect formation: Sarah Palin's speech. *Journal of English Linguistics*, 37(4), 331–355.

Purpura, S., & Hillard, D. (2006). Automated classification of congressional legislation. *Proceedings of the 2006 International Conference on Digital Government Research*, 219–225.

Quinn, K. M., Monroe, B. L., Colaresi, M., Crespin, M. H., & Radev, D. R. (2010).

How to analyze political attention with minimal assumptions and costs. *American Journal of Political Science, 54*(1), 209–228.

Radio audience trends: 2006 annual report (2006, March 13). Journalism.org: Pew Research Center's Project for Excellence in Journalism. Retrieved from http://www.journalism.org/node/836

Rae, N. C. (2010). Review of *Going rogue: An American life* by Sarah Palin. *Forum, 8*(2), article 9. Retrieved from http://www.degruyter.com

Rahn, W. M. (1993). The role of partisan stereotypes in information processing about political candidates. *American Journal of Political Science, 37*(2), 472–496.

Rapoport, R., & Stone, W. J. (2005). *Three's a crowd: The dynamic of third parties, Ross Perot, and Republican resurgence.* Ann Arbor: University of Michigan Press.

Reagan, R. (1982, September 18). Weekly radio address to the nation. Retrieved from *The American presidency project:* http://www.presidency.ucsb.edu/ws/?pid=43011

Reagan, R. (1982, November 6). Weekly radio address to the nation. Retrieved from *The American presidency project:* http://www.presidency.ucsb.edu/ws/?pid= 41959

Reagan, R. (1982, November 20). Weekly radio address to the nation. Retrieved from http://www.reagan.utexas.edu/archives/speeches/1982/112082a.htm

Reagan, R. (1985, August 10). Weekly radio address to the nation. Retrieved from *The American presidency project:* http://www.presidency.ucsb.edu/ws/?pid= 38989

Reagan, R. (1986, October 4). Weekly radio address to the nation. Retrieved from *The American presidency project:* http://www.presidency.ucsb.edu/ws/?pid= 36544

Reagan, R. (1987, January 17). Weekly radio address to the nation. Retrieved from *The American presidency project:* http://www.presidency.ucsb.edu/ws/?pid= 34008

Reed, J. (1973). *Faulkner's narrative.* New Haven: Yale University Press.

Renshon, S. A. (2000). After the fall: The Clinton presidency in psychological perspective. *Political Science Quarterly, 115*, 41–65.

Renshon, S. A. (2001). America at a crossroads: Political leadership, national identity, and the decline of common culture. In S. A. Renshon (Ed.), *One America? Political leadership, national identity, and the dilemmas of diversity* (pp. 3–27). Washington: Georgetown University Press.

Renshon, S. A. (2008). Psychological reflections on Barack Obama and John McCain: Assessing the contours of a new presidential administration. *Political Science Quarterly, 123*, 391–433.

Ridout, T. N., & Franz, M. (2008). Evaluating measures of campaign tone. *Political Communication, 25*, 158–179.

Rieder, J. (2003). "The fractious nation?" In J. Rieder & S. Steinlight (Eds.), *The fractious nation? Unity and division in contemporary American life* (pp. 1–12). Berkeley: University of California Press.

Roanoke Tea Party, Inc. (n.d.). Company overview. Retrieved from http://www.facebook.com/pages/Roanoke-Tea-Party-Inc/213650083901?ref=ts

Rockwell Corporation (1995). *Annual letter to shareholders*. Housed in the Campaign Mapping database at http://keywords.communication.utexas.edu/keywords/

Rodgers, D. T. (2011). *Age of fracture*. Cambridge, MA: Belknap Press.

Rolle, R. (1340/1863). *The pricke of conscience*. Berlin. A. Asher & Company.

Rosenblum, N. (2008). *On the side of the angels: An appreciation of parties and partisanship*. Princeton: Princeton University Press.

Rosenstone, S. J., Behr, R. L., & Lazarus, E. H. (1996). *Third parties in America* (2nd ed.). Princeton: Princeton University Press.

Rotter, J. B. (1990). Internal versus external control of reinforcement: A case history of a variable. *American Psychologist, 45*, 489–93.

Rousseau, J. J. (1998). *Essay on the origin of languages and writings related to music* (J. T. Scott, Trans.). Hanover, NH: University Press of New England.

Rowland, R., & Jones, J. (2002). "Until next week": The Saturday radio addresses of Ronald Reagan. *Presidential Studies Quarterly, 32*(1), 84–110.

Rowland, R., & Jones, J. (2007). Recasting the American dream and American politics: Barack Obama's keynote address to the 2004 Democratic National Convention. *Quarterly Journal of Speech, 93*, 425–448.

Ryfe, D. M. (1999). Franklin Roosevelt and the fireside chats. *Journal of Communication, 49*, 80–103.

Sanbonmatsu, K. (2002). Political parties and the recruitment of women to state legislatures. *Journal of Politics, 64*(3), 791–809.

Sandburg, C. (1954). *Abraham Lincoln: The prairie years and the war years*. New York: Harcourt.

Sandefur, A. G. (2003). *Narrative immediacy and first-person voice in contemporary novels*. Ph.D. dissertation, Louisiana State University.

Sands, P. (2002). World wide words: A rationale and preliminary report on a publishing project for an advanced writing workshop. *Academic Writing*. Retrieved from http://wac.colostate.edu/aw/articles/sands_2002.htm

San Jose mayor's proposed ethics reforms have political overtones (editorial) (2009, Dec. 11). *San Jose Mercury News*. Retrieved from http://www.lexisnexis.com

Savage, L. C. (2005, June 27). The right court. *Maclean's, 118*(26), 20.

Scacco, J. (2010). *A weekly genre: The rhetorical content and persuasive effects of the Saturday presidential address in the Obama administration*. Paper presented at the annual meeting of the American Political Science Association's Preconference on Political Communication, Washington.

Scharnhorst, G. (Ed.). (2006). Mark Twain: The complete interviews. Tuscaloosa: University of Alabama Press.

Schlesinger, A. M. (1998). *The disuniting of America: Reflections on a multicultural society* (Rev. ed.). New York: Norton.

Schlesinger, R. (2011, January 31). Obama has mentioned "American exceptionalism" more than Bush. *U.S. News and World Report*. Retrieved from http://www .usnews.com/opinion/blogs/robert-schlesinger/2011/01/31

Schneck, S. F. (2001). Political parties and democracy's citizens. In J. K. White & J. C. Green (Eds.), *The politics of ideas: Intellectual challenges facing the American political parties* (pp. 133–154). Albany: State University of New York.

Schneider, G. L. (2010, November 19). Tea for 2010, and beyond? *Chronicle Review*. B10–B11.

Schulz, K. (2011, June 24). What is distant reading? *New York Times*. Retrieved from http://www.nytimes.com/2011/06/26/books/review/the-mechanic-muse -what-is-distant-reading.html

Schutz, A. (1995). Entertainers, experts, or public servants? Politicians' self-presentation on television talk shows. *Political Communication, 12*, 211–221.

Seelye, K. Q. (2008, September 11). Palin interview: She didn't blink when asked to run. *New York Times*. Retrieved from http://thecaucus.blogs.nytimes.com /2008/09/11/palin-interview-she-didnt-blink-when-asked-to-run/

Seelye, K. Q. (2009, January 17). The past as a guide for Obama's address. *New York Times*. January 17. Retrieved from http://www.nytimes.com/2009/01/18/us /politics/18speech.html

Seligman, M. E. P. (1998). *Learned optimism*. New York: Pocket Books.

Senior, J. (2009, August 2). The message is the message. *New York Magazine*. Retrieved from http://nymag.com/news/politics/58199/

Sennett, R. (1978). *The fall of public man*. New York: Vintage Books.

Sheafer, T. (2007). How to evaluate it: The role of story-evaluative tone in agenda setting and priming. *Journal of Communication, 57*, 21–39.

Sheldon, K., & Nichols, C. (2009). Comparing Democrats and Republicans on intrinsic and extrinsic values. *Journal of Applied Social Psychology, 39*(3), 589–623.

Sheridan, T. (2001). A course of lectures on elocution. In P. Bizzell & B. Herzberg (Eds.), *The rhetorical tradition: Readings from classical times to the present* (2nd ed., pp. 879–888). Boston: Bedford/St. Martin's.

Shirley, C., & Devine, D. (2010, April 10). Karl Rove is no conservative, as his memoir shows. *Washington Post*. Retrieved from http://www.washingtonpost .com/wp-dyn/content/article/2010/03/31/AR2010033102630.html

Shome, R. (2003). Space matters: The power and practice of space. *Communication Theory, 13*, 39–56.

Sigelman, L., & Whissell, C. (2002). Projecting presidential personas on the radio: An addendum on the Bushes. *Presidential Studies Quarterly, 32*, 572–576.

Silva, C. L., Jenkins-Smith, H. C., & Waterman, R. (2007). Why did Clinton survive the impeachment crisis? A test of three explanations. *Presidential Studies Quarterly, 37*, 468–485.

Simendinger, A. (2008). Lessons learned the hard way: Questioning presidents. *Presidential Studies Quarterly, 38*(4), 693–699.

Simons, H. W. (2000). A dilemma-centered analysis of Clinton's August 17th apologia: Implication for rhetorical theory and method. *Quarterly Journal of Speech, 86*, 438–453.

Sinclair, B. (2000). Hostile partners: The President, Congress, and lawmaking in the partisan 1990s. In J. R. Bond & R. Fleisher (Eds.), *Polarized politics: Congress and the President in a partisan era* (pp. 134–153). Washington, DC: CQ Press.

Sinclair, B. (2005). Patriotism, partisanship, and institutional protection: The congressional response to 9/11. In R. S. Conley (Ed.), *Transforming the American polity: The presidency of George W. Bush and the war on terrorism* (pp. 121–134). Upper Saddle River, N.J.: Pearson.

Sirota, D. (2011, Nov 18). Palin embraces OWS? *Salon.*

Skinner, R. M. (2008). George W. Bush and the partisan presidency. *Political Science Quarterly, 123*(4), 605–622.

Skitka, L., & Tetlock, P. (1993). Providing public assistance: Cognitive and motivational processes underlying liberal and conservative policy preferences. *Journal of Personality and Social Psychology, 65*(6), 1205–1223.

Smith, M. A. (2007). *The right talk: How conservatives transformed the Great Society into the economic society.* Princeton: Princeton University Press.

Smith, R. M. (2008). Religious rhetoric and the ethics of public discourse: The case of George W. Bush. *Political Theory. 36*(2), 272–300.

Smith, S. (2010). Autobiographical discourse in the theaters of politics. *Biography: An Interdisciplinary Quarterly, 33*(1), v–xxvi.

Smith, Z. (2009, February 26). Speaking in tongues. *New York Review of Books.* Retrieved from http://www.nybooks.com/articles/archives/2009/feb/26/speaking -in-tongues-2/?pagination=false

Smitherman, G. (1977). *Talkin and testifyin: The language of Black America.* Boston: Houghton Mifflin.

Spring, S. E., & Packer, J. (2009). George W. Bush, "An address to a joint session of Congress and the American people." *Voices of Democracy, 4*, 120–131.

Stahl, R. (2008). A clockwork war: Rhetorics of time in a time of terror. *Quarterly Journal of Speech, 94*, 73–99.

Starr, A., & Dunham, R. S. (2003, June 30). Washington's other tough Texan. *Business Week*, p. 80.

Stein, S. (2008, January 16). Obama compares himself to Reagan, JFK ... but not Bill Clinton. *Huffington Post.* Retrieved from http://www.huffingtonpost .com/2008/01/16/obama-compares-himself-to_n_81835.html

Stein, S. (2008, October 17). Palin explains what parts of country not "pro-

America." Retrieved from http://www.huffingtonpost.com/2008/10/17/palin
-clarifies-what-part_n_135641.html

Stevenson, N. (2010). Chatting the news: The democratic discourse qualities of non-
market and market political talk television. *Journalism Studies*, *11*(6), 852–873.

Stigler, G. J. (1975). *The citizen and the state: Essays on regulation*. Chicago: University of Chicago Press.

Stone, W., & Maisel, S. (2003). The not-so-simple calculus of winning: Potential U.S.
House candidates' nominations and general election prospects. *Journal of Politics*, *65*(4), 951–77.

Strolovitch, D., McHeaney, M., Masket, S., Miller, J., & Skarrow, E. (2010). *Gen-
der consciousness through a partisan lens: Convention delegates' evaluation of
Hillary Clinton and Sarah Palin*. Paper presented at the annual meeting of the
American Political Science Association, Washington.

Stuckey, M. E. (2005). One nation (pretty darn) divisible: National identity in the
2004 conventions. *Rhetoric and Public Affairs*, *8*(4), 639–656.

Stuckey, M. E., Curry, K. E., & Barnes, A. D. (2010). Bringing candidacies in from
the cold: mainstreaming minority candidates, 1960 and 2008. *Presidential Studies Quarterly*, *40*(3), 414–430.

Stuckey, M. E., & Wabshall, S. (2000). Sex, lies, and presidential leadership: Interpretations of the office. *Presidential Studies Quarterly*, *30*, 514–533.

Sturm, S. (2010, July 18). Hypotaxis and parataxis; periodic and running style (blog
post). *Te ipu pakore: The broken vessel*. Retrieved from http://seansturm.word
press.com/2010/07/18/parataxis-and-hypotaxis/

Sullivan, A. (2009, November) Deconstructing Sarah, ctd. *Atlantic*. Retrieved from
http://www.theatlantic.com/daily-dish/archive/2009/11/deconstructing-sarah
-ctd/193876/

Suskind, R. (2011). *The confidence men: Wall Street, Washington, and the education
of a president*. New York: Harper Collins.

Suskind, R. (2004, October 17). Without a doubt. *The New York Times Magazine*,
p. 44.

Svandoren (2009, July 21). Comment to "Palin needs a good editor" (comment on
blog post). *Bob Cesca's Awesome Blog*. Retrieved from http://www.bobcesca
.com/blog-archives/2009/07/palin_needs_a_g.html

Sydserff, R., & Weetman, P. (2002). Developments in content analysis: A transitiv-
ity index and scores. *Accounting, Auditing and Accountability Journal*, *15*, 523–
545.

Tanenhaus, S. (2009, Dec 7). North star: Populism, politics, and the power of Sarah
Palin. *New Yorker*, p. 84.

Tannen, D. (1994). Interpreting interruption in conversation. In D. Tannen (Ed.),
Gender and discourse (pp. 53–79). New York: Oxford University Press.

Tavits, M. (2009). The making of mavericks. *Comparative Political Studies*, *42*(6),
793–815.

Taylor, S., Jr. (2008, June 14). Overplaying its hand. *Newsweek*. Retreived from http://www.newsweek.com/2008/06/14/overplaying-its-hand.html

Terkildsen, N. (1993). When white voters evaluate Black candidates: The processing implications of candidate skin color, prejudice, and self-monitoring. *American Journal of Political Science. 37*(4), 1032–1053.

Terrill, R. E. (2009). Unity and duality in Barack Obama's "A more perfect union." *Quarterly Journal of Speech, 95*(4), 363–386.

Theriault, S. M. (2008). *Party polarization in Congress*. New York: Cambridge University Press.

Thomas, M., Pang, B., & Lee, L. (2006). Get out the vote: Determining support or opposition from congressional floor-debate transcripts. *Proceedings of the 2006 Conference on Empirical Methods in Natural Language Processing*, 327–335.

Tocqueville, de A. (2000). *Democracy in America* (H. C. Mansfield & D. Winthrop, Trans.). Chicago: University of Chicago Press.

Travers, K. (2010, January 20). Exclusive: President Obama: We lost touch with American people last year. *ABC World News*. Retrieved from http://abcnews.go.com/WN/Politics/president-obama-lost-touch-american-people-year/story?id=9613462.

Tross, OC (n.d.). Defining the Tea Party, *Ezine Articles*. Retrieved from http://EzineArticles.com/?expert=OC_Tross

The 2000 campaign; excerpts from interview with Bush on campaign issues and election strategy. (2000, March 16). *The New York Times*, p. A20.

Urban, G. (2010). A method for measuring the motion of culture. *American Anthropologist. 112*(1), 122–139.

Van den Haag, E. (1960). A dissent from consensus society. *Daedalus, 89*, 315–324.

Vavreck, L. (2009). *The message matters: The economy and presidential campaigns*. Princeton: Princeton University Press.

Velasco, A. (2010). *Centrist rhetoric: The production of political transcendence in the Clinton presidency*. Lanham, MD.: Rowman and Littlefield.

Viroli, M. (1992). The revolution in the concept of politics. *Political Theory, 20*, 473–495.

Wade, M. E., Jr. (1988). The lantern of ethics. *Vital Speeches of the Day, 54*, 340–343.

Walker, S. (2007). *Style and status: Selling beauty to African American women, 1920–1975*. Lexington: University Press of Kentucky.

Walsh, K. C. (2003). *Talking about politics: Informal groups and social identity in American life*. Chicago: University of Chicago Press.

Ware, B., & Linkugel, W. (1973). They spoke in defense of themselves: On the generic criticism of apologia. *Quarterly Journal of Speech, 54*, 273–283.

Watts, S. (1991). The idiocy of American Studies: Poststructuralism, language and politics in the age of self-fulfillment. *American Quarterly, 43*, 625–660.

Weaver, M. R. (2001). *Re-placing politics: The politics of place in Gary Snyder and Wendell Berry*. Paper presented at the annual meeting of the American Political Science Association, San Francisco.

Weaver, R. (1953). *The ethics of rhetoric*. New York: Henry Regnery.

Webb, S. (2008). Providence and the president (or, the new Eusebius). *Reviews in Religion and Theology, 15*(4), 622–629.

Weispfenning, J. (2003). Cultural functions of reruns: Time, memory, and television. *Journal of Communication, 53*, 165–177.

White, J. K., & Zogby, J. J. (2004). The likable partisan: George W. Bush and the transformation of the American presidency. In S. E. Schier (Ed.), *High risk and big ambition: The presidency of George W. Bush* (pp. 79- 96). Pittsburgh: University of Pittsburgh Press.

Whitman, W. (1986). *Leaves of grass*. New York: Penguin.

Wilkins, A. C. (2008). *Wannabes, goths, and Christians: The boundaries of sex, style, and status*. Chicago: University of Chicago Press.

Williams, J. L. (2011, January 7). The statistical turn in literary studies. *Chronicle of Higher Education*. Retrieved from http://chronicle.com/article/The-Statistical -Turn-in/125751/

Wills, G. (1999). *A necessary evil: A history of American distrust of government*. New York: Simon & Schuster.

Wilson, E. O. (1998). *Consilience: The unity of knowledge*. New York: Knopf.

Winokur, J. (Ed.). (1990). *Writers on writing*. Pp. 89–109. Philadelphia: Running Press.

Winter, D. (2009). Predicting the Obama presidency. *International Society for Political Psychology News, 20*, 7.

Wolfe, A. (1998). *One nation, after all: What Americans really think*. New York: Penguin.

Wolin, S. (1960). *Politics and vision*. Boston: Little Brown.

Wood, D. (2009). *The myth of presidential representation*. New York: Cambridge University Press.

Woods, S. (2009, March 5). Bill Maher's life after W. *Rolling Stone*, pp. 36–37. Retrieved from http://www.ebscohost.com

Woodson, B. (2010). *The role of congressional polarization and divided government in the new ideological partisanship*. Paper presented at the annual meeting of the American Political Science Association, Washington.

Yip, M. (2007). Tone. In P. de Lacy (Ed.). *Cambridge Handbook of Phonology* (pp. 229–251). Cambridge: Cambridge University Press.

York, B. (2009). Bush 43: Conservative movement is inconsequential. *Washingotn Examiner*. Retrieved from http://washingtonexaminer.com/politics/2009/09 /bush-43-conservative-movement-inconsequential#ixzz1LyecPItK

Young, J. (2011, April 27). New director of MIT media lab talks of encouraging openness. *Chronicle of Higher Education*. Retrieved from http://chronicle

.com/blogs/wiredcampus/new-director-of-mit-media-lab-talks-of-encouraging
-openness/31112

Yu, B., Kaufmann, S., & Diermeier, D. (2008). Classifying party affiliation from political speech. *Journal of Information Technology and Politics,* 5(1), 33–48.

Zaller, J. R. (1998). Monica Lewinsky's contribution to political science. *PS: Political Science and Politics, 31,* 182–189.

Zarefsky, D. (2004). George W. Bush discovers rhetoric: September 20, 2001, and the U.S. response to terrorism. In M. Hyde (Ed.), *The Ethos of Rhetoric* (pp. 136–155). Columbia: University of South Carolina Press.

Zarefsky, D. (2008). Two faces of democratic rhetoric. In T. F. McDorman & D. M. Timmerman (Eds.), *Rhetoric and democracy: Pedagogical and political practices* (pp. 115–138). East Lansing: Michigan State University Press.

Zeleny, J. (2007, July 29). Obama and Clinton trading more jabs on foreign policy. *New York Times,* p. A22.

Zeleny, J. (2011, December 20). Perry dismisses Gingrich's complaint of "negative campaigning." *New York Times.* Retrieved from http://thecaucus.blogs.nytimes.com/2011/12/20/perry-not-concerned-about-negative-tone-of-campaign/?scp=1&sq=perry%20dismisses%20gingrich%27s%20complaint&st=cse

Zeleny, J., & Healy, P. (2008, Jan 16). Obama and Clinton seek a softer tone in Democratic presidential debate. *New York Times,* January 16, p. A19.

Zhu, L. (2010). *Computational political science: A literature survey.* An occasional paper from the College of Information Sciences and Technology, Pennsylvania State University. Retrieved from http://www.personal.psu.edu/luz113

Zillman, C. (2011, February). A big hole in the federal bench. *American Lawyer, 33*(2), 22.

Index

A page number followed by f *refers to a figure, and a page number followed by* t *indicates a table.*

① What instances of political comm do "the people" eg?
attend? Not the average stump speech/polly pulpit —
the less ordinary --

memory – repetition — but then ..

② accommodation — the linguistic/lexical equivalent of
the successful (skilled/experienced) river boat captain
adjust/adapt to "new" situations

① middle not "static" --   but not doing a Schlesinger
                                   "dynamic middle"
        ↓
    contested

Ⓑ middles are created → how we establish/posit
    the "extremes" we reject

avoidable
accommodate +
descriptives concept of
shell situation

→ ① How to react to
situation — trade high/ go one
way

trade low/ go another

will high, etc

② How to
control situation

No Bakhtin — maybe approach...

chech BO —
kanon speed

(assertive

tone — tonalitie
[BO tone re. GOP/convenche]

accommodation —→ distance
↘ diversity